PENGUIN BOOKS

CHARLES I

Christopher Hibbert was born in Leicestershire in 1924 and educated at Radley and Oriel College, Oxford. He served as an infantry officer during the war, was twice wounded and was awarded the Military Cross in 1945. Described by Professor J. H. Plumb as a 'writer of the highest ability' and in the *New Statesman* as a 'pearl of biographers', he is, in the words of *The Times Educational Supplement*, 'perhaps the most gifted popular historian we have'. His much-acclaimed books include the following, all of which have been published by Penguin: *The Destruction of Lord Raglan* (which won the Heinemann Award for Literature in 1962); *Benito Mussolini*; *The Court at Windsor*; *The Making of Charles Dickens*; *London: The Biography of a City*; *The Dragon Wakes: China and the West, 1793–1911*; *George IV*; *The Rise and Fall of the House of Medici*; *Edward VII: A Portrait*; *The Great Mutiny: India 1857*; *The French Revolution*; *The Personal History of Samuel Johnson*; *Africa Explored*; *Rome: The Biography of a City*; *The Virgin Queen: The Personal History of Elizabeth I*; *Florence: The Biography of a City*; *Nelson: A Personal History*; *Redcoats and Rebels*; *The Road to Tyburn* and *George III*.

Christopher Hibbert is a Fellow of the Royal Society of Literature. He is married with two sons and a daughter, and lives in Henley-on-Thames.

Christopher Hibbert

Charles I

PENGUIN BOOKS

PENGUIN BOOKS

Published by the Penguin Group
Penguin Books Ltd, 27 Wrights Lane, London w8 5tz, England
Penguin Putnam Inc., 375 Hudson Street, New York, New York 10014, USA
Penguin Books Australia Ltd, Ringwood, Victoria, Australia
Penguin Books Canada Ltd, 10 Alcorn Avenue, Toronto, Ontario, Canada m4v 3b2
Penguin Books India (P) Ltd, 11, Community Centre, Panchsheel Park, New Delhi – 110 017, India
Penguin Books (NZ) Ltd, Private Bag 102902, NSMC, Auckland, New Zealand
Penguin Books (South Africa) (Pty) Ltd, 5 Watkins Street, Denver Ext 4, Johannesburg 2094, South Africa

Penguin Books Ltd, Registered Offices: Harmondsworth, Middlesex, England

First published by Weidenfeld and Nicolson 1968
Published as a Classic Penguin 2001
1

Copyright © Christopher Hibbert, 1968
All rights reserved

Printed and bound in Great Britain by The Bath Press, Bath

For Rupert and Ann

Contents

List of Illustrations

CHARLES I

Reverse of the medal struck to commemorate Charles's return to London in 1633 (British Museum)

The gold ampulla used at Charles's Scottish coronation (National Museum of Antiquities of Scotland)

New Palace Yard with Westminster Hall and the Clock House by Hollar (British Museum)

The Tower of London by Hollar (British Museum)

Old London Bridge by Claude de Jongh (Iveagh Bequest, Kenwood, London)

Westminster, with Parliament House, Westminster Hall and the Abbey by Hollar (British Museum)

Westminster, showing the Palace, Hall and Abbey by Hollar (Victoria and Albert Museum)

Engraving of Charles I and his queen (Radio Times Hulton Picture Library)

MONARCH AND HUSBAND: COURT AND DOMESTIC LIFE [*pages 65–80*]

An engraving, after Van Dyck's 1634 portrait of Charles and Henrietta Maria, by R. V. Voerst (British Museum – Freeman)

Charles I and his Court in Greenwich Park by Adrian van Stalbent (Reproduced by Gracious Permission of Her Majesty the Queen)

An early 17th-century portrait of Charles embroidered on satin with painted silk (Victoria and Albert Museum)

An early 17th-century white satin stump-work panel with the figures of Charles and his queen (Victoria and Albert Museum)

Henrietta Maria's dwarf, Jeffery Hudson, at the age of twenty-eight (National Portrait Gallery)

Marble bust of Charles by Hubert le Sueur, 1631 (Victoria and Albert Museum)

Etching by Hollar of Le Sueur's equestrian statue of Charles at Charing Cross (Peter Jackson Collection – Freeman)

Charles I as depicted in an illumination on a patent (Mansell Collection, London)

Van Dyck's 1637 portrait of Charles I 'in Three Positions' (Mansell Collection)

The three elder children of Charles and Henrietta Maria by Van Dyck (Mansell Collection)

The model of a ship made in about 1634 and given to the Prince of Wales, the future Charles II (Ashmolean Museum, Oxford)

Charles I dining in State at Whitehall Palace by Houckgeest (Reproduced by Gracious Permission of Her Majesty the Queen)

A bronze bust of Charles I copied from the Le Sueur bust in the Bodleian, Oxford (Victoria and Albert Museum)

A cabinet bearing the monogram of Henrietta Maria (Reproduced by Gracious Permission of Her Majesty the Queen)

A book cushion of canvas embroidered in silk (Victoria and Albert Museum)

Bellarmines discovered at Oxford (Ashmolean Museum

Trenchers from the Royal Household used at banquets in the late 15th and early 16th centuries (Ashmolean Museum)

A tin-glazed earthenware wine bottle in use during the Civil War (Victoria and Albert Museum)

Pottery discovered at Broad Street, Oxford (Ashmolean Museum)

Enamelled earthenware dish, Lambeth 1637 (Victoria and Albert Museum)

Household utensils from 17th-century Oxford (Ashmolean Museum)

A watch said to have been given by Charles I to his fourth child, Princess Elizabeth (Victoria and Albert Museum)

CHARLES I

THE LAST YEARS: PRISONER AND VICTIM [*pages 257–72*]

CHARLES I

Title page and explanation of its symbolism from the copy of *Eikon Basilike* at Carisbrooke Castle (Reproduced by permission of the Trustees of Carisbrooke Castle – Magnus Bartlett)
'The Blessed King Charles the Martyr' as he appeared to 18th-century Tories, an engraving of 1717 by Faber

Author's Note

I am most grateful to Dr
Maurice Ashley for having read
the manuscript and for having
given me much useful advice,
and to my wife for having read
the proofs and prepared the
detailed index.   C.H.

I

The Child and His Parents
1600–16

IN her great bedchamber at Richmond Palace, between two and three o'clock in the morning of 24 March 1603, Queen Elizabeth turned her white and wrinkled face to the wall, and died. Three hours later, soon after it was light, Sir Robert Carey, a grandson of her aunt, Mary Boleyn, stole out of the palace grounds and galloped off towards the Great North Road.

Carey was a man of great strength and stamina. Some years before, he had won a wager of two thousand pounds by walking from Plymouth to Berwick-upon-Tweed in twelve days, an average of thirty-nine miles a day. His feat this March was scarcely less remarkable. On the evening of the 26 March, having ridden 397 miles in less than sixty hours, he brought his last panting relay horse into the courtyard of Holyrood Palace in Edinburgh and, spattered with mud, 'be-blooded with great falls and bruises', he dropped wearily from his saddle. He was the first – as he had been determined to be in the hope of reward – to bring the long-awaited news to James VI, King of Scotland, that he was King now, too, of England.

Within a week King James had formally bidden farewell to the Scottish people and soon, accompanied by numerous courtiers and retainers who hoped to share with him some of the profits of his new inheritance, he was riding for the border. The farther south he reached the more his welcome excited him. The people 'of all sorts rode and ran, nay, rather flew' to meet him, he afterwards remembered with characteristic self-congratulation, 'their eyes flaming nothing but sparkles of affection, their mouths and tongues uttering nothing but sounds of joy'.

A closer inspection of the new King came, however, as something of a disappointment, even as a shock. His eyes, blue and watery, were too large and too protuberant, 'ever rolling after any stranger that came in his presence'; his nose was too fleshy and too long; the skin of his cheeks was slightly pitted by the marks of smallpox;

his hair was of a pale brown colour and very sparse; his trowel-shaped beard was 'scattering on his chin and very thin'. When he dismounted from his horse it was noticed how ungainly he was, how ill-matched were his broad, rather plump body and his weak, thin, strangely erratic legs; when he spoke it was in a loud and unattractive voice 'in the full dialect of his country'; when he ate and drank he made a distasteful splashing noise, dribbling the gravy into his beard and the wine down each side of the cup, for his tongue was too big and his jaw too narrow. It seemed scarcely possible that this was the son of the fascinating and passionate Mary Queen of Scots and her second husband, Lord Darnley – the 'lustiest and best proportioned long man' that his wife had ever seen – that this was the great-great-grandson of Henry VII and Elizabeth of York, a man who had been a king since his mother had been forced to abdicate thirty-six years before when he was but one year old.

Those who had heard reports about him from Scotland could scarcely comfort themselves that this unprepossessing appearance, this slovenly manner and dress, concealed a character of either charm or distinction. He was said to be a coward and a pedant, lazy, conceited, dogmatic and vulgar, delighting in lewd stories, tales of sexual perversions and accounts of the anatomical details of freaks and monstrosities. He swore with a disconcertingly lurid zest for obscenity and blasphemy in the presence both of his servants, with whom he was 'extremely familiar' – and extremely mean – and of the young ladies of his court whose intellects he derided and to whose physical attractions he was not so noticeably partial as to those of such charming young men as the Duke of Lennox. He seemed almost grotesquely susceptible to flattery, and dedicated to the belief that, since kingship was divine, he was God's lieutenant on earth.

Although most of these highly disturbing reports from Scotland were exaggerated in the telling – and although there could not but be some sympathy for a man who had endured such an appalling childhood as his – the Englishmen whose duties now brought themselves into direct contact with James for the first time, realised how difficult their future might well prove to be. His early actions had seemed to confirm their worst fears: on arriving at York he had immediately sent off a demand to the Privy Council in London for more money for the rest of his journey; shortly after his arrival in London he had exploded in nervous irritation at the people who crowded round him in the street to stare at him. What did they want? he demanded, frightened as well as exasperated by their importunity and noisy curiosity. They came merely out of love, he was assured, to see his face. 'God's wounds!' he cried out with his wonted vulgarity, 'I will pull down my breeches and they shall also see my arse.'

Yet the new King had many virtues; and the English, disillusioned in recent years with Queen Elizabeth's government, were anxious to recognise them. Rising prices, costly wars, unpopular taxes, rebellions and executions had overcast the glory of the Queen's golden and triumphant age. The people looked in relief to her heir, a confirmed Protestant and a King who would bring them a new government, a new security and a new dynasty. James was not, as all had to agree, an attractive man; but he was fundamentally good-natured. His slavering speech and thick Scottish accent made him difficult to understand, but there could be no doubt that he had a quick, shrewd, perceptive mind and remarkable knowledge. He was accused of being a poltroon, and certainly his abject terror of naked steel which induced him to wear his clothes padded and stuffed as a precaution against assassination, leant weight to the accusation, but he was a fearless, not to say reckless, rider. His taste for coarse jokes, for rowdy, obstreperous bawdy, and for heavily facetious puns did not prevent him from being on occasions genuinely funny. 'He was very witty,' said Sir Anthony Weldon who cannot be accused of the least prejudice in his favour, 'and had as many jests as any man living, at which he would not smile himself, but deliver them in a grave and serious manner.' Nor did his inherent laziness prevent him from settling down to work when he had to with a will to get it done quickly and well: he boasted that he could do a whole day's business in an hour or two, and his ability to make up his canny mind with speed and decision could not but recommend itself to men who had had to contend with the old Queen's wearisome prevarications, hesitations and evasions. Above all, the King's healthy Danish wife, Anne, had borne him heirs which secured the succession and which neither Elizabeth, nor either of Henry VIII's two other children, had been able to provide.

Queen Anne had been born in 1574, the youngest daughter of King Frederick II of Denmark and Norway and of his German-born

Queen, Sophia. Lively, handsome, cheerful and well made, she had been married to James by proxy when she was fourteen. She sailed for Scotland soon after her marriage, but a violent storm – for which several Scottish and Scandinavian witches were not merely blamed but burned to death – forced her ship back across the North sea and into a Norwegian harbour. So James, impatient to be with her, set off for Norway himself and married his blonde, slim and shapely bride at Oslo on 23 November. After touring Denmark they sailed together for Scotland early the next year. This time, also, there was a fearful storm and James, whose fear of witches was intense, had no doubt that they were to blame once again. He was there and then inspired to demonstrate their danger and reality in a book which he later published under the title, *Daemonologie*.

Anne did not share his obsession. Nor did she settle down happily in the dour, forbidding atmosphere of Scottish Calvinism, far more repressive than the undemanding Lutheranism of the Danish Court and – to a high-spirited, pleasure-loving fifteen-year-old girl – far more provocative. She soon found herself roundly condemned for her Roman Catholic leanings, her extravagance and profligacy, her 'night waking and balling'.

When her first son, Henry, was born in 1594, it was as much because of her irresponsible way of life and her suspect religion as because James wanted to get the boy as far as possible away from the rough, unscrupulous nobles of the Scottish Court, that the Prince was entrusted to the care of the Earl and Countess of Mar at Stirling Castle. Anne was furiously indignant; but James would not give way. When the boy was five, his father repeated his determination in writing: in the event of King James's death, Prince Henry was not to be handed over to the care of his mother until he had passed his eighteenth birthday. He was nine when his father set off for England to claim his new kingdom. His mother, who was left behind, renewed her claim to have her son come to live with her. But no, the Countess of Mar flatly refused to consider such a thing; his Majesty would never allow it. The Queen, who was pregnant again, became so angry and distraught that she had a miscarriage and almost died.

No one who knew the boy was surprised that the Queen was so dismayed not to be allowed to have him with her or that the Countess of Mar was so reluctant to let him go. He was good-looking, athletic, intelligent and charming, while her younger son, Charles, was a poor little sickly thing who was not expected to live long.

Charles was born on 19 November 1600 at Dunfermline Palace, twelve miles outside Edinburgh, in a bedroom overshadowed by the great stone tower of Dunfermline Abbey. When his father became King of England he was still there; and when his mother, his brother and elder sister Elizabeth all moved south across the border, never to return, Charles stayed behind, in the care of nurses, servants and guards, at Dunfermline. He was three years old then; yet he had not the strength to walk and he could not speak.

In April 1604 a doctor and an apothecary came up from London to examine the child, to determine whether or not he was capable of withstanding the strain of the journey south. They decided that he might be moved when the warmer weather came; so in July, by easy stages, he was brought down in a curtained litter to England. His parents went up to meet him at Northampton.

His immediate future had already been decided: he was to be placed in the care of Sir Robert Carey's wife, a kind and under-standing, yet practical and resourceful Cornish woman who could be trusted to do all that anyone could to ensure that the pale, pathetic creature survived and gathered the strength to walk and the ability to talk. Perhaps, his father suggested, the boy might walk if his weak legs and ankles were placed in irons; perhaps he might talk if a surgeon were to cut the ligament at the base of his tongue. No, said Lady Carey, such drastic measures would do more harm than good. If he were left alone to her capable care, living in the country away from the flurry of the Court, nature and love would do their work. Lady Carey was trusted and allowed to have her way. Her husband, rewarded now for his arduous ride to Holyrood, was given the control of the Prince's Household and a generous salary to maintain it and his own family in comfort.

Once, a few days after his fifth birthday, in a dazzling suit and gleaming with jewels, Prince Charles was taken to Court, carried by lords and attendants into the Palace of Whitehall. Here he was created Duke of York, and at a great feast in the banqueting hall he sat at the head of a special table in his high chair. But for the rest of these days of early childhood he led a quiet country life, moving from one of the royal palaces to another, in the care of the Careys and his tutors; trying to walk without fear of falling down, to speak without fear that the sounds he made would be misunderstood, to learn well his lessons and how to behave as befitted the brother of that glowingly vital Henry, Prince of Wales.

Charles did not appear to be in the least jealous of Henry. Indeed, the older he grew the more devoted to his brilliant brother he seemed to become. 'Sweet, sweet brother,' he wrote to him in his first letter, 'I will give anything that I have to you: both my horse and my books and my pieces and my cross-bows or anything that you would have. Good brother, love me and I shall ever love and serve you.' No doubt the letter was written under the eyes of a tutor and with more than assurances of affection in mind, but the sentiment behind it was unfeigned. Nothing would make him more happy, he wrote in another letter, than that Henry should come for another visit, 'for to enjoy your company, to ride with you, to hunt with you,' Charles went on, 'will give me the greatest of pleasure'.

The letter was written in Latin; its author was eight. By then, under his sensible governess's care, he had improved beyond all recognition both in health and liveliness. He was still very pale and very small for his age, but he could walk with perfect steadiness now, and his speech – Scottish in accent like his father's though not so strongly so – was less impeded by his stammer. His tutor, Thomas Murray, a Scottish Presbyterian, found his charge an easy and conscientious pupil. His Latin and Greek were satisfactory; he spoke French, Italian and some Spanish; he mastered mathematics; enjoyed music, both practice and theory; showed a precocious appreciation of painting and a more than dutiful interest in theology. He would never, it was clear, be as clever as his father was; but already he gave signs of becoming more intellectual than most royal princes ever had been, or ever were to be.

Despite his small size he was also demonstrating some ability as a sportsman. The decision to become one was as much his as anyone else's. He practised hard and long; and in the end he could not only ride with all his father's nerve and with none of his clumsiness, but could even take part in jousts without appearing ridiculous. He was an excellent shot; at the age of ten he began to learn tennis; and he proved his fondness for all things Scottish by taking up golf, a game, curious English observers decided, which was not unlike pall-mall, consisting in the wielding of a crooked club (its curved end strengthened with horn and lead) to drive a little ball (of hard leather stuffed with feathers) into certain holes made in the ground.

It required a good deal of skill and strength to hit the ball high, far and straight, and Charles spent long hours in practising: it was a game his brother much enjoyed.

There was still no open rivalry between the two boys. Charles had no hope of reaching Henry's high standard; merely he strove to make himself worthy of being considered good enough to play with his brother, so strong and so very much taller than himself. Yet on occasions there were hints of a more troubled relationship that later adolescence might exacerbate. Once, for example, the two princes were together in a room next door to which their father was consulting the Archbishop of Canterbury. His Grace's hat lay on a table. Henry picked it up and, teasing him for his learning and virtuous earnestness, placed it on his brother's head with the promise that when he was king he would make Charles an archbishop; Charles, humiliated by the joke, tore it off, threw it to the ground and furiously trampled it underfoot, 'not without much difficulty and some force being taken off from that eagerness'.

Henry, though, was not to be king. In the autumn of 1612 he fell ill with a mysterious fever. He had not been feeling well for some days; but he had refused to go to bed, believing that the best cure for most complaints was violent exercise. He insisted on playing tennis, did not trouble to wrap himself up well after the game, caught a chill and collapsed. The doctors disagreed in their diagnoses of his complaint – it was probably the then unknown disease, porphyria – and they prescribed a variety of contradictory cures and remedies, at one moment bleeding him, at another applying a pigeon to his head, then placing a cock, split down the back, against his feet to draw down the evil humours from his brain. Sir Walter Raleigh – whose continued imprisonment in the Tower of London had once caused the Prince to express his astonishment that his father could keep so beautiful a bird in such a cage – sent him a phial of medicine which, after being tested, he was allowed to take by permission of the Privy Council. It did him a little temporary good. But the days passed and the boy's condition deteriorated; his headaches and the buzzing in his ears grew worse; he fell into delirium and then into convulsive ravings. His father came to see him, but the doctors would not let him into the room; the Prince called out for his sister, Elizabeth, who, knowing that visits from members of the family had been proscribed, came disguised as a country girl, but she was recognised and turned away. On 6

November Prince Henry died in a coma. He was eighteen.

Within a few months of this tragedy, Charles had to face another. Princess Elizabeth, by now a beautiful, affectionate girl of eighteen to whom he was deeply attached, was taken away from him. Her suitors had already included the Dauphin, the Prince of Orange, Gustavus Adolphus and the King of Spain; but it was in order to strengthen the alliance with the Protestant powers in Germany that she was eventually betrothed at Whitehall Palace – wearing black satin in mourning for her brother, silver lace and a plume of white feathers in honour of her future husband – to Frederick, the Elector Palatine, one of the leading Protestant princes. She was married in February and sailed for Heidelberg. Charles never saw her again.

He was alone now, the King's only surviving son, England's only royal child. His mother had had other children, but they had all died; and Charles, twelve years old at the time of his sister's marriage, turned ever more deeply in upon himself. He had been considered old enough the year before to leave the comforting care of Lady Carey and to pass into a harsher, male environment. Of those he had known in happier days few other than his tutor, Murray, now remained. His shyness, detachment and grave reserve became more noticeable and deeply marked; his replies to questions increasingly delayed and hesitant, whether from shyness or sluggishness of thought it was difficult to say; when addressed by strangers he would often blush and drop his heavy-lidded eyes; only rarely did his quiet docility break forth into a sudden flash of anger to reveal a resentment and determined will which for the rest of the time lay hidden. Yet there *was* determination and a kind of mournful courage behind that façade of innocence, that trembling insecurity. He tried, by talking to himself with his mouth full of pebbles, to cure his stammer, and when that proved ineffective he tried to form each sentence in his mind before attempting to utter it; he concentrated on his lessons to make himself a better scholar than Henry would ever have become; he forced himself to be almost as good a rider as Henry had ever been. Every morning from St James's Palace he went out running in the park.

In November 1616, just before his sixteenth birthday, he was created Prince of Wales, coming up by river from Richmond for the ceremony, attended by the Lord Mayor and all the City companies in their barges 'in very good order which made a goodly show'. Thereafter his appearances at Court became more regular. But they were a duty, not a pleasure; for the life that was led there was not in the least to his taste.

2

The Prince and The Courtiers
1617–22

SIR John Harington, once one of Prince Henry's tutors, described
a characteristic evening at King James's Court on the occasion of
a visit by Queen Anne's brother, the pleasure-loving King Christian
IV of Denmark. The scene was Theobalds, Lord Salisbury's house
near Cheshunt in Hertfordshire, which was later acquired by King
James, who liked the hunting there, in exchange for Hatfield.

After dinner the ladies and gentlemen of the Court enacted for
the royal guest the Queen of Sheba's coming to Solomon's Temple.
The lady who took the part of the Queen of Sheba was, however,
too drunk to keep her balance on the steps and fell over onto King
Christian's lap covering him with 'wine, cream, jelly, beverages,
cakes, spices and other good matters' which she was carrying in her
hands. The King, even more drunk than Sheba, struggled to his
feet, took her round the waist and would have danced away with
her had he not collapsed to the floor and been carried off to recover
on a bed of state in an inner chamber. The performance continued,
but the players stumbled and fell about to such an extent that it was
impossible to discover what they were endeavouring to represent.
Three ladies, gorgeously dressed as Hope, Faith and Charity, made
a brief appearance but then promptly withdrew. Hope returned,
tried to speak, failed, and staggered out of the room again. Faith
was no more successful. Charity did manage to kneel down in
front of King James at her second attempt and to mumble a few
words before following her companions down into the lower hall
where they were both being sick. Victory 'after much lamentable
utterance' was 'led away like a silly captive, and laid to sleep in the
outer steps of the ante chamber'. Peace, boisterous and argumenta-
tive, endeavoured to take her place and 'most rudely made war with
her olive branches' on those, less drunk than she was, who interfered
with her progress.

At Christmas, a few years before, Sir Dudley Carleton had been
shocked by similar revels, by the King and Queen and some of the
noblest of their courtiers painting themselves black to play the part

of Ethiopians, and by ladies whose dresses were as inordinately expensive as they were indecently revealing. The Queen's passion for dressing up and her wild extravagance were at least partly to blame, such critics as Carleton contended, for the sad contrast between the English Court and the ideal decorousness propounded in Castiglione's *Book of the Courtier*. A Court entertainment might well cost as much as ten thousand pounds to produce; the Queen might well appear in it, expensively and provocatively dressed and covered in precious stones worth a hundred thousand pounds. Her allowances were considerable yet her debts ever increased and her appetite for jewelry was insatiable. Between her confinements, her life was one long 'continued maskarado'.

But, apart from suggesting that she ought to make do with the two thousand outmoded dresses which had been discovered in his predecessor's wardrobes, the King appeared to do nothing to check his wife's wanton extravagance. Indeed, he was quite as improvident himself. He bought jewels and plate indiscriminately and, as indiscriminately, gave them away, bestowing gifts upon those whose affection he craved with such abandonment to the pleasures of generosity that Sir Dudley Carleton calculated he made presents of more plate in a single year than Queen Elizabeth had done in her entire reign. One day he made out an order for £20,000 for one of his numerous Scottish courtiers; another time, while walking down a corridor, leaning on the shoulder of one of the forty-eight Gentlemen of the Bedchamber, he passed some servants carrying three thousand pounds' worth of gold, and when his companion remarked that he wished he had as much as that to spend, James ordered the servants to take the gold to the Gentleman's lodgings.

His attentions to handsome young Gentlemen like this were not limited to sudden bursts of generosity. He patted their cheeks, petted and fondled them in public as though they were lapdogs, seemingly unconscious of the distaste he aroused by his almost abject devotion to their beauty. Although he rarely got drunk himself, preferring to sip throughout the day at sweet Greek wines and Scottish ale, he encouraged his young men to drink too much, just as he encouraged the young ladies of the Court to wear scanty clothes and to behave lasciviously. When drunk the men, vying for the King's attention, would parade about the Court, exceeding 'any part of woman kind', so one observer put it, 'with their

mincing gait and wanton gestures'. Practical jokes and horseplay
were also encouraged. The Earl of Pembroke disliked frogs, so the
King put one down his neck. The King disliked pigs, so Pembroke
put one in his bedroom. The 'master of the game for fooleries', Sir
George Goring, went even further than Pembroke by leading into
a party 'four brawny pigs, piping hot, bitted and harnessed with
ropes of sausages, all tied to a monstrous pudding'. While the
sausages were being thrown about the room, the Court fools and
dwarfs darted around charging from wall to wall on each other's
shoulders.

Conspicuous among the King's young friends on these occasions was
Robert Carr, who had come from Scotland as the King's page and
had been knighted in 1607 and created Viscount Rochester in 1611.
In 1613 Carr became the lover of the sultry, sensual and unbalanced
daughter of the Earl of Suffolk, Frances Howard, who had been
married at the age of thirteen to the Earl of Essex. The Countess,
with the help of her powerful family, managed to obtain an
annulment of her marriage to Essex who was alleged by his wife to
be impotent. She then married Carr who, two months later,
was created Earl of Somerset. Before the wedding, however, she
had arranged for the murder of her bridegroom's secretary, Thomas
Overbury, who had strongly opposed it and who knew so much
about her past life that he might well have been able to prevent it.
In 1616 the deathbed confessions of an apothecary's apprentice
forced the King to order an investigation into the circumstances of
the crime. Lady Somerset confessed, but her husband denied his
complicity and as he left to stand trial, the King, so Anthony
Weldon reported, 'hung about his neck, slabbering his cheeks,
saying, "For God's sake, when shall I see thee again? On my soul I
shall neither eat nor sleep until you come again . . . For God's sake
let me, shall I, shall I?" – then lolled about his neck. "Then, for
God's sake give thy lady this kiss for me", in the same manner at
the stair's head, at the middle of the stairs, and at the stair's foot.'
    Dismayed by scenes like these, disgusted by the continual
drunkenness of the Court and by his father's close involvement with
such recurrent scandals as the Overbury murder and Lady Roos's
well-publicised accusation that her husband was in the habit of
making incestuous love to his step-grandmother, the Prince of
Wales kept as far away from the Court as he reasonably could. He

made no open criticism, it seems, either then or later; but he cannot have been left unaffected, nor can he have been less than deeply embarrassed by his father's coarse and blasphemous jokes. Certainly the conversation of the courtiers made him blush and the behaviour of the Queen's ladies horrified his rigid sense of propriety. And when the place of the Earl of Somerset – condemned to death by his peers but reprieved by the King – was taken by the even more physically attractive George Villiers, Charles was lonelier than ever.

For Villiers, astonishingly good-looking, irresistibly charming and glowingly virile, seems to have taken as little notice of Charles as any one else in his father's Court. It was quite impossible, on the contrary, for anyone to overlook Villiers. He had first come to the King's notice at Sir Anthony Mildmay's country house at Apthorpe in Northamptonshire, a favourite haunt of the King whose devotion to hunting was almost obsessional. Villiers was the second son of an impoverished Leicestershire squire whose calculating and ambitious widow had spent much of her money on giving the boy a costly education which included a visit to France of three years' duration. He had returned with charming manners and faultless French, an expert swordsman, dancer and rider, a delightful conversationalist, graceful, poised and entertaining. He was tall and lithe with deep blue eyes and a beautifully shaped face framed by dark, smooth hair that fell in elegant curls onto his broad and exquisitely tailored shoulders.

James was immediately captivated. Deciding that the boy bore a strong resemblance to St Stephen, whose angelic features were represented on a miniature in the royal collection, he gave him the Scottish nickname, Steenie; and soon the King's 'kinde dogge Steenie' and Villiers's 'dear dad and gossip' were inseparable. Villiers's rise to fortune and rank was swifter than even Somerset's had been. In 1614 he was appointed Cupbearer, in 1615 Gentleman of the Bedchamber with a grant of a thousand pounds a year, the next January he became Master of the Horse, the following May, at the age of twenty-four, he was dubbed a Knight of the Garter, given land to support the dignity of such a title, and created Baron Whaddon and Viscount Villiers. In 1617 he was made Earl of Buckingham and a Privy Councillor, in 1619 Marquess of Buckingham. The rise to such heights of a man who five years before had been seen at a horse race in Cambridgeshire 'in an old black suit broken out in divers places' was astounding. Apart from Somerset,

29

who, before his disgrace, had threatened to break Buckingham's neck, everyone at Court seems to have been so overwhelmed by the young man's brilliance and charm that his sudden elevation was at first rather welcomed than deprecated. The Earls of Bedford, Pembroke, Hertford and Suffolk, and Lord Lisle all encouraged his advancement; the Archbishop of Canterbury had recommended his knighthood; even the Queen – grateful enough to be left behind at Denmark House in the Strand whenever Buckingham accompanied the King on one of his country progresses – fostered the relationship between her husband and his new friend. 'My Kind Dog,' she wrote to him, 'you do very well in lugging the sowe's [King's] eare, and I thank you for it, and would have you do so still, upon condition that you continue a watchful dog to him and be always true to him. So wishing you all happiness . . . '

There was one person, however, who stood stubbornly aside from this benevolence towards the rising star; and that was Prince Charles. At the time of Buckingham's elevation to a marquessate, Charles was nineteen, and had stopped growing. He was only about 5 ft 4 in tall, and although by dint of continual exercise he had managed to overcome the weakness in his legs, they were still slightly bowed. There was nothing undignified about him as there was about his father, but he did not possess Buckingham's commanding presence. His forehead was high, his light brown hair long and full, falling in a thick cluster onto the back of his wide, lace ruff, his slightly prominent eyes looked sad, dispirited and remote, his hands were small and delicate. Desperately he needed love and admiration, and Buckingham seemed the last person likely to accord him either. Sometimes, as though determined at least to be noticed, he would turn on Buckingham in a kind of petulant resentment. Once he twisted the angle of a water spout so that it played on the favourite's splendidly clothed back; on another occasion he quarrelled with him on the tennis court and they almost came to blows.

But so susceptible a nature as Charles's could not for ever resist Buckingham's disarming personality. Soon it was noticed at Court that the friction between the two men was no longer apparent, that they were often to be found in each other's company, and that a friendship was forming between 'Sweet Steenie' and 'Baby Charles' which promised to be as emotionally intense, if not as sensually provoked, as that between Buckingham and the King.

The Queen's death at Hampton Court in March 1619 strengthened the newly formed friendship. For whatever their relationship may have been in Charles's early adolescence – nothing is known of it – the Prince and his mother seemed to have been close to each other during the last years of her life when failing health induced by dropsical swellings prevented her spending so much time and energy on the frivolities of Court life. He was with her when she died and was deeply affected. Steenie's warm sympathy was a comfort and a strengthening bond.

The increasing affection of Charles for Buckingham was not, however, universally shared, either at Court or in the country at large. The richer and more powerful the favourite became, the more jealousy he aroused; the greater his patronage, the more enemies he was bound to make; the more besotted by him the King became, the more the Council began to fear the power of his influence. After the marriage of Buckingham's abysmally stupid brother, John, to the intelligent daughter of Sir Edward Coke, the King, who had given the unwilling bride away, confessed in a speech that he loved Buckingham 'more than anyone else' and more, he added, 'than you who are here assembled. I wish to speak on my own behalf, and not to have it thought to be a defect, for Jesus Christ did the same and therefore I cannot be blamed. Christ had his John and I have my George'.

By now the way to most offices of importance or high remuneration lay through Buckingham's favour, and the enmity which his growing power naturally aroused grew to a new height when, though already Master of the Horse, he was given the additional appointment of Lord High Admiral, in place of the old Earl of Nottingham whose profitable office was bought from him for three thousand pounds and a pension for life of a thousand a year. Then, when the Queen's death brought jewels and plate worth nearly half a million pounds into the King's possession, he bestowed a large part of them on Buckingham, together with more land and the Keepership of Denmark House.

It was not that Buckingham was considered incompetent either as a businessman and estate owner or as a servant of the Crown; the main burden of the complaints about him was that his collection of so many offices made it quite impossible for him to give to any one of them his proper attention. What time he could give to the direction of the Navy Commissioners, for instance, was well enough spent, but he had no sooner scratched the surface of the Navy's problems than he was off again to undertake some other enterprise. Also, those appointed to positions by him or on his recommendation were denied the exercise of any independent judgement. Often, indeed, they were incapable of exercising it, for they were, as often as not, men of little or no talent who happened to have married into his big family or who had won his affection by flattery. He wanted his own way and if he did not get it he arose in indignant fury against those who had thwarted him. He was a genuinely good-natured man and always remained so; but his power, though it never corrupted his unfeigned kindness and generosity, brought out all that was most vain and arrogant in his character.

Yet neither his growing unpopularity nor his marriage in May 1620 in any way affected Prince Charles's devotion to him. His bride, Lady Katherine Manners, being the only child of the Earl of Rutland, was able to bring to him a considerable dowry extricated from Rutland by Buckingham's greedy and extortionate mother. But Buckingham married her because he loved her rather than because she was rich; and she, deeply in love with him, agreed to the King's demand that before the wedding took place she should abandon the Roman Catholic Church and publicly conform to the rites of the Church of England. She made Buckingham an excellent wife, and although he was soon 'winking and smiling at comely and beautiful young women', she remained devoted to him to the end, as he did to her. 'There never was a woman loved a man as I do you,' she told him, and when he was away from her she kept the portrait of her 'sweet saint' always by her bed. The King as constantly wore his 'Steenie's picture in a blue ribbon' under his waistcoat next to his heart. Charles's devotion to Buckingham was quite as great as theirs.

The Early Years:
Prince and Bridegroom

James I (1566–1625). A portrait by the Flemish artist, Daniel Mytens, Court Painter to the King, done when James was fifty-five.

Anne of Denmark (1574–1619), Queen of James I, mother of Charles I and daughter of Frederick II of Denmark and Norway. A portrait, painted in 1617, from the studio of Van Somer.

(*opposite*) Elizabeth of Bohemia (1596–1662) by the Dutch artist Gerard van Honthorst. Elizabeth was Charles I's only surviving sister. She married the Elector Palatine in 1613 and her brother never saw her again.

Henry, Prince of Wales (1594–1612), elder son of James I. A portrait attributed to Robert Peake, done two years before the Prince died, aged eighteen.

of Bohemia.

Hampton Court Palace in the seventeenth century by Henry Danckerts.
It was one of Charles I's favourite palaces.

Interior of the Queen's House at Greenwich.
Charles I spent a considerable part of his childhood here.

Richmond Palace. An engraving by Michael van der Gucht. It was settled on Prince Henry by James I, after whose death Charles spent much of his youth here and later added to it the 2,250 acres of the deer park.

A chimney piece designed by Inigo Jones in 1636 for Oatlands, Surrey. Acquired and rebuilt by Henry VIII, Oatlands was renovated by Inigo Jones and became a favoured residence of both Anne of Denmark and Henrietta Maria. It was to a great extent destroyed in the Civil War.

George Villiers, Ist Duke of
Buckingham (1592–1628), the
adored favourite of Charles and
his father, by an unknown artist.

Charles I as Prince of Wales, from the
engraving by Elstracke in Taylor's *Brief
Remembrance of All the English Monarchs*.

Charles I when Prince of Wales by Daniel Mytens.

Armour made for the young
Charles I now in the
Tower of London.

James I and Charles, Prince of Wales since 1616, feasting with envoys from Spain during the negotiations for Charles's marriage to the sister of the King of Spain in November 1622.

The Infanta Donna Maria (1606–46), daughter of Philip III of Spain, and sister of Philip IV, by Balthazar Gerbier.

Spanien geſcheben.

Konigs Pallaſt

Der Statt Steep terdrager
Halfreich- ten
Capitan der Teutsche
Ihrer Majeſtet Steep terdrager
Der Spaniſche Lebt Guardi Leut tenant

Groſe Herrn van Spamen oder Titulati.
Der Printz von Gualles
Ihr Kongl: M: in Hiſpanien
Graff von Olivares Admiral zu Eugell
Extraordinari Abgeſandten.

Der Statt Madrill Obrigkeit ſo den hinmel dragen.

The ceremonial entry of Prince
Charles into Madrid in March 1623.
He proceeded to the Palacio Real under
a canopy carried over his head by
attendants dressed in cloth of gold.

Prince Charles welcomed home
from Spain by his father after the
breakdown of the marriage
negotiations in Madrid.

The
High and mighty
and most vertuous
Princesse MARY Queene
of Great Brittaine
France and Ireland

The Daughter, Wife, and Sister to a King:
Greatnesse and Goodnesse from thy Grace doth spring

Henry Rich Earl of
Holland

Henrietta Maria, like her husband,
was a skilful rider.

(*above right*) Henry Rich, 1st Earl of
Holland (1590–1649), from the studio
of Daniel Mytens. Lord Holland, at that
time Lord Kensington, was England's
'wooing Ambassador' in the negotiations
for Charles's marriage to Henrietta Maria.

(*right*) Anne, the eldest sister of the
Infanta Donna Maria and the neglected
wife of Louis XIII of France (1601–66).
The Duke of Buckingham's advances to
her created a scandal at the French court.

(*opposite*) Henrietta Maria (1609–69), by
Gerard van Honthorst. The daughter of
Henri IV of France and Marie de'
Medici. she was married to Charles by
proxy at Notre Dame on May Day 1625.

An etching by James Basire of
Cheapside in the City of London on
the occasion of the visit to England
of Marie de' Medici, the Queen's
mother, in the autumn of 1638.

(*left*) Marie de' Medici (1573–1642),
daughter of Francis de' Medici,
Grand Duke of Tuscany, second
wife of Henri IV of France, and
mother of Louis XIII and of Henrietta
Maria. Depicted by Rubens on her
landing at Marseilles shortly after
her marriage to Henri IV by proxy
in Florence in October 1600.

(*opposite*) The reverse side of the
medal celebrating Charles I's return
from Scotland in 1633, showing
the City of London.

A medal struck in commemoration of Charles I's Scottish coronation, 1633.

The gold ampulla used at Charles's coronation at Edinburgh where the ceremony gave offence to the Presbyterians.

An etching of
New Palace
Yard with
Westminster
Hall and the
Clock House
by Wenceslaus
Hollar, who
was brought
to England
from Bohemia
in 1637 by the
Earl of
Arundel.

Castrum Royale Londinense, vulgo the TOWER

The Tower of
London by
Hollar.

Old London
Bridge by
Claude de
Jongh. One of
the most cele-
brated sights in
Europe.

Hollar's etching of Westminster, with Parliament House, Westminster Hall and the Abbey.

Another view of Westminster by Hollar, showing the Palace, Hall and Abbey.

Greate Brittaynes hope, and Joy of this ower land
It is heauen on earth, heere holdeth in his hand
Which sweete coniunction, of two mightie powers
Presageth both of peace, and plenty showers
To this oure blessed Iland to oure foes
Warr famin ruin and there ower throws

Lee heere, doth stand, the glory of her sex:
Vntz. whose beauty, vertue grace doth nex:
Whose haert, as well as hand, to him she giues
In, whom the halfe part, of her soule heere liues
Long: may thy happy liue, and when they dye
Yet liue, agayne, with god, eternally

Charles I and his Queen from an engraving illustrative of the happiness of their
marriage after the Duke of Buckingham's death.

3

Sweet Boys and Ventrous Knights
1623

THE harmony that existed between the royal family and
Buckingham was in no sense reflected in the monarchy's
relationship with the country gentry, professional men, merchants
and well-to-do yeomen who constituted the House of Commons.
In 1614 James had dissolved a difficult Parliament remarking in
private that he was surprised that his 'ancestors should have permitted such an institution to come into existence'. He could not
govern indefinitely without Parliament, however, for he needed the
money that only Parliament could provide. He needed it particularly
after the outbreak of the Thirty Years War between Protestants
and Catholics in Germany was followed by the rash acceptance by
his son-in-law, the Elector Palatine, of the throne of predominantly
Protestant Bohemia. The Elector Palatine had accepted the throne
in defiance of the wishes of the Austrian Habsburg Emperor whose
Catholic deputy governors in Prague had recently been attacked in
the Hradshin palace by Protestant rebels who threw them out of the
windows onto a dunghill in the palace moat. Catholic armies from
Spain and Austria at once combined to drive the Elector from
Bohemia, forced him and his wife, the Protestant heroine, Elizabeth,
into exile in Holland, and occupied the Palatinate.

Immediately there were demonstrations in England in support
of the popular Elizabeth, 'The Queen of Hearts', so recently an
English princess. Crowds demanded action against the Catholic
coalition which had overrun her country; and Parliament – when
it was summoned again in January 1621 to provide funds for the
Government's foreign policy – advocated a declaration of war on
Spain.

James had for some time, however, been pursuing a quite
contrary policy. He had made peace with Spain soon after coming
to the throne, and more recently, tempted by the possibility of a
large dowry and a profitable alliance with what was still considered
the most powerful state in the world, he had been trying to bring
about a marriage between Prince Charles and the Infanta Donna

c

Maria, sister of King Philip IV. Such an alliance, urged on him by Roman Catholic members of the Howard family and by the wily Spanish envoy, the Count of Gondomar, would, he hoped, result in the Spanish Habsburgs abandoning their support of the Austrian branch of the family and allowing the restoration of his daughter and son-in-law, if not to the throne of Bohemia, at least to their palace in Heidelberg. The Commons would have none of this: they wanted a Protestant alliance not a Catholic one, an offensive against Spain and an immediate end to the marriage negotiations.

Once again the King had come into direct conflict with Parliament. James refused to admit that the Commons had a right to question his policy, to interfere with his inherited prerogative powers. Their privileges depended upon *him*, he wrote to the Speaker, denying that they had any business meddling with matters of state; and when they entered in their journal a protestation that their privileges did not depend upon the King but were the 'ancient and undoubted birthright of the subjects of England', he dissolved Parliament, tore the protestation from the book with his own hand, and ordered the arrest of those Members whom he took to be the trouble-makers.

The marriage negotiations then proceeded, the Spaniards believing that they would lead to the return of England to Roman Catholicism, James and the Earl of Bristol, his ambassador extraordinary in Madrid, hoping that they would result in Spain's support of his son-in-law's return to the Palatinate. The difficulties in the way of the match were so considerable as to appear at times insuperable. Not only did the still continuing war against the German Protestants inflame the passions of English opinion, but when the beleaguered Heidelberg fell to the troops of Count Tilly the demand for war against Spain grew to such a pitch that Prince Charles himself begged the King to let him lead an army in defence of his sister's religion and rights.

The poor Infanta, moreover, was aghast at the thought of marrying a Protestant; reserved and devout she would far rather, she protested, go into a monastery. Eventually she was unwillingly persuaded that to help in bringing a husband and a country back into the true faith was a mission worthy of a saint; while Charles, for his part, though at first he could not bring himself to face marriage to this girl with her pale skin, reddish hair, pouting lower lip and heavy jaw, was brought to the belief that his sister's cause, his father's wishes and his country's future must come before his personal distaste. Then suddenly his resigned acceptance of his duty was transformed into a burning eagerness: an idea, first planted in Buckingham's mind by Gondomar, had fired the impressionable Prince's romantic fancy, and he became so anxious to marry the Infanta that it seemed almost as though he had fallen in love.

The idea, daring and quixotic, was that he and Buckingham with but two companions should secretly travel to Madrid in disguise and there win the Infanta's heart and hand and with them the Spanish alliance. Exciting and ingenious as the plan seemed to Charles and Buckingham, it could scarcely be expected to recommend itself to the more cautious and sensible mind of the King; and, of course, it did not. But the two young men waited until James was in a good temper, then Charles, falling on his knees before him while Buckingham stood to one side, begged for his permission to set out upon their venture. Before his son's pleadings and dear Steenie's arguments, James's resistance collapsed. He had always found it difficult to deny these boys anything they wanted; and he could not deny them this. He gave his permission.

As soon as they had gone, however, his better judgement warned him of the danger and folly of such an enterprise. Later when they returned to make more detailed arrangements he broke down and wept, telling them that if they 'pursued their resolution' he was 'undone and it would break his heart'. He warned them that once they had arrived in Spain every pressure would be exerted upon them and upon himself to make promises about Roman Catholic relief to which Parliament would never agree, that Buckingham would raise against himself a torrent of abuse from which it would be impossible to protect him. Yet no advice, no warnings, no pleas could lessen their determination to carry out their plan; and by alternatively cajoling, bullying and flattering the poor, ageing man they forced him tearfully to give way.

It was settled that their two companions should be Sir Francis Cottington, who had been English agent at the Spanish Court and consul at Seville, and Endymion Porter, a Groom of the Prince's Bedchamber, who had relatives in Spain and had been brought up there as page in the household of the Count of Olivarez, the King of Spain's favourite and chief minister. The plan was that the Prince and Buckingham would say goodbye to the King in front of witnesses at Theobalds, that the King would say 'See that you be with me on Friday night', and that Buckingham would reply, 'Sir, if we should stay a day or two later, I hope your Majesty would pardon us'. They would then set out for Buckingham's house at Newhall, finding excuses on the way to get rid of all their various companions except one trusted attendant, Sir Richard Graham; and early in the morning of Tuesday 18 February 1623, in the characters of two unremarkable brothers, Thomas and John Smith, their faces disguised with false beards and concealed by big hoods, they would ride down to Dover where Cottington and Porter would be waiting to meet them.

All this they managed to do without being detected, though when crossing the river at Gravesend they had to give the ferryman a twenty-two shilling piece, having forgotten to supply themselves with any small change, and the ferryman – his suspicions aroused by this and by the theatrically mysterious appearance of the gentlemen who, with pistols in their belts, looked to him as though they were off to fight a duel – gave warning to the authorities in Gravesend. They managed to evade arrest there, but they were stopped at Canterbury as they were changing horses at the posthouse. This time they had been seen in the fields outside Rochester, leaping across ditches and hedges beside the Dover road in their efforts to avoid the suite of the Spanish Ambassador who, by a strange unfortunate chance, had recently landed and was making his way to London. The Mayor of Canterbury questioned them, and Buckingham, giving away part of the secret so as to conceal the whole truth, tore off his beard, confessed his identity, and told the Mayor that he was going to the coast to make an unexpected inspection of the Channel fleet. Pointing to Prince Charles and Sir Richard Graham, he explained that his two companions were secretaries from the Lord High Admiral's office. Released with apologies by the Mayor they rode on without further mishap to Dover where Cottington and Porter were waiting for them as arranged.

They set sail at six the next morning and after a rough crossing of eight hours, during which the Prince was very seasick, they landed at Boulogne in the early afternoon. They were in Paris two days later; and it was from here on Saturday, 22 February, that the 'obedient son and servant, Charles' and the 'humble slave and dog, Steenie' wrote to their 'dear dad and gossip' to recount their adventures: how they had ridden post through Breteuil and how, although Charles had fallen off his horse four times, he had arrived without hurt. 'Your son's horses stumble as fast as any man's,' the letter continued: 'but he is so much more stronger . . . than he was. He holds them up by main strength of mastery, and cries still on! on!! on!!! This day we went to a perriwig-maker, where we disguised ourselves so artificially that we adventured to see the King . . . I am sure now you fear we shall be discovered, but do not fright yourself; for I warrant you the contrary. And finding this might be done with safety, we had a great tickling to add it to the history of our adventures.'

They were not discovered. They managed to gain admittance to the Louvre and from a gallery saw not only the young Louis XIII but also his mother Queen Marie de'Medici whose husband, Henri IV, had been stabbed to death in his coach in the Rue de la Ferronerie thirteen years before. That evening they went from their lodgings in the Rue St Jacques to Court and saw the young Queen – daughter of Philip III of Spain and sister of the Infanta Donna Maria – the Queen's brother-in-law, the Duke of Orleans, and her sister-in-law, Henrietta Maria, rehearsing a masque. There were 'nineteen fair dancing ladies' attending them but the Queen was 'the handsomest' which 'wrought' in Charles 'a greater desire to see her sister'.

They left before dawn next morning in quest of her, riding fast for Bordeaux and then on to Bayonne which they reached on 28 February. Just beyond Bayonne they met an English courier returning to London with despatches from the Earl of Bristol. They stopped him and, as Charles confessed to his father, 'saucily opened' his letters which were, annoyingly, for the most part, in code. The courier noticed, and reported later in London, that the Marquess of Buckingham looked very tired after his long ride, but that the Prince of Wales was in the best of spirits.

It was certainly true. Charles was obviously happy, perhaps for the first time in his life. What he had been able to read of Bristol's letters had not been in the least encouraging, but he remained as cheerful as ever after seeing them. It being Lent when they rode through Guienne and Gascony, no meat was to be had at any of the inns, and Charles and his companions had paid a *chevrier* for one of his goats which Charles, in great good humour, watched

Buckingham, Porter and Cottington chasing all over the country-side until the Prince brought it to earth by a well-aimed shot through the head. Now when they rode down past Guethary and crossed the Bidassoa river into Spain, Charles actually danced with happiness. He arrived in Madrid full of hope and excitement on the evening of 7 March.

Charles and Buckingham made straight for Bristol's house in a side street off the Calle de Alcala where Buckingham, introducing himself as Thomas Smith, asked permission to come inside with his brother John who was waiting on the other side of the street holding the horses. Bristol had already heard that the two men were on their way and so was not surprised when Thomas Smith threw back his all-concealing hood to reveal himself as the Marquess of Buckingham. Nor when Count Gondomar – who had now returned to Madrid from the Spanish Embassy in London – arrived at Bristol's house the following morning was he surprised to see the English Ambassador's two uninvited guests, for his ubiquitous spies had reported their presence within an hour of their arrival in the capital.

It was arranged that Buckingham should be introduced to the Count of Olivarez in the park that afternoon and then conducted by the Count to the royal palace to be presented to the King. Nothing was said, however, about a meeting between the Prince and the King's sister, the Infanta.

Buckingham brought up this delicate but vital matter later when Olivarez went back with him to Bristol's house to be presented to Prince Charles. It was a difficult time, Olivarez said, it was Lent and at that season the Infanta spent much of the day with her priest and confessor; but he would see what he could do.

The best that he could do for the time being turned out to be the arrangement of a kind of mutual inspection in the Prado where the royal family was in the habit of taking a ride most afternoons in an open coach. He hoped that the Prince would not be seen to be looking at her too intently, but the Infanta would be distinguished by a blue ribbon tied round her arm. Whether or not Charles did manage to get a good view of her on this occasion does not appear – he can scarcely have used the 'perspective glasses' with which the Marchioness of Buckingham had supplied him – but the Infanta, it seems, looked up at him and her pale skin flushed deeply. It was not until a month later, on 7 April, that he was permitted to see her face to face.

By then the private visit of the brothers Smith had turned into a brilliant state occasion conducted by the Spanish Court with exquisite courtesy, and witnessed by the people of Madrid in high excitement. The first interview between King Philip and the Prince of Wales had been distinguished throughout by its grace and tact; Olivarez was kind and complimentary, Gondomar helpful and hopeful, the King and his brothers polite and discreet. In honour of Charles a general pardon had been proclaimed and all Englishmen serving in the galleys had been released.

On 16 March Charles, accompanied by the King and a glittering procession of grandees, ministers, court officials and guards, made his ceremonial entry into a Madrid decorated in his honour. Under a canopy carried over his head by twenty-four attendants dressed in cloth of gold, he proceeded to the palace where the Queen was waiting to receive him. Holding hands with the King he walked into the state room and she came forward to meet them. Later in his private apartments he received a present from her of a golden bowl so heavy that it took two men to carry it into the room.

That night, and for three nights more, the streets were crowded with excited crowds watching the firework-displays and torchlight-processions, hurrying to the bull-ring to watch the special fights in honour of the Infanta and her English suitor, shouting '*Viva! Viva! Viva! el Principe de Galles*' and singing the song that Lope de Vega had written in honour of Carlos Estuardo whose love had drawn him to Maria, the star of the Spanish sky.

When he met her on 7 April, he was so excited that, forgetting or rejecting the formal speech that had been written for him, he blurted out his love for her in words that left the astonished Court aghast. The only person who remained unmoved by his outburst seems to have been the Infanta herself. She replied to him composedly, remembering her conventional text, and then turned away.

It was as though she already understood that her suitor's hopes would never be realised. For despite his obvious anxiety to marry her, despite the flattering attentions her family and the Court were paying to him, the likelihood of the marriage ever taking place seemed even more remote now than when the Prince had first arrived in Spain.

On 10 March the Prince and Buckingham had written home to King James to say that the Count of Olivarez was 'so overvaluing' of their journey, 'so full of real courtesy' that the 'kindest letter of thanks and acknowledgment' that the King could devise should be sent to him. Olivarez had even suggested, they went on, that if the Pope would not give his consent to the marriage the Spanish Government would give the Infanta to Charles 'as a wench'.

It was becoming ever clearer, though, that Charles would certainly not obtain Maria either as a wife or as a wench unless he were prepared to change his religion or at least, in his father's name, make more promises about Roman Catholics in England than had ever been suggested previously.

The morning after Charles's arrival, King Philip, remembering his own father's dying declaration that it had never been his intention to marry his daughter to the Prince of Wales, had sworn before a crucifix that he would not give way in the marriage negotiations on any religious matter, however small; and at first it had seemed that no religious concessions would be necessary. The Marquess of Buckingham, clearly a man not much concerned with the niceties of conscience or doctrine, had gone out of his way to demonstrate how pliable he was; he made a point of not attending the Protestant services in the British Embassy's chapel, and whenever he entered a Catholic church he behaved with the utmost reverence. Also, neither King Philip nor Olivarez could believe that the Prince had undertaken the journey without intending to become a Catholic at the end of it, nor that in acknowledgment of the favour bestowed upon him by their agreement to his marrying the Infanta, he would not also be prepared to grant more freedom to English Catholics. Surely he could not have expected to have the girl on any other terms? The only stumbling-block, as Philip and Olivarez saw it, was the Earl of Bristol. So Gondomar had been sent to Bristol's house to beg him not to interfere. But Bristol had never presumed to interfere; he was as much at a loss as the Spaniards to understand the Prince's motives in coming to Madrid, if he did not intend to make some important gesture. 'What might be the true motive and cause of your Highness's coming hither?' Bristol asked Charles one day, respectfully dropping to one knee in front of him.

'Why, my Lord, do you not know?'

'No, in truth nor cannot imagine. The match would have been no sufficient cause, for it might have been transacted in your

absence and much cost and labour have been spared. But although
I cannot imagine the cause myself, yet I will tell you what others
report – that your Highness hath intent to change your religion,
which if your Highness should do, I shall do my best endeavour that
things may be carried out in the discreetest manner.'

The Prince, evidently alarmed by the suggestion, hastily assured
Bristol that he had never had the slightest intention of doing such a
thing. It was a reply that would have relieved his father; for James
had been recently shocked to receive from Buckingham a suggestion
that the match might be speedily concluded if the King of England
would but 'acknowledge the Pope chief head under Christ'.

'I am sure ye would not have me renounce my religion for all the
world', James replied firmly and immediately. 'I am not a Monsieur
who can shift his religion as easily as he can shift his shirt when he
comes in from tennis.'

Already James was becoming frightened by the consequences of
the mad escapade to which he had given his reluctant consent. His
first thoughts after the departure of his 'sweet boys and dear
ventrous Knights' had been that they were 'worthy to be put in a
new Romanso'; but when rumours of their departure spread
throughout England and a number of Privy Councillors hastened to
Newmarket to beseech the King on their knees for an assurance that
the stories were not true, James became almost distracted by worry.
He had been ill for some time with chronic indigestion and torturing
pain in his leg, and this unnerving crisis agitated him beyond
measure, aggravating his complaints and driving him to seek the
refuge of his bed. Within a week of his boys' departure, he was
longing for their return. 'I must command you, my Baby,' he wrote
to his son in his first letter, 'to hasten Steenie home.' Within a few
days he was begging them again not to forget their 'olde Dad' in all
the excitement of their reception in Madrid, and urging them again
to make haste and come home. 'Alas, I now repent me sore that I
ever suffered you to go away,' he later lamented, as though there
were tears in his eyes as he wrote, 'I care for match nor nothing, so I
may once have you in my arms again; God grant it, God grant it!
Amen, amen, amen . . . God bless you both, my only sweet son and
my only best sweet servant and God send you a happy and joyful
meeting in the arms of your dear dad.'

His melancholy and anxiety were increased by the changing tone of Steenie's letters. In the beginning Steenie had assured him he was losing no time 'in hastening the conjunction' of the Infanta and Baby Charles, 'in which,' he added, 'I shall please him, her, you, and myself most of all, in thereby getting liberty to make the speedier haste to lay myself at your feet, for never none longed more to be in the arms of his mistress'. But as the weeks passed Buckingham's letters became more and more brusque. Finding that the jewels that had been sent out to him were outmatched and outshone by those that glittered on the sumptuous clothes and smooth brown skins of the Spaniards, Buckingham demanded more. Charles told his father that in Steenie's opinion the jewels that had arrived for presentation to the Infanta were 'not fit to be given to her'. Buckingham later warned that unless finer jewels arrived he would not send James any more animals for his menagerie – 'therefore look to it'.

'I your dog, says you have many jewels, neither fit for your son's nor your daughter's wearing, but, very fit to bestow on those who must necessarily have presents.' Also, he needed more jewels himself, otherwise James's 'Dog would want a collar'. 'So, craving your blessing,' ended a further letter, adding insult to importunity, 'I kiss your dirty hands.'

The jewels arrived, jewels for Steenie and Baby Charles and jewels for the Spanish Court, swords 'fully garnished with dyamondes of severall bignes', pearl necklaces and gold chains, jewelled rings, bracelets and hatbands, the Portugal Diamond and the Cobham Pearl. Charles and Buckingham adorned themselves with what they fancied and handed the rest over as presents.

So the charade went on, receptions, parades, banquets and entertainments providing an exotic and incongruous background to the negotiations which remained as far as ever from conclusion. At the end of April the Pope's dispensation arrived in Madrid but, as Buckingham himself said, it was 'clogged' with conditions. The Infanta must be allowed to supervise the education of all children of the marriage until they were twelve; and there must be liberty of conscience for all Roman Catholics in England. Buckingham began to realise now how unlikely it was his mission would succeed. He had long since stopped bothering to flash his charm upon the Spaniards who now condemned his easy affectation of their religious customs as revolting cynicism and who shuddered at the condescending familiarity with which he treated everyone around him, including the Prince of Wales himself. At the Prince's table, it was rumoured, he would slouch at his ease, 'in indecent manner without breeches, only in [his] nightgown; and in public places at the feasts stood with [his] back towards the Infanta'. He quarrelled openly with Olivarez and for two days refused to speak to him; more than once he lost control of his suddenly flaring temper, and so offended the grandees generally that one of them was heard to say that it would be better to drop the Infanta down a well than to let the English get their hands on her.

Prince Charles, nevertheless, continued to long for the day when he could get his hands on her. Frustrated and thwarted, he confessed to Buckingham that all the girls he had ever seen were 'as nothing to her', and swore that if he did not get her 'there shall be blows'. According to Olivarez he watched her as a cat watches a mouse; and an Englishman reported that he had seen the Prince staring at her for half an hour at a stretch, his eye 'unmovably fixed'. Not once had he been allowed to see her alone. He was always accompanied by Bristol as his interpreter; she was always surrounded by her family and ladies. Once, so it was later said, driven to desperation he climbed a high wall to jump down into an orchard near the Caso del Campo where she had repaired to gather flowers. He ran towards her; but she, with a terrified scream, fled away from him into the arms of her ladies.

Provoked, exasperated and over-wrought, and, at the same time, fearing the scorn he would arouse in England if he returned without her, Charles decided to try to win her by deceit. Making all sorts of promises about the future position of English Catholics to which Parliament, so he assured the Spanish Commissioners, could be persuaded to agree, he so convinced them of his determination to marry the Infanta that Olivarez raised his terms. It was now proposed that the bride should remain in Spain for a year after the wedding and that within this time all anti-Catholic laws must be suspended; the King, Prince and Council must solemnly swear never again to impose them, and Parliament must confirm its assent. Buckingham flew into a fresh rage at Olivarez after hearing these impossible proposals; and even Charles decided that no purpose could be served by his remaining any longer in Madrid. But soon, although Buckingham became more than ever anxious to go home, Charles changed his mind: he would stay and continue, by guile and promises, to win Maria on more promising terms.

While the hot summer weeks passed in agonisingly protracted and absurdly inconsequential negotiations, preparations to receive the Infanta in England continued unabated. Builders, decorators and furnishers were hard at work at St James's Palace making extensions, redecorating rooms, bringing in new hangings and furniture, finishing a chapel which the King's Surveyor, Inigo Jones, had designed for the Infanta's personal use; a large fleet – whose cost incessantly worried the King with fears that it would make him and his Baby 'bankrupt for ever' – lay at anchor at Dover waiting to sail for Spain under the command of Buckingham's father-in-law, the Earl of Rutland. Buckingham himself, as an ultimate reward for his services and in order to give him greater authority at the Spanish Court, was created Earl of Coventry and Duke of Buckingham, the first man outside the royal family to be made a duke since the Wars of the Roses. But then the King had long since grown accustomed to the fancy that Buckingham *was* a member of the royal family. He referred to him as his 'bastard brat' and to his baby, Mary Villiers, as his own dear 'grand-chylde', his darling Moll. He spent hours playing with her and talking to her mother, having his meals with them, taking as much interest in their personal affairs, in the weaning of the child and her four little pebbly teeth, as in affairs of state, deriving comfort from their presence, these living links with Steenie whose continuing absence was making his life a misery. The arrival of Steenie's letters caused them all the wildest excitement. His father-in-law recorded how the arrival of a messenger from Spain would so overjoy his family that they 'could eat no meat . . . forgot to eat' and 'sweet Moll, as she was undressing cried nothing but "Dad! Dad!"'

The object of this devotion was delighted with his new titles and wrote to tell his master that nothing he could ever do for him in future could possibly increase the love and duty which he bore him, and, at the same time, he assured him, 'I am confident you will never love none of your sevants (I will be saucy here) better than Steenie'. James confessed that this letter gave him the deepest pleasure, and when, soon afterwards, he heard that there had been a suggestion that his two 'sweet Boys' should stay another year in Madrid, he wrote, in an almost hysterical letter, the news 'hath strucken me dead. I fear it shall very much shorten my days . . . come speedily away . . . give over all treaty. And this I speak without respect of any security they can offer you, except ye never look to see your old Dad again.'

In his by now frantic anxiety to see them both back in England he was even prepared, against all his better judgement, to give way to the Spaniards on the religious issue. His son urged him to do so, or at least to pretend to do so; and he wrote to his father, pointing out with consummate disingenuousness that the oath to 'swear that Parliament shall revoke all the penal laws against the Papists in three years' need not necessarily be considered binding, because 'if you *think* you may do it in that time, if you do your best and it take not effect you have not broken your word'.

In Madrid Charles certainly seemed to be adopting this attitude to oaths and promises himself. On 7 July he told Philip that he was perfectly prepared to accede to the Spanish proposals; and although Olivarez doubted that Parliament would prove as amenable as the Prince of Wales suggested, it was agreed that the difficulties were now virtually resolved, and the marriage was spoken of as being settled.

Defying all the opposition in England, James formally accepted the Spanish terms at Whitehall Palace, and the Earl of Rutland was given orders to set sail at last. But then there were further delays: the Pope died, and the marriage could not proceed until the new Pope had given his approval to its conditions; then Philip objected to the departure of his sister for England before the spring; the inconvenient subject of Spanish support for the return of the Elector Frederick to the Palatinate was raised by the English side only to be hastily dismissed by the Spanish who showed how little intention they really had of offending the Austrian Emperor. Finally there was an embarrassing scene when a priest trying to enter the sick room of one of the Prince of Wales's Catholic servants to administer the sacrament found his path blocked by several of the Protestant attendants who – accompanied by the Court jester, Archie Armstrong – had now come out to Madrid to wait upon him. One of these attendants, Sir Edmund Verney, slapped the priest across the face. On the priest's complaint being heard at Court, Philip immediately ordered all the offending Protestants to leave Madrid. Charles apologised and dismissed Verney; but the Spaniards' honour was not satisfied: every one of them must go, if the Prince of Wales wanted to stay.

This scandal helped Charles to make up his mind that he did not want to stay. Up till then stubbornly refusing to believe that he could not gain this bride by idle promises, he now agreed with Buckingham that there was no purpose in remaining in Spain any longer. When the King and Prince said goodbye outside the Escurial on the last day of August the pretence that the negotiations had even then not broken down, that the Infanta would be sailing for England later was still maintained. Buckingham was more explicit. He angrily told Olivarez that he blamed him entirely for the outcome of the sad, undignified affair; and then he rode off towards Santander, profoundly relieved to be on his way home at last.

Charles caught up with him the next day and they were riding on together when a messenger galloped up to them from Santander to report that the Earl of Rutland's fleet was waiting for them in the bay. Buckingham was so exhilarated by the news that he threw his arms round the messenger's neck, kissed him, and presented him with a valuable diamond ring which he had excitedly drawn from his own finger.

4

The Husband and His Wife
1624–6

ON Sunday afternoon 15 October 1623 the Prince of Wales and the Duke of Buckingham landed at Portsmouth as happy to be home as the English people were to have them back. Rumours that the Prince had been doped and married to the Infanta during High Mass, that he had been forced by the Inquisition to embrace the Catholic faith, that he had been murdered by Spanish agents were all confounded. He was at home with Buckingham in England, and the Infanta was not with them. Their welcome was ecstatic. Church bells clanged, drums were beaten, organs played; tables were carried out of kitchen doors and piled high with food and barrels of wine and beer; bonfires were burned in the streets and the carts carrying loads of fuel to feed the flames were broken up and thrown on top of them. All the way from Portsmouth to Guildford, through London and along the road to Royston, crowds cheered the Prince and the Duke, his honest gallant saviour, England's hero.

At Royston King James anxiously awaited their arrival, looking out for them from an upper storey window, and, as soon as he caught sight of them, he hurried down the stairs as fast as his weak legs would take him. In the hall they sank to their knees before him, and he fell on their necks and, putting his arms around their shoulders, burst into tears.

The brief Spanish love affair was over. The honest Earl of Bristol, left behind in Madrid to sweep up the wreckage, might well protest that the Infanta could not but feel dishonoured now that he was instructed to proceed no further in the matter even after the Pope's ratification arrived; he might well complain that the negotiations could still continue in perfect amity and mutual sympathy as they had done before the Prince and the Duke had arrived. But the Prince and the Duke, conscious of their mission's failure and exhilarated by their sudden, intoxicating popularity, turned on Spain and all things Spanish with a hostility fired by pique. They insisted that James should make Spanish support of the Elector a *sine qua non* of all future discussions, knowing well that this was something to which Philip and Olivarez would not and could not agree; they accused Bristol of being an abject Hispanophil, attaching to him most of the blame for the shameful way in which they had been treated; they viewed with disdain the antics of such members of their retinue as Sir Francis Cottington, who had actually admired the Spaniards and adopted many of their manners and customs, and of Archie Armstrong who, in token of his respect for the young Spanish King, decided to call his own son Philip. The heavy gold bowl that the Queen of Spain had presented to Charles in Madrid was handed over to a footman; some sweets that later arrived for him from the Infanta, as though she wished to suggest that at least there need be no hard feelings between herself and the Prince, were immediately given away to another servant. And when the Earl of Middlesex, the Lord Treasurer, a man who had started life as Lionel Cranfield, apprentice to a City businessman, had the temerity to say that he thought that the Prince of Wales was in honour bound to proceed with the marriage, Charles turned on him in fury, advising him to stick to money matters of which he presumably had some knowledge and not to talk of honour to a gentleman.

It was partly to bring about the downfall of this dislikeable but highly efficient public servant that Buckingham now advised James to call another Parliament which could be persuaded to impeach Middlesex on the familiar charge that in administering the treasury he had accumulated a vast private fortune. The ruin of Middlesex, who was closely identified with the pro-Spanish party in the country, would make Buckingham's triumph complete.

'My God, Steenie, you are a fool and will shortly repent this folly,' James told Buckingham when he realised what was in his mind. 'You are making a rod with which you will be scourged yourself.' And to his son he said, 'You will live to have your bellyful of impeachments.' They were prophetic utterances.

But James was a dying man. What little will he had formerly been able to exert in face of the perverse wishes of his two sweet boys he could no longer summon. He gave way. A Parliament was called; Middlesex was destroyed; the whole foreign policy of the country was reversed; and, since Parliament supported the new hostile stand against Spain, its advice was sought as to whether diplomatic relations with Madrid should be broken off – although the King's insistence that it had no right to be consulted on foreign

Monarch and Husband:
Court and Domestic Life

An engraving by R. V. Voerst after Vandyck's 1634 portrait of Charles I and
Henrietta Maria.

Charles I and his
Court in Greenwich
Park by Adrian van
Stalbent. Greenwich
Palace, part of the town
and the Thames can be
seen in the background.

(*right*) An early seven-
teenth-century
portrait of Charles I
embroidered on satin in
painted silk.

An early seventeenth-century white satin panel, chiefly in stump work, embroidered with the figures of Charles and the Queen.

(*left*) A portrait by an unknown artist of Henrietta Maria's dwarf Jeffrey Hudson at the age of twenty-eight. The son of a butcher from Oakham in Rutland, he was three feet nine inches in height.

A marble bust of Charles
dated 1631 by the sculptor
Hubert le Sueur who
came to England in 1628.

(*opposite*) Charles as depicted
in an illumination on a patent.

An etching by Wenceslaus
Hollar of Hubert le Sueur's
bronze equestrian statue of
Charles at Charing Cross
executed in 1633. At this
time it was surrounded by
the stables of the royal mews
which were demolished in
the early nineteenth century.

Van Dyck's 1637 portrait of 'Charles I in Three Positions' which was sent to Rome to help the sculptor, Bernini, in the execution of a bust. When Bernini saw it he described the countenance depicted as that of a man 'doomed'. 'Never', he said, 'have I beheld features more unfortunate.' The finished bust is lost, believed to have been destroyed in the fire that consumed Whitehall Palace in 1698.

The three elder children of Charles and Henrietta Maria as portrayed by Van Dyck, Prince Charles (born in 1630 and later to become Charles II), Princess Mary (born in 1631 and as wife of the Prince of Orange, to be mother of the future William III), and Prince James (born in 1633, and to succeed his brother as James II in 1685).

(*left*) The model of a ship made in about 1634, given to the Prince of Wales, the future Charles II.

Charles dining in state in the hall at Whitehall Palace, by Houckgeest, waited upon by numerous attendants and watched by members of the public.

(*right*) A bronze bust of Charles copied from the Le Sueur bust in the Bodleian, Oxford.

Cabinet bearing the monogram of Henrietta Maria.

A book cushion of the period, of silk embroidery in tent-stitch on canvas.

Trenchers from the Royal Household, used at banquets in the late sixteenth
and early seventeenth centuries, for fruit, cheese and sweetmeats.

(*opposite*) Bellarmines discovered at Oxford.

(*left*) A tin-glazed earthenware wine bottle in use during the Civil War.

(*lower left*) Another find from the Broad Street site in Oxford.

(*lower right*) An enamelled earthenware dish such as those in use at Whitehall Palace in the 1630s.

Household utensils from seventeenth-century Oxford.

(*upper left*) A watch, in a silver case, with a movement signed Edward East
Landine, said to have been given by Charles to his fourth child, Princess Elizabeth.
(*upper right*) A jewel spray believed to have been given as a present by Charles
to a friend. There is a miniature of the King in the heart of the central flower.
(*above*) Gloves, hat and pieces of a cloak of Charles, and Henrietta Maria's slippers.

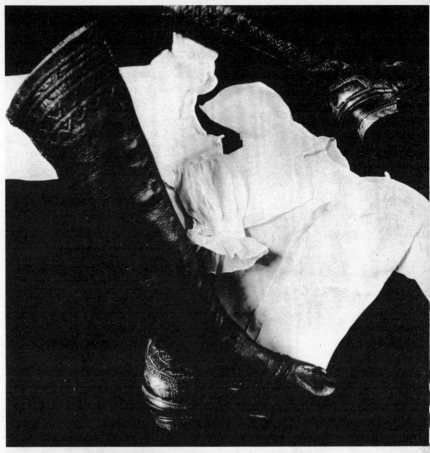

Early seventeenth-century shirts and boots which were worn by Charles as a boy.

(*left*) The knitted silk vest worn by Charles at his execution.

Three etchings by Wenceslaus Hollar of
ladies' attire in 1644 at different
seasons of the year, (*above*) 'Autumn',
(*upper right*) 'Winter', (*right*), 'Spring'.

(*below*) An embroidered early seventeenth-
century purse.

Abraham Bosse's engraving of a cavalier in the characteristically flamboyant dress of the early 1640s.

Hollar's etching of 'Summer', with the Banqueting House seen across St James's Park in the background.

affairs was one of the main reasons why its predecessor had been dissolved three years before.

In preparation for a future war against Spain, alliances were sought not only with the Dutch but also with the French whose policy, now directed by Cardinal Richelieu, was to oppose the Austrian Emperor; and an expeditionary army, mostly vagabonds and mercenaries, was gathered under the command of the egregious *condottiere*, Count Mansfeld, who was lodged in the apartments which had been specially prepared for the Infanta.

Parliament's ideas on how the war should be conducted and how much money should be voted for its prosecution were, however, very different from those entertained by the Prince and the Duke of Buckingham. The Commons, ignoring now the question of the Palatinate, advocated a naval war against Spain – together, of course, with a new campaign against the English papists – and voted, with many provisos and limitations, the sum of £300,000.

James – well knowing how utterly inadequate the money was for the sort of full-scale war in Germany which, ignoring the Commons' provisos, the Prince and Buckingham had in mind – begged them not to push him into declaring war. It was pathetic to see him now, looking so very old at fifty-eight. He had lost all his teeth and so, as he bolted his food, his indigestion was worse than ever. He had a passion for fruit and when the first cherries or strawberries of the season were presented to him he would plunge his hands impatiently into the basket, so he suffered from diarrhoea as well. He also suffered from what was diagnosed as arthritis, nephritis and colic, and from gout which he tried vainly to cure by standing in the bellies of bucks freshly slaughtered in the hunting field. 'His skin was as soft as taffeta sarsnet,' Anthony Weldon said, 'because he never washed his hands, but only rubbed his fingers' ends slightly with the wet end of a napkin'. He was always scratching himself, fiddling about with his codpiece, hiccupping, and belching. His clothes were so stuffed and padded as a precaution against assassins that he was frequently too hot; then he would throw the outer garments off and catch a cold which made him sneeze continually. There were stones in his bladder, he had decided, disease in his liver, and the sores on his lips were due to the 'bitter humours boiling from his mouth'. He was subject to fits of overwhelming sadness and of unconsciousness, accompanied by the passage of urine 'red like Alicante wine'. Modern research has suggested that,

D

like his elder son, he was suffering from porphyria. It was difficult not to be repelled by him in his illness, but impossible not to feel pity for him. His clever mind had not degenerated in the way that his body had; yet as he doddered about the Court he appeared to be in his dotage.

Terrified of losing Buckingham now that his body was collapsing and he had so little more to offer him in riches, power or honour, he entirely abandoned his struggle against his policies, and became more pitiably maudlin than ever in his abject devotion to him. 'I desired only to live in this world for your sake,' he wrote to him during the last Christmas of his life. 'I had rather live banished in any part of the world with you, than live a sorrowful widow-life without you. And so God bless you, my sweet child and wife, and grant that ye may ever be a comfort to your dear Dad and husband.'

Three months later he fell into his last painful illness at Theobalds. A gaggle of doctors, ordered about by Buckingham and Buckingham's bossy, fussy mother, disagreed as to the best treatment. A local doctor advocated the application of plasters to his wrists and stomach and these were stuck on by Buckingham and the old beldame who, when the King shortly afterwards expired, were naturally accused of having killed him. Yet when the surgeons opened the body they found no poison. All the vitals were 'sound, as also his head, which was very full of brains; but his blood was wonderfully tainted with melancholy'.

It was not only the powerful will of Buckingham and his sudden flashes of passionate temper that the old King had had to contend with since his boys had come back from Spain – these were bad enough: James had felt constrained to complain to the Spanish Ambassador that he did not know how many devils Buckingham had in him 'since that journey'. But there was also the changed character of the Prince. He was still reserved, still liable to shrink into an embarrassed or wary silence in the middle of a conversation. But that almost docile obedience and nervous insecurity which had characterised his early years had now been replaced by a variable but none the less real self-confidence. His time in Spain away from the sheltering atmosphere of his Household, and his so close and constant association with the romantic, volatile and forceful personality of Buckingham, had turned a shy and hesitant boy into a young man whose spirit could for the first time be sensed behind that usually so courteous manner, that automatic grace and slow, sad, distant smile. His sudden outbursts of temper, as when he had told the Earl of Middlesex to mind his own business, were both more vehement and more frequent than before.

This change in him was widely noticed. His journey to Spain had greatly improved him, one observer thought. His self-assurance, though he was still young for his years, was much increased. He even spoke confidently in Parliament, disingenuously putting the Members' minds at rest as to how the King intended to spend the money for which they had been asked to vote. It was usually Buckingham's ideas and schemes he was putting forward, but so convinced was he of their rightness that they seemed to be his own. 'He is grown a fine gentleman,' another of his contemporaries decided, 'and beyond all expectation I had of him when I saw him last, which was not these seven years; and, indeed, I think he never looked nor became himself better in all his life.'

In Paris such reports were delighting the little Princess whom it was now intended that this eligible Prince should marry.

Lord Kensington, soon to be created Earl of Holland, had arrived in Paris in February 1624, as England's 'wooing Ambassador', to use his own description of his status. He was confident that he could present an appealing picture of the Prince of Wales without the pious perjury which envoys on such a mission as his so often had to commit. He could honestly describe a courteous young man, kind and considerate, rather delicate, even feminine in appearance, it was true, and by no means tall, but healthy, with limbs made strong by manly exercise. He was thoughtful and studious; he read often from a little book, written out by hand and containing – though Lord Kensington, nor anyone else for that matter, had ever looked closely inside it – noble sentiments and spiritual advice; he was most regular in his religious observances. Yet he was a young man of action, too, and of physical courage; he hunted with fine spirit and was known to have a deep interest in military affairs, even once to have asked his father permission to go off and fight in the service of the Venetian State.

He was temperate in all things. He had a good appetite but never ate greedily, preferring plain food to rich, simple to elaborate dishes; he enjoyed a glass of wine or ale but never drank to excess, often, indeed, contenting himself with a glass of water or fruit juice. There had never been any suspicion of his misbehaving with any of the young ladies of the English Court.

There would, of course, be no cause for Lord Kensington to emphasise this chastity, this demure purity which seemed to some of the more uncharitable gossips in England to suggest that the Prince, now twenty-five years old, might well turn out to be 'less than man'. Nor would there be need for Kensington to lay too much emphasis on the Prince's serious nature, the rarity of those occasions upon which a smile of amusement rather than politeness lit up that small, pale, wistful face, the even rarer occasions upon which he had been heard to laugh. There need be no mention of those flashes of petulant temper.

But whatever disadvantages there might be in being married to him there was no doubt that the Princess was far more anxious to become his wife than the Infanta had ever been.

She was fourteen years old. Named Henriette after her father, Henri IV, who had been assassinated when she was only a few months old, and Marie after her mother, the stout, managing and formidable Marie de' Medici, the Princess was very small and dark, and walked about with the quick, sudden movements of a sparrow. She spoke quickly, too, and had a quick temper. She had thick and curly black hair, which fell below her shoulders at the back and was arranged in a fringe of tight rings along her forehead; her long nose had a slight bump in it below the bridge; her eyes, particularly her left eye – so most of her portraits seem to suggest – were hooded by heavy lids; her upper lip – as even Van Dyck was to indicate – was noticeably protuberant, in consequence of her projecting teeth; her complexion was sallow. Yet, despite the unpromising impression that a catalogue of her adolescent features was bound to give, she was not an unattractive girl. Only the most extravagant of her flatterers ever claimed for her great beauty; but she was too eager and vivacious to be considered plain; her face always expressive of some emotion, of excitement, sorrow, happiness or anger, was appealing in its responsiveness and childish candour.

Certainly, Lord Kensington found much to praise. She was, he reported, giving way to what even the child's mother must have considered hyperbole, 'the loveliest creature in France and the sweetest thing in nature . . . for Beauty and Goodness an Angel . . . Her growth,' he added, though she would scarcely reach her bridegroom's shoulder, 'is very little short of her age; and her Wisdom infinitely beyond it . . . her shape is perfect'. He went on to speak of her conversational powers, her 'extraordinary discretion and quickness', and then returned, with fresh emphasis, to the delicate matter of her height. Her sister, the Princess of Piedmont, he was assured, had been no taller than she at her age and was 'now grown a tall and goodly Lady'. Moreover, Henrietta Maria was not only an accomplished dancer and singer, but an excellent horsewoman, too. Above all, she had been entranced by the portrait of Charles which Lord Kensington wore in a locket round his neck. Naturally she had not been so immodest and impolite as to inspect the miniature in his presence; but she had asked the lady of the house where he was staying to enquire whether it might be borrowed for a time. The lady, who had once been in the Princess's service, brought the locket to her, Holland told the Prince, and Henrietta Maria 'retired into her Cabinet, calling only her in; where she opened the picture in such haste as shewed a true picture of her passion, blushing in the instant at her own guiltiness. She kept it an hour in her hands and when she returned it she gave it many praises of your Person'.

In May a large portrait arrived and a letter from Charles which Henrietta Maria read, it was noticed, with tears in her eyes before refolding it and pushing it into the bodice of her dress. Now, in accordance with the traditional pattern of such courtly wooings, it was time for Lord Kensington to seek a private conversation with the hoped-for bride. He asked her mother for permission to see her alone. What exactly would he say to her, the Queen Mother wanted to know. Nothing improper, Kensington assured her. But Marie de' Medici insisted on hearing some of the 'more free and amorous kind of language' herself before she could permit the ambassador to repeat it to her innocent child.

Kensington, a vain but charming man with 'an amorous tongue' and such dark and handsome features that he was known as *El Conde*, could 'court it as smoothly as any man with the ladies'. With the true courtier's nicely calculated balance of self-assurance and deferential respect, he must have done well with the Queen, for she greeted his vicarious rhapsodies with a delighted assent, '*Allez! Allez!* Off you go! There is no danger in any of that. I put my trust in you! I put my trust in you!'

The trust was evidently not misplaced; for the Princess, when she heard them herself in private, drank the ambassador's words 'down with Joy, and, with a low Courtesie, acknowledged [them] to the Prince, adding that she was extremely obliged to his Highness'.

While the wooing of the Princess was going on favourably enough, the settlement of the political and religious conditions which were necessarily attached to the marriage was less straightforward. As, when negotiations with Madrid were in progress, more was asked for Roman Catholics in England than the English negotiators could very well concede, so now more help over the Palatinate question was expected from the French than Richelieu – although he supported the English alliance as a balance against Austria and Spain – felt able to give. The Pope now was unwilling to grant a dispensation for the Princess's marriage to a Protestant; Louis XIII, having closed the port of Calais to Count Mansfeld's army, had proved to be equally unwilling to make any effort to support it in its defence of the Elector's rights or even to save it from starvation and disintegration in Holland. By the end of 1624 it was reported in London that the French match was going on 'only by fits'.

Within a few weeks of Charles's accession, however, he had cut through all the difficulties by giving a secret guarantee to allow the English Roman Catholics freedom of worship. At the same time he undertook to ensure that nothing would be put in the way of his wife continuing in her faith, that her children's education would be entrusted to her keeping until they were thirteen years old. She was to have her own chapels and chaplains in every royal palace; she would be accompanied to England by a bishop and twenty-eight priests; all her private attendants were to be French and Catholic. She was not as innately pious and devotional as the Infanta, but she was – and remained – a determined, uncompromising Catholic. Her religious education had been strictly supervised by the Mother Superior of the Carmelite convent in the Faubourg St Jacques; and it was an education whose mark was everlasting. The day before her wedding was spent within the walls of the convent where it had taken place.

The marriage was celebrated on a platform outside the west door of Notre Dame on May Day 1625, the Duc de Chevreuse standing in for the absent Protestant bridegroom to whom he was distantly related. The Princess wore a bridal dress of cloth of silver and gold, decorated with gold fleurs-de-lis, and a diamond crown; her train was so heavy that its three bearers could not manage to lift it off the ground and a man was required to walk beneath it taking the weight on his head. As soon as the wedding was over, an English messenger who had been watching the ceremony in the cathedral square turned and galloped across the Seine towards Boulogne, taking the news to the English Court that the King was married.

A few days later the Duke of Buckingham arrived in Paris to escort the new Queen to England. He had prepared for the journey some weeks before by equipping himself with twenty-nine suits, one of them purple satin embroidered with pearls, another of white satin and velvet 'set all over both suit and cloak with diamonds, the value whereof thought to be fourscore thousand pounds'. He had also had a new hat made with a diamond-studded band and a diamond-encrusted feather, and had arranged to be accompanied by nearly seven hundred attendants, to be driven to Paris in a coach upholstered in crimson velvet and covered with gold lace.

King James's death had interfered with these splendid arrangements; but when the Duke arrived in Paris at the end of May – although not escorted by the impressive entourage he had planned should accompany him – he was at least wearing the most magnificent of his suits. He was determined to astound the French Court by his brilliance; and he succeeded. The King himself was ill; but the Queen responded to his charm with a flattering and provocative susceptibility. Neglected by her husband who blamed her for a recent miscarriage, she could not fail to be struck by this most attractive of men, so refreshingly different from her swarthy, graceless, sullen husband who seemed so much fonder of his animals than of her.

Already angered by France's refusal to co-operate in the Mansfeld expedition, Buckingham was now increasingly infuriated by Louis's apparent lack of any real interest in his further grandiose schemes for the reorganisation of Europe. He decided to exploit the attraction he had aroused in the Queen and to behave as though he had fallen in love with her. One evening when they were walking together in a riverside garden the Queen suddenly began to scream. Her ladies rushed towards her; they found the Duke scowling, the Queen trembling; but when they asked if she were all right, she replied that there was nothing the matter, it was just that she had been momentarily alarmed. Two days later, when the Duke said goodbye to her – for it was time to take her sister-in-law to the coast – he parted from her with a display of unseemly devotion; and rode off as though deeply disturbed. Soon he was back again. Leaving his charge at Abbeville in the care of her younger brother, he returned to the Queen's palace and, entering her bedchamber, he sank to his knees by her bed and, while her ladies watched in consternation, he put his head on her pillow and began whispering in her ear. She made a mild protest, yet seemed reluctant to stop him or to have him led away. It was an episode her husband never forgot or forgave; it was to lead to a troubled future.

For Henrietta trouble seemed far away when she arrived at Boulogne on the evening of 8 June. An English sailor saw her there as she stood on the shore gazing out to sea, venturing so close to the water that the waves lapped over her shoes. A Roman Catholic gentleman who had sailed over from England to catch a sight of her was delighted with her appearance, thankful to discover that although she was certainly very small she did not look as much like a little girl as he had been led to believe she did. She seemed to him a 'most sweet, lovely Creature', simply dressed and gracious. Another witness admired her 'dark brown' complexion and her eyes that sparkled 'like Stars'.

The day before her arrival at Boulogne had been stormy, and it was still so rough when she set sail on 11 June that the crossing took twenty-four hours. It was raining hard when the ship came ashore and the Queen was carried up the quayside in a chair to Dover Castle. She went to bed straight after supper; and Charles arrived while she was having breakfast at ten o'clock the next morning. He said he would wait until she had finished; but she came running down to him, knelt before him and began – in French, for she could speak no English yet – the speech that she had learned it was her duty to make to him: 'Sir, I am come into your Majesty's country to be used by you and commanded by you . . .' She faltered, seemed to forget the words, and burst into tears. Charles, almost as nervous now as she was herself, bent down and kissed her, told her that he would go on kissing her until she felt better, that she had not fallen into the hands of enemies or strangers but into the care of God who would 'have her leave her kindred and cleave to her spouse'.

They stood up together and he asked her politely about her

journey. His gaze kept returning to her feet and this she thought must be because he found her taller than he had expected; he was so slight himself she did, indeed, not feel so small as she had done beside Lord Kensington and the Duke of Buckingham. Suddenly she pulled up the hem of her dress to show him that she was not wearing pattens. 'Sir,' she said, 'I stand upon mine own feet; I have no helps by art; thus high am I; neither higher nor lower.'

Charles seemed to be enchanted by his first sight of her; and so, too, did the people who lined their route to Canterbury, smiling and cheering. On Barham Downs two long rows of villagers were drawn up on the bowling green, and here the royal carriages stopped. The King helped his wife down and led her along the ranks, while her ladies watched the simple ceremony with an austere disdain which was to become only too familiar. A Kentish man, returning their disapproving gaze, decided they were 'a poor lot, not one worth the looking after', except the Duchesse de Chevreuse, and she painted her face 'foully'. The little Queen, though, he excepted from his strictures without reservation: she *was* worth looking at.

That evening at Canterbury her second wedding took place, this time with her husband standing beside her instead of the Duc de Chevreuse; and, after the wedding banquet was over, she was taken to her bedchamber by the 'foully' painted Duchess. Charles joined her there when she had been undressed and was himself undressed by two Gentlemen of the Bedchamber. Then, asking everyone to leave the room, he shut the doors and pushed home their seven bolts.

Two days later, on 16 June – though the plague that had infested London with exceptional virulence that summer was not yet over, though church bells still dismally tolled, mourning the latest deaths, and though ıe deadcarts still made their harrowing rounds – the bride and bridegroom set out by barge for London followed by hundreds of boats whose numbers grew ever greater as they approached the roaring cannon of the Tower. One boat capsized, toppling its crew and passengers into the water, and this served but to increase the people's cheerfulness which neither the plague nor the steadily falling rain could dampen. The King and Queen, both dressed in green, stood by the open windows of the barge, bowing and waving politely to the crowds who waved back with complimentary vigour, shouting and cheering, clinging

to the sides of the surrounding boats, jostling each other along the
riverside stairs and on top of the Tower walls, leaning out of the
windows of the bulging buildings on London Bridge which seemed
on the point of tumbling outwards and falling into the water that
roared past the huge starlings built round the bases of the piers. All
the way from the Tower, past Old Swan Stairs and Dowgate
Wharf, Queenhythe Dock and Puddle Dock, past the outflow of
the Fleet and the timber yard at the bottom of Dorset Street, past
the gardens of the Temple and the vast riverside mansions of the
Earls of Essex and Arundel, the cheering and shouting continued,
the boom of the Tower's cannon echoed by the roar of the guns of
the armed vessels on the river.

At five o'clock the royal barge drew up at the watergate of
Denmark House, the London home of which the King's mother
had been so fond. This was to be the new Queen's London home,
too. Since the late Queen's death it had been restored by the great
Inigo Jones whose chapel at St James's Palace was being completed
in her honour. Denmark House was also to have a chapel built by
Inigo Jones who was soon to re-design the whole of the river
front of the palace with a fine sweep of arches sheltering a covered
walk in the manner of the great Italian architect, Sebastiano Serlio.
But although chapels had been built for her and priests had come
with her, the people were ready to overlook the Queen's Catholic
background and to hope that she would soon outgrow her foreign
ways: after all, she was but a child and, so it was reported on every
side, on being asked if she could abide a Huguenot she had sturdily
replied, 'Why not. Was not my father one?'

The people's enthusiasm for their young Queen did not, however,
last long. It was soon noticed that she responded to their acclamations, if at all, with a sulky ill grace. When they crowded round
her and stared at her, she turned away or even scowled at them.
Particularly she disliked being watched with gaping curiosity when
she had her meals at Whitehall Palace. 'Divers of us being at
Whitehall to see her being at dinner,' one of her critics reported,
'and the room somewhat overheated with a fire and company, she
drove us all out of the chamber. I suppose none but a Queen could
have cast such a scowl!'

One day while shopping in the City, she escaped recognition
for a time as she hurried about with those quick, bird-like move-

ments of hers from stall to shop and shop to stall; but then a hard, prolonged stare warned her that she had been recognised and immediately she flounced away. Not only had she taken no trouble to learn any English, but she showed no inclination to talk to anyone except the French women who constantly surrounded her. She even refused to attend her husband's coronation, though a special place had been prepared for her in the Abbey where she could watch the ceremony from behind a grille without having to take any part in it. Instead she and her ladies chose to peer down on the King from a window in Old Palace Yard, as, under a dark and threatening sky, wearing white, not purple – the robes of innocence rather than of majesty – he walked towards the Abbey, accompanied by the Duke of Buckingham for whom the ancient office of Lord High Constable had been especially revived.

It was the leader of her ecclesiastical retinue, the young Bishop of Mende, who had forbidden her to accept the crown from the Protestant Archbishop of Canterbury. Indeed, the influence which her confessor, and all her chaplains, priests and their acolytes, held over her seemed to the English excessive and alarming. Ignorant of the secret promises which their King had made to the French, the presumptions of the Queen's entourage appeared to them all the more outrageous.

Charles had been given hope in the beginning that all would turn out well. Before their first meal together her confessor had reminded her that it was the Eve of St John and that accordingly she must fast. But although he had stood by her chair throughout the meal, she had remained quite uninhibited by his disapproving presence and had enjoyed generous platefuls of pheasant and venison. Such gratifying independence did not last; and the more Henrietta came to dislike England and the English people and to shrink from a husband she could not yet begin to understand or even to like, the more obedient she became to her priests' injunctions, as though taking a perverse pleasure in flaunting her Catholicism in the face of Protestant susceptibility. One well-remembered morning, when the Court was in progress and for the time being staying at Lord Southampton's mansion at Titchfield, she and her ladies had strolled casually back and forth through the hall, laughing and talking amongst themselves, while a Protestant service was being held there. The King had been out hunting in the New Forest that day; but on another occasion at Titchfield there had been a most disagreeable scene in his presence. It occurred before dinner. The King's chaplain was finishing grace and Charles was preparing to begin his meal, when the Bishop of Mende began to say another grace more acceptable to the Catholic conscience. Raising their voices above the protests and the angry conversation he and the Protestant chaplain ended in shouting at each other. The same scene was repeated at the end of the meal, and Charles left the table without a word, overcome with anger.

His usual reaction was cold, disapproving silence. Yet occasionally he appears to have burst out in one of those sudden flashes of rage which overwhelmed him when he felt his dignity or authority to have been slighted, as when, on hearing that a Catholic courtier declined to attend the Anglican services in the royal chapel, he furiously exclaimed, 'If he will not come to my prayers, let him get out of my house!' On another occasion his sense of dignity was outraged by the insistent importunities of the Queen's priests. They had been complaining that the Queen's chapel at St Jame's Palace was not yet finished and that the Queen's Closet where they were obliged to say Mass was far too small. Well, then, replied the King dismissively, if the Queen's Closet were too small, they could use 'the Great Chamber; and if the Great Chamber were not wide enough, they might use the Garden; and if the Garden would not serve them, then was the Park the fittest place.'

Nor was it only the Bishop of Mende and his priests whom the King found so insupportable. Even closer to Henrietta were the eccentric Duchesse de Chevreuse (who had established herself in the royal palace at Richmond where her shocking antics included swimming across the Thames) the Queen's Chamberlain, the supercillious Comte de Tillières, and her intimate friend, the beautiful Mme de Saint-Georges, whose mother, a distant relative of Marie de' Medici, had been Henrietta's governess. This Mme de Saint-Georges had placed herself in the royal carriage with the King and Queen on their journey from Dover Castle and since then had rarely left Henrietta's side, insisting that her duty to care for her, and having loved her since she was a baby, entitled her to precedence over the English ladies of the Court.

For her part, Henrietta liked her husband's friends and attendants no better than he liked hers. Above all she detested the Duke of Buckingham, who treated her as though she were a little girl, inexperienced and simple, in need of his worldly advice on how to behave and how to dress, how to conduct herself in English society and at the English Court. He disparaged her in the eyes of the King, just as her French attendants disparaged Charles in the eyes of the Queen. And Charles himself complained to Buckingham, both in conversation and in writing, of the Queen's misbehaviour and failings, her lack of due respect for him, her 'eschewing' to be in his company, and the mounting insults offered to him by her priests and ladies. The first time she had come to Hampton Court, he wrote indignantly, she had publicly flouted his orders. He had sent a message to her asking her to instruct her chamberlain, the 'Count of Tilliers', to ensure that the same regulations were observed in the running of her Household as had been observed in his mother's time. 'Her answer was that she hoped I would give her leave to order her house as she list herself . . . I could not imagine that she would have affronted me in such a thing publicly. After I heard this answer, I took a time when I thought we had both best leisure to dispute it, to tell her calmly both her fault in the public denial and [in] the business itself. She, instead of acknowledging her fault, gave me so ill an answer that I omit (not to be tedious) the relation of that discourse, having too much of that nature hereafter to relate.'

He would not trouble to set down, Charles plaintively continued, 'all her various neglects', the way she tried to avoid being alone with him, how he had to communicate with her through a servant, how she still had made no effort to learn English or to understand the English people. But he could not forbear to record his profound displeasure at the reports – which she denied – that she had made a pilgrimage to Tyburn to pray for the souls of the Roman Catholic priests who had been executed there, nor to recount the history of a quarrel about the people, nearly all of them French, whom she had chosen to appoint to profitable appointments in connection with the landed estates which were held by the Crown in her name. She had handed him the list when he was in bed; he had agreed to read it in the morning but had reminded her that the appointments were his to make, not hers; she had replied that there were English names on it as well as French; Charles had then pointed out that Frenchmen were not entitled to hold such positions, and she had told him that all the names had been selected by her mother and herself and they would have no others. Increasingly angry. Charles had insisted that it was nothing to do either with her or her mother, that if she persisted he would strike out any name either of them suggested.

Very well then , she snapped, he could keep all the land and houses himself for if she could not choose who was to look after them she did not want any of them.

'I bade her then remember to whom she spoke,' Charles concluded his long account of the quarrel, 'and told her she ought not to use me so. Then she fell into a passionate discourse, how miserable she was . . . When I offered to answer, she would not so much as hear me. Then she went on saying, she was not of that base quality to be used so ill. Then I made her both hear me and end that discourse.'

It was certain that the poor girl was profoundly unhappy and desperately homesick. In her misery she even brought herself to ask his overbearing friend, Buckingham, if he would persuade her husband to let her go home to France for a time; if he would, then *she* would persuade her mother to let the Duke go as her escort, and in Paris he would be able to see her sister-in-law again. But Richelieu and Louis, neither forgetting nor forgiving the Duke's gross behaviour on his previous visit, would not entertain the idea of allowing him anywhere near Queen Anne, so the proposal came to nothing and Henrietta was made more unhappy than ever. A good part of the trouble, no doubt, was her physical aversion to a husband without either the imagination or the humour, the experience or the sensuality to overcome the nervousness and shrinking reluctance of an unawakened and underdeveloped girl. On the morning after their first night together an inquisitive observer had noticed that while her husband looked cheerful enough, Henrietta appeared 'very melancholy'. It may not, then, have appeared strange to the more understanding members of the Court that the young Queen should react against an incompatibility which distressed and perhaps even frightened her with a pert, combative and sometimes almost hysterical self-will.

Charles, himself – having conceived, since his Spanish experiences, an aversion to all foreigners which never entirely left him – was convinced that the cause of his unhappy marriage was 'the maliciousness of the monsieurs'. It was surely not in the Queen's nature to behave as she did; her 'unkind usages' must have been instigated by 'ill instruments'. Few if any of her servants were blameless, he thought, and they must collectively be responsible for the 'ill crafty counsels' which was poisoning his wife against him. The more he thought about it, the more insults he had to bear from them, the more determined he became to rid himself of them.

The crisis came on the afternoon of 26 June 1626 when, accompanied by the Duke of Buckingham he walked into her room at Whitehall Palace. Her attendants, some of whom, at the moment of his entrance, had been 'unreverently dancing and curvetting' in front of her, watched in awed silence as he sharply told her to come outside with him for a moment. The Queen replied that if he had anything to say to her he could say it where they were. Angrily he took hold of her hand, pulled her after him to his own apartments, pushed her inside, locked the door and told her that he had had enough of her French attendants and all of them were to be sent home. She burst into tears, then fell to her knees in supplication, then lost her temper with him and, running to the window, smashed her fist through the glass and began to shout to the people gathered in the courtyard below. Charles pulled her back, bruising her hands and tearing her dress.

Later, he gave instructions to Lord Conway, Secretary of State, to issue orders for all Her Majesty's French attendants to leave England immediately. They refused at first to believe that such orders could ever have been issued, and the Yeomen of the Guard had to be called in to 'thrust them and all their countryfolk out of the Queen's lodgings . . . The women howled and lamented as if they had been going to execution'.

They went, however, only as far as Denmark House; and over a month later, Charles was writing crossly to Buckingham: 'I command you to send all the French away to-morrow out of the town. If you can by fair means (but stick not long in disputing), otherwise force them away; driving them away like so many wild beasts, until you have shipped them; and so the devil go with them! Let me hear no answer but of the performance of my command.'

The command was obeyed. All her ladies, except the Duchesse de Thouars, who had been born a Dutch Protestant, and two others, and nearly all her French servants and priests were soon afterwards seen off at the river stairs by Denmark House by a delighted, hooting mob of Londoners, one of whom threw a stone at Mme de Saint-Georges and knocked her hat off.

5

Devils and Martyrs
1627–9

BY the time he had brought himself to expel from the country his
wife's French attendants, Charles's unhappy marriage was but
the most personal of the depressing problems that faced him on
every side. Buckingham – who 'lay on the first night of the reign in
the King's bedcamber and three nights after in the next lodgings' –
was still his adored Steenie, his constant companion and adviser,
influencing him and moulding him, urging him by the force of a
far more dynamic personality to adopt poses that were foreign to
his true nature, to pursue policies which were as disastrous as they
were financially ruinous.

The war with Spain had proved a tragic fiasco. Count Mansfeld's
twelve thousand men, from the first a lamentable army 'showing
nothing but deadly unwillingness to the service', had disintegrated
and been finally annihilated by the ruthless Von Wallenstein;
while a second expeditionary force of fifteen thousand men, pressed
into the service for an attack on the Spanish coast, fared no better.
Most of the soldiers in this second army were rogues and vagabonds,
an appalled diarist recorded; they were half-starved and dressed in
rags, some were lame, many were usually drunk. Yet they were
packed off to sea, under command of an admiral, created Lord
Wimbledon in honour of his first and only maritime command,
and they were landed on the Andalusian shore after a bombardment
of Fort Puntal. They marched on Cadiz in the blazing October sun
with empty knapsacks and through a countryside able to supply
nothing but wine. Their officers watched helplessly as they drank
themselves insensible; and while the Cadiz garrison was reinforced,
the Spaniards tumbled them back into the boats. The fleet then set
sail for deeper waters, hoping to intercept the treasure ships on their
way back from Mexico. But after a few days it was forced to turn
back, for the ropes and sails – some of which had been in use at the
time of the Armada – were rotten, the victuals aboard would not
have tempted a stray London dog, and the men were dying in such
numbers that corpses were tipped wholesale into the water every

hour. When the survivors returned, bleeding, barefoot, lice-ridden and scarcely able to walk, they were billeted upon the respectable citizens of the south coast ports upon whom they vented their desperate resentment.

The Spanish war, marked by such disgraceful incidents as these, dragged on for four years. Yet before it was ended Britain drifted into war with France as well. It was a war which Richelieu had striven to avoid, for it had been his hope that he could keep on friendly terms with the English while acting against Austria. But Buckingham's passionate overtures to the Queen of France and Charles's dismissal of Henrietta's French attendants were two final insults which brought the relations between the two countries to breaking point. Already there had been quarrels over trade and shipping, over the French refusal to become involved in the war in Germany, over the English support of the Huguenot rebels.

In 1626 Spain and France resolved their differences, and the following summer an expedition, under the command of the Duke of Buckingham, as Lord High Admiral, sailed from Stokes Bay at the mouth of Portsmouth harbour to relieve the Huguenot rebels in the town of La Rochelle then being besieged by the Catholic forces of the French King. Buckingham's intention was to capture the Île de Ré, a long narrow island whose south-eastern tip is separated from La Rochelle by a strait two miles wide. Once captured, the island would provide an excellent base for operations against French and Spanish shipping as well as for sallies in support of the Huguenots on the mainland. When Buckingham gave the order for the invasion of the Île de Ré, however, he found that his army shared none of his own enthusiasm, while the Huguenots, for their part, greeted their self-appointed champion with sobering reserve. Buckingham proved himself a brave commander, but his venture was no more successful than Count Mansfeld's expedition or the attack on Cadiz. The main fortress on the island was strongly defended and with little support either from the Huguenots or from his own half-hearted men, he could not take it. While he was trying to starve it into submission, a strong French force landed on the island; and Buckingham, after a desperate attempt to storm the citadel with scaling-ladders too short to reach the top of the walls, was forced to march back to his boats. His army badly mauled during its retreat was brought back to Plymouth, 'with no little dishonour to our nation, excessive charge to our treasury, and great slaughter of our men'.

Before Buckingham had been long ashore a messenger rode up to him with urgent advice from London: if he valued his life, he would avoid the main roads to the capital. He ignored the message; but when he arrived in London on the evening of 17 November 1627, though he had escaped the hands of assassins, he was soon made to realise that Charles, who received him 'most joyfully and graciously', was almost the only friend he had left.

Parliament had already tried to ruin him; and Charles had had due cause to remember the warning his father had given him upon his return from Spain. The first Parliament of the new reign had failed to provide him with the financial support he had asked of it. Exasperated by his unwillingness to explain to them exactly what his foreign policy was or for what purposes the money would be used, and distrusting Buckingham's capacity to put it to good use, the Members of the Commons had voted to give him less than a quarter of what was needed for the prosecution of the war. They had also refused to grant him for more than a single year the right to collect those customs duties which his predecessors had been granted for life. Displaying more interest in religion at home than in dynasties abroad, they had gone on to urge stronger measures against Roman Catholicism, fresh support of Puritanism and the public disgrace of a clergyman who had denied that the Pope was anti-Christ. Charles had replied by dissolving Parliament and appointing the clergyman one of his own chaplains.

Charles's second Parliament had proved no more satisfactory than the first. In order to make it more tractable, Charles had rendered those Members who had proved most tiresome in 1625 ineligible for election by appointing them sheriffs. This manoeuvre had, however, merely resulted in the elevation to the leadership of the Commons of a Member far more dangerous than the relatively moderate men who had been excluded.

This man was Sir John Eliot. The son of a rich Cornish squire, Eliot had spent three years at Exeter College, Oxford, before embarking on a prolonged tour of Europe during which he had met and been befriended by the young and strikingly beautiful George Villiers. After his return, while Villiers had risen so rapidly to success as the Marquess of Buckingham, Eliot had settled down to the quiet life of a west country gentleman making occasional

visits to London as Member of Parliament for Newport and later
St Germans. On one of these visits to the capital he had once again
met Buckingham who used his influence to secure for him the post
of Vice Admiral of Devon; and it was while serving in this capacity
that Eliot had witnessed at Plymouth the harrowing return of the
men from the Cadiz expedition. It was an experience he never
forgot. His uncompromisingly anti-papist feelings already affronted
by the shamefully unsound religious principles and policies of the
King and Buckingham, he determined to bring about the downfall
of the man whom he blamed for the disastrous course upon which
the Government was headed and to whose unworthy patronage he
owed his own advancement. Emotional, excitable, narrow and
vehement, he harangued the Commons in a loud, harsh voice,
protesting that he and his fellow Members were not creatures of
the King elected to approve his policies and vote him supplies but
men with individual consciences and a duty to act only in
accordance with what they knew to be right. He demanded an
enquiry into Buckingham's conduct and went so far as to urge his
impeachment.

Charles reacted as though in panic. He had Eliot arrested and
imprisoned in the Tower; yet when the House, refusing to be
intimidated, declined to do any further business until Eliot was
released, Charles did release him, at the same time despatching a
curt and provocative message to the House enjoining it to lose no
more time in voting him the money for which he was tired of
waiting.

Eliot immediately rejoined the attack. In the middle of a violent
storm that dashed the rain against the windows of the chamber and
hurled the waters of the Thames across the river steps, he demanded
that the complaints of the Commons should be heard and registered
before financial matters were discussed. Attacking the Duke of
Buckingham in the most extravagant terms, he accused him of all
manner of follies and crimes, compared him to Sejanus the evil
counsellor of the Emperor Tiberius and shouted his belief that the
Duke's mind, 'full of collusion and deceit' could best be likened to
the 'beast called by the ancients stellionatus, a beast so blurred, so
spotted, so full of foul lines that they knew not what to make of it'.

While Eliot was haranguing the Commons, a less wild but not
less formidable opponent of Buckingham had appeared in the
House of Lords. This was the Earl of Bristol who had been

rancorously blamed by the Duke and the King for all that had gone wrong in Madrid and who, on his return from Spain, had been told to consider himself a prisoner on his country estate at Sherborne and informed that he would not be returned to favour until he admitted his mistakes. Curtly refusing to acknowledge faults he had not committed, and strongly denying the King's charge that he had tried to convert him to Catholicism in order to further the Spanish match, Bristol had demanded a trial by his peers and, in contravention of a royal warning, appeared in London where he presented himself before the Lords. He told them that he had been kept a prisoner for two years in Dorset because Buckingham was afraid of him, and that he had now come to lay an accusation against his tormentor. Reacting with that sudden, ill-considered desperation which always overcame him whenever Steenie was threatened, Charles ordered the Attorney General to bring against the Earl a charge of high treason.

Undaunted, Bristol turned the tables on the King and sternly told the Lords, 'I accuse that man, the Duke of Buckingham, of high treason and I will prove it'. He had scarcely had time to open his case, however, when his accusations were interrupted by an urgent message from the King which announced that His Majesty himself would answer and contradict all the charges made. The Lords – increasingly aware that the King, while a man of impeccable virtue in his private life, did not scruple to abandon honesty when dealing with political opponents – politely rejected the royal message and declared themselves of the opinion that it would scarcely be seemly for His Majesty to give evidence in such a case as this. But, as it happened, Buckingham was saved from the humiliation of Bristol's further accusations by the impeachment of the Duke by the Commons, and by the King's dissolution of Parliament before the proceedings against him had been completed.

Already the King had shown himself incapable of managing Parliament. It had been his father's practice to make long speeches to both Houses, to send them frequent messages, to remind them constantly of his theory of kingship. This theory, as propounded in his *Trew Law of Free Monarchies*, was that there were no legal limits to the power of kings, that Parliaments had no function but to give advice. It was a theory upon which Charles had been brought up. For the benefit of his heir, James had explained it in a little manual,

Basilikon Doron, which showed how kings, like fathers, derived their authority from God and had a Divine Right to demand obedience and honour. A few months before his accession Charles had heard his father tell Parliament – and he himself believed it absolutely – that the King of England sat in Jesus Christ's throne in 'this part of the earth'. But although James so often informed Parliament that he was outside or above the law, he was always careful, in practice, to act according to the law; although he believed that theoretically he had no duty to communicate with Parliament at all unless he wished to do so, in practice he was in almost constant communication with it.

Charles, on the other hand, affronted Parliament by virtually ignoring it. When he addressed it he did so in the briefest, curtest way. He had no doubt that it was Parliament's duty, as it was all his subjects' duty, to recognise his absolute authority, to trust him to do what was best for them of his own good will. He could not and would not be forced to act by legal obligations which did not exist.

Unable now to raise money through the House of Commons, Charles was reduced to finding other, more direct means of support. He ordered the collection of customs duties even though Parliament had not granted him the right to them, he imposed a capital levy, had those who refused to pay it imprisoned, and dismissed the Lord Chief Justice for questioning its lawfulness.

Buckingham's expensive failure on the Île de Ré, however, forced Charles's hand. He was obliged to summon Parliament again, and to trust that even those gentry who had been imprisoned for failing to pay his forced loan and who were sure to be elected, would this time be reasonable and recognise 'the common danger'. But the danger, as the Commons saw it, came not from France and Spain, but from the tyranny of the King. They refused to grant money to him until they had set out their complaints about his conduct, until they had registered their condemnation of taxation without Parliamentary consent, of imprisonment without due cause, of the practice of billeting soldiers on unwilling citizens – as had happened in the west country after the Cadiz expedition – and of the subjection of civilians to martial law – which the King had proclaimed to suppress the disturbances that this billeting had provoked. These and other of the nation's grievances were incorporated in a Petition of Right which was presented to the King for his assent as though it were a statute. Charles declined to bestow upon it such authority, and, hoping to nullify its force, he said that he would be graciously pleased to accord it his 'royal word'. The Commons – as unwilling to trust his royal word as the Lords had been to accept his testimony in the Bristol case – expressed their dissatisfaction with the formula, and returned with renewed vigour to their condemnation of the Minister who was seen as the chief source of all their misfortunes. In an effort to save Buckingham from further attack, Charles at length gave way and summoned the Commons to attend him in the House of Lords where he signified his assent to the petition with the traditional words, '*soit droit fait comme est desiré*', adding impenitently, with that petulant self-justification which never failed to stir his listeners to irritation, 'This I am sure is full, yet no more than I granted you on my first answer. And I assure you that my maxim is that the people's liberties strengthen the King's prerogative and that the King's prerogative is to defend the people's liberties . . . I have done my part, wherefore if the Parliament have not a happy conclusion the sin is yours. I am free of it'.

Despite his weary ill grace, the Commons were prepared to be generous in their triumph. Overcoming their irritation at his implied rebuke, they rose to their feet and accorded him 'such an acclamation as made the House ring several times'. Their cheers were repeated in the streets outside where a 'general joy in all faces spread itself suddenly and broke out into ringing of bells and bonfires miraculous'.

If the King was momentarily forgiven, the Duke of Buckingham was not. The charges against him, voiced by the indefatigable Eliot and his supporters, continued to ring through the House and were echoed and embellished in the workshops and taverns beyond its walls. Hundreds of handbills were printed and passed from hand to hand in the streets: 'Who rules the Kingdom? The King. Who rules the King? The Duke. Who the Duke? The Devil.'

The Devil, in some eyes, was incarnate in the shape of one Dr Lambe, a physician and astrologer whom the Duke was known to consult and with whom – so it was maliciously rumoured – he engaged in various iniquitous practices. This Dr Lambe was seen leaving the Fortune Theatre one evening in June 1628 by a crowd of apprentices who greeted his appearance with cries of 'The Duke's Devil! The Duke's Devil!' The mob followed him, taunting him and throwing lumps of filth at him, to a cookshop where he had his supper while a guard of sailors was collected for his defence. As he ate the size of the mob increased until there were hundreds of ruffians and rowdies outside the doors. When the doctor reappeared they shouted at him anew and followed him all the way to the Windmill Tavern in Lothbury, pushing aside the sailors who had been employed to guard him, and pelting him now with stones. Before he could reach the Windmill door some of the mob leaped at him, beat him to the ground, battered his head on the cobbles, kicked out one of his eyes, and left him unconscious where he lay. He died a few hours later. Next day the unrepentant mob went singing and shouting through the streets,

> 'Let Charles and George do what they can,
> The Duke shall die like Dr Lambe.'

As week passed week that hot summer, the rage of the people against Buckingham grew more and more intense. Scarcely a day went by without some new prophecy of his imminent, untimely end; there were stories of his portrait falling from the wall, of his ghost walking in a shroud, of a dagger hovering above the door of his house in the Strand. His wife was tearful and in constant fear for him; and even he himself seemed unwontedly nervous, though he refused to wear a steel jacket under his coat as a friend suggested.

On 17 August, accompanied by his devoted wife who now refused to be parted from him, he left London for Portsmouth where another expedition in relief of La Rochelle was being prepared. He made his will before starting out and went to call on the Bishop of London to ask him to make sure that the Duchess and their children were well cared for by the King should anything happen to him. Did he think anything *would* happen to him? the Bishop asked him. No, Buckingham said; but after all, he was just as likely to die as the next man.

Two days after the Duke's departure, one of his former officers, to whom he had refused promotion, entered a cutler's shop on Tower Hill and, with tenpence he had borrowed from his mother, bought a dagger, and sewed its sheath firmly into the lining of his right hand pocket. His left hand had been crippled by an old wound and he wanted to be able to draw the dagger quickly without fumbling. He was a lonely, embittered man of about thirty, much given to ruminating, praying, harbouring grievances and listening to sermons. Inside his hat he had stuck a piece of paper on which was inscribed the motto, 'That man is cowardly, base, and deserveth not the name of a gentleman or soldier that is not willing to sacrifice his life for the honour of his God, his King and his Country . . . signed, John Felton.'

Felton set off to walk to Portsmouth on 18 August and arrived four days later at about nine o'clock in the morning. He made straight for the house in the high street where the Duke and Duchess were lodging. The Duke, after a very disturbed night, was having breakfast, surrounded by servants, attendants, messengers, officers and orderlies. Felton had no difficulty in gaining access to the house and concealing himself behind a hanging which covered an entrance to a passage leading off the hall. Buckingham, as he ate in the breakfast-room, was given the exciting, but unfortunately ill-founded, news that La Rochelle had been relieved. Keeping watch from behind his velvet curtain, Felton saw the Duke rise from the table and eagerly walk in the direction of the passage where he was hiding, followed by a group of Huguenot officers loudly protesting that the news about the relief of La Rochelle could not possibly be true. Within a few feet of him Buckingham stopped, detained by an army officer, who asked to speak to him. The Duke bent his head to listen to what the man had to say, and as he did so Felton appeared with his dagger in his hand. Praying, 'God have mercy upon thy soul!' Felton plunged the blade with all his strength into Buckingham's left breast. Lord Cleveland who was standing nearby clearly heard the 'thump' of the blow and turned round to see Buckingham pull out the dagger, reach for the handle of his sword and stagger into the hall, crying out in a choking voice. 'The villain hath killed me'. He collapsed against a table with the blood pouring out of his mouth.

The attendants in the breakfast-room, supposing that the Duke had been struck by one of the Huguenot officers who had followed him out, shouted 'A Frenchman! A Frenchman!' While Felton, believing they were calling his name and gratified, no doubt, that his martyrdom had so soon been recognised, came forward with the words, 'Here I am!' – holding out the message inside his hat. As his victim died in the arms of a doctor, the Duchess, called from her bed by her sister-in-law, rushed out onto the balcony above the hall and began to scream with such hysterical grief that a witness afterwards said he had never heard more pitiable 'screechings, tears and distractions' and hoped that he would 'never hear the like again'.

A messenger galloped off to convey the bitter news of the Duke's death to the King who was staying nearby at Southwick. Charles was at prayers when the message reached him; but he did not interrupt the service; he remained kneeling where he was, his pale face, drawn and tight, as his chaplain continued with the service. As soon as his prayers were over he went to his room where he threw himself across the bed, sobbing uncontrollably. All that day he remained in the room, abandoning himself to his grief. He had loved Steenie with all his heart. There had never been any other man who had meant so much to him; nor was there ever to be.

The next morning Charles came down from his room and as though he knew that this would be the only anodyne, he threw himself into his work with a resolute energy that left no time for sorrowful reflection. Within the next fortnight, his secretaries said, he despatched more business than the Duke had done in three months, dealing with all his friend's public and private affairs as well as his own. He wanted to build a tomb of colossal proportions in which the remains of the hero might be laid to rest; he wanted to follow him to the grave in a state funeral of magnificent pomp. But he was dissuaded: the times were not right for such a display; the people had not known the Duke's greatness; they were not to be trusted; there was the danger of riots.

It was no less than the truth. Indeed, the people were rejoicing, congratulating each other on deliverance from the Duke and all his devilish works. Felton was greeted as the hero he had always wanted to be; and Londoners outside his cell in the Tower toasted the 'little Goliath, God bless him'. It was, for Charles, a display of malevolence and blind cruelty which he could never forgive or forget. Nor could he ever forgive the man whom he blamed for it. Felton himself was not important. There must have been accomplices; and the King commanded the lawyers to put him to 'the question' to discover who these accomplices were. The lawyers declined to sanction the use of torture; and Felton was executed at Tyburn protesting that he had acted alone 'not maliciously but with love of his country'. Yet looming behind Felton in the King's mind was the sinister figure of Sir John Eliot. Even if he had not been directly involved in the foul crime of the murder, his was the ultimate responsibility. He would soon be made to pay for it.

Eliot came to take his seat in Parliament once again in the January following the Duke's death. Although his arch enemy, the beast 'so blurred and spotted', had been removed, the general principle of the Commons' right to criticise the King's Ministers had not yet been conceded and must be firmly pursued. Eliot pursued it. Sensing the advantages of allying the growing force of Puritan enthusiasm in the country with demands for political change, he and his friends changed the emphasis of their attack. They now moved against the King on religious grounds.

They had cause enough, they considered, for their complaints. Not content with appointing the High Church Richard Montague to be one of his chaplains, the King had now compounded his folly by transferring him to the see of Chichester. Worse than this he had presented Roger Manwaring to a crown living; and Manwaring had been impeached by the previous Parliament for declaring that the refusal to pay forced loans was not merely a crime against the state but a sin against God. Then there was the appointment of William Laud, an opponent of Puritanism and an advocate of the scandalous doctrine that the Roman Church was one of the true churches of Christendom, to be Bishop of London. As a final provocation to the Puritan gentry in the House, the King declared that the reform of the English Church was nothing to do with Parliament.

The House of Commons responded to this provocation by refusing to confirm the Crown's right to its traditional revenue in the form of customs duties until they had debated a resolution that 'the affairs of the King of Earth must give way to the affairs of the King of Heaven'. While Eliot belaboured the High Church bishops who were poisoning the purity of the true faith and were not to be trusted with the interpretation of the Thirty-Nine Articles, other Members who shared his views accused the High Churchmen of being Jesuits at heart, ranted against the new paintings 'laid on the old face of the whore of Babylon' and accused the Bishop of Winchester of preaching 'flat popery'.

Charles felt his duty to be clear and forceful. He had read with admiration Richard Montague's *Appelo Caesarem* which identified popery with tyranny, and puritanism with anarchy, and which concluded 'poperie is originall of Superstition; puritanisme, the high-way unto prophaneness; both alike [are] enemies unto piety'. This stated the King's own views precisely. He had abhorred the behaviour and beliefs of the Queen's priests; he regarded with even more distaste the opinion of the Puritan landowners and merchants in the House of Commons and the Puritan preachers whose disrupting sermons could be heard all over London. It was his belief, no less than it had been his father's, that an attack on the bishops was an attack on the King.

He sent orders to the Speaker to ask the House to adjourn. Its militant Members refused to accept the request, shouting defiantly 'No! No!' in the Speaker's face. Sir John Eliot rose to insist that it was for the Commons to adjourn themselves. But, protested the Speaker, it had been the King's command: the House must adjourn; there could be no more speeches, and if there were he would leave the chair. So saying, he stood up and prepared to leave the chamber; but immediately two of Eliot's supporters sprang at him and forced him back into his seat. 'God's wounds!' one of them, Denzil Holles, a childhood friend of the King and now the impetuous Member for Dorchester, bellowed above the roar, 'God's wounds! You shall sit till we please to rise.' Another Member locked the door and put the key in his pocket.

In growing pandemonium, which on occasions came close to hysteria, the House passed resolutions against the religious policy of the Government and against both the levy and the payment of the customs duties, known as tonnage and poundage, without Parliamentary sanction. Each resolution was met by deafening shouts of 'Aye! Aye!' Then the doors were unlocked and the Members emerged, some of them elated by their bold defiance, many others, who would have slipped away earlier had the door not been locked, in nervous apprehension.

Charles was at once appalled and indignant. Unable to recognise the depth or the sincerity of Puritan feeling, or the respect in which most of his people held their Parliament, he condemned the 'undutiful and seditious' behaviour of the Commons in uncompromising terms, referring to Sir John Eliot's headstrong supporters as 'vipers', and ordering the arrest of Eliot himself. But if few others could share the strength of the King's feelings, there were those, even among the Puritans, who agreed with the diarist Simonds D'Ewes that 'divers fiery spirits in the house of commons' had been 'very faulty' and that their conduct could not be excused. For

D'Ewes the day of this latest clash between King and Parliament in 1629 was the 'most gloomy, sad, and dismal day for England that [had] happened in five hundred years'. There were many who shared this view, who believed that the King had been disgracefully wronged and were prepared to give him their sympathy and their support.

Charles himself, remembering always the violent death of his dear friend, Steenie, could never bring himself to change his opinion of Sir John Eliot who was left to languish in the Tower comforted only by his writing and his books. Depressed and resentful, deprived of fresh air and exercise, Eliot contracted tuberculosis. He wrote to the King, after nearly three years' close confinement, 'By reason of the quality of the air, I am fallen into a dangerous disease. I humbly beseech Your Majesty you will command your judges to set me at liberty that, for the recovery of my health, I may take some fresh air.' The King, noting the absence or remorse or even of apology for his vendetta against Buckingham or for what he took to be Eliot's crime against the state, refused the request. A second petition received no answer. On 27 November 1632 Eliot died. He was just forty years old. The eldest of his five sons asked permission to remove his father's body for burial in the Cornish churchyard where his family and ancestors lay. This request received a short reply: 'Let Sir John Eliot be buried in that parish wherein he died.' The Parliamentarians were given their first martyr.

6

The Patron and His Artists
1625–41

ON a warm August day in 1629, when Sir John Eliot was still incarcerated in the Tower whiling away the wearying hours in the compilation of a political tract, the King hurried to the royal palace of Oatlands to meet the Queen who had herself gone there from Tunbridge Wells, 'suddenly, by great journeys' in order to be close to him.

. Such impulsive displays of affection on both their parts had for some time now been a delightful, and touching feature of Court life; for even the most misanthropic observer could not but admit – however cynical his interpretation of the phenomenon – that after four years of marriage the King and Queen had fallen in love. They had reached 'such a degree of kindness', Archie Armstrong told the Earl of Carlisle, that the King was 'a wooer again'. He gazed at his wife with the sort of soulful desire with which he had regarded the Infanta in Madrid, repeatedly gave her presents, kissed her – so an ambassador reported to his government – 'a hundred times' in an hour, felt restless and unfulfilled when they were apart.

There had been a minor improvement in their relationship after the French attendants had been sent home in 1626. He had allowed her to keep her old nurse and her faithful dresser, her bakers and cooks, and had placed at the head of her Household the charming Lord Holland who had wooed her in Paris. Amongst her English ladies, both older and more experienced than herself, were the good-natured Kate Buckingham, whose love and championship of her wayward husband had made even the Duke less dislikeable in her eyes, and the lively and lovely, constantly entertaining Lucy, Countess of Carlisle.

Another comforting and benign influence upon the disgruntled young Queen was the French Ambassador, the Marshal de Bassompierre, who had been sent over from Paris after Henrietta's dismissed attendants had returned there. A brave soldier and voracious lover, Bassompierre was a man of tact and discrimination. His mission had been peculiarly difficult. He had been granted a public reception in London only on the understanding that he did not mention the matter of the French retinue – the cause, after all, of his visit – as this would make the King cross and the Queen cry; and the Queen almost did cry when she later saw her with the King in a private audience at Hampton Court. Charles, however, behaved with quiet decorum; and Bassompierre felt inclined to conclude that the fault of the matter lay not so much with the husband as with the emotional, impulsive and quick-tempered wife. On one occasion he told her so and, threatening to report as much to her family in Paris, he refused to have anything more to do with her for two days. By the time of his return to France, Bassompierre had helped not merely to gain some concessions for English Catholics but also to bring about some sort of reconciliation between the estranged pair.

This reconciliation had become surer and firmer when Buckingham's campaign on the Île de Ré had deprived Charles of his friend's companionship for a longer period than he had ever previously had to bear. He had been driven to seek consolation in his loneliness in the company of his now less cantankerous wife. But it was Buckingham's murder which had brought about the transformation in the marriage; and in the comfort her fond presence gave him in the agony of his grief was conceived a new love.

Henrietta was soon pregnant; and on 13 May 1629 the baby, a boy, was born at Greenwich Palace. It was a difficult, premature birth; the local midwife had fainted in the royal bedchamber, overcome by her responsibility; the father had paced back and forth urging that at all costs the mother's life must be saved. The baby, weak and small, died within an hour of its christening.

But Henrietta soon recovered; her husband was so kind and considerate, so different from her brother, Louis XIII, when *his* wife through carelessness had miscarried his heir. 'As to my loss,' she said, 'I wish to forget it.' She was, she decided, 'not only the happiest princess, but the happiest woman in the world.' By the middle of October she was pregnant again, with a pre-natal craving for shell-fish.

She wore a trinket around her neck which her mother had sent her with an assurance that, wearing it always, she would not miscarry again. She placed such great faith in it that once when she lost it she could not stop trembling; but she had no cause for worry. The baby, born on 29 May 1630, another boy, was big and healthy. Very dark, to be sure, and, as even she had to admit, extremely ugly; but so fat and healthy. One day, she felt sure he would grow a 'little fairer'. They christened him Charles.

Other children followed him with the most satisfying regularity, a princess, Mary, the next year, another son, Prince James, in 1633, a second daughter, Princess Elizabeth in 1635, then a third daughter in 1636 and a third son in 1640. A fourth daughter, born at Whitehall, died within a few minutes of her birth; but all the others were healthy children; and their mother, her years of unhappiness now far behind her, settled down to a life of full contentment.

The Court which formed the background to the Queen's life was very much changed since the days when Christian of Denmark had visited King James and, smeared with wine and jelly, had collapsed at the feet of one of Queen Anne's drunken ladies.

In sharp contrast, King Charles's Court was decorous, orderly, elegant and ceremonial. Foreign observers were astonished by its almost ritualistic formality. Not even the King of Spain was waited upon with such devoted subservience and minute regard to a drill-like and unchanging custom as was the King of England. The French Ambassador discovered with some indignation that his wife was obliged to remain standing in the King's presence for, on formal occasions, no lady at the English Court, other than the Queen was permitted to sit down in His Majesty's sight.

There were rumours in London, of course, that all was not as demure as it seemed: merchants' young wives, foolish enough to accept an invitation to some Court entertainment, were not safe there – 'not a lobby nor chamber, if it could speak, but would verify this'. Yet, in fact, as the widow of a Parliamentarian later confirmed, the 'fools and bawds, mimics and catamites of the former Court' had grown out of fashion 'and the nobility and courtiers who did not quite abandon their debaucheries, yet so reverenced the King as to retire into corners to practice them.'

But although severely and exactly formal, the Court was not always dull. The Queen ensured that. She loved dancing and colourful clothes, and the company of dashing handsome and rather disreputable men like Henry Jermyn, her Master of the Horse, and of nubile women as beautiful as Lady Mary Villiers; she loved to surround herself with fashionable young poets, to be gay with them and to show that she understood their wit, to act with them, even to go to the theatre with them, which was something no one could remember a Queen ever having done before. Ignoring the horror of the London citizens, she went so far as to watch the performances of a French company which had women on the stage playing the parts of women. She took a special pleasure in her monkeys, blackamoors and dwarfs, in all the freaks and follies of a Court which let Archie Armstrong make jokes about William Laud, Archbishop of Canterbury – whom she, like most women, did not like – and which provided the spectacle of the absurdly tiny figure of the dwarf Jeffrey Hudson – who had once, in full armour, jumped out of a pie and bowed to her on the Duke of Buckingham's dining-table – being picked up between the two halves of a loaf of bread as a tasty morsel by the gigantic porter at the palace gate.

The King complaisant and loving, indulged Henrietta's frivolities and extravagance. She had lost by now what little claim to beauty she had ever possessed. Yet, delighting in the knowledge of his love for her and in her happy fortune, she had that quick and charming gaiety that can dispense with beauty for its effects. She succeeded so well in rescuing the Court from the dullness which the King's tastes and temperament might have imposed upon it, that the Venetian envoy could write of it as '*la piu sontuosa e la piu allegra del mondo*'.

It was certainly sumptuous. Every day the King's table – where he sat in state and in public, served by attendants on bended knee – was provided with twenty-eight dishes, brought in to a fanfare of trumpets that temporarily stilled the less strident notes of his private orchestra. The Queen's table had twenty-four dishes; the other eighty-four had over four hundred dishes between them. Each year, in addition to vast quantities of pigs, fish, boars, game and bacon, three thousand carcasses of beef were consumed in Whitehall Palace alone, fourteen thousand sheep and lambs, twenty-four thousand birds.

The staff necessary to maintain the huge and complicated organisation of Whitehall – more, in fact, a rambling village than a palace – was immense. The numbers of those employed in the various departments in the King's Household, the Queen's Household, the Households of the Prince of Wales and of the other royal children was probably not less than 1,700. Almost half of all peacetime royal expenditure was devoted to this labyrinthine complex known vaguely as the Court.

Art and Architecture

A detail, showing Morris dancers, from *The Thames at Richmond*, a painting of the Flemish school, formerly attributed to David Vinckeboons (1578–1629).

Ben Jonson (1572–1637) by an unknown artist, painted during the years when he and Inigo Jones were co-operating with each other in the production of court masques.

A drawing of Inigo Jones (1573–1652), Surveyor of the King's Works, by Van Dyck.

Designs for masques by Inigo Jones: (*above*) *Chloridia* scene I (*below*) *Salmacida Spolia* scene V.

Costume designs by Inigo Jones for the masque
The Fortunate Isles: an 'Airy Spirit', 'Scogano',
'Skelton' and a 'Brother of the Rosy Cross'.

Two figures designed by
Inigo Jones for a masque.

Two figures from a masque by
Inigo Jones. (*below left*)
Charles I in Davenant's
Salmacida Spolia of 1640 and
(*right*) Henrietta Maria as
'Chloris' in *Chloridia* of 1631.
Both costume designs are by
Inigo Jones.

An etching by Wenceslaus Hollar of Covent Garden, the Earl of Bedford's estate developed under the supervison of Inigo Jones in the 1630s.

Whitehall as seen from the river in an etching by Hollar.

(*right*) The interior of Inigo Jones's Queen's Chapel St James's Palace, 1623–27, shows how strongly the architect was influenced by his years of study in Italy. The chapel, the first to be built in England in the classical rather than the gothic taste, was begun for the Infanta Maria and finished for Henrietta Maria.

(*opposite*) Henrietta Maria's bedroom in the Queen's House, Greenwich (now the National Maritime Museum), which was started by Inigo Jones in 1616 for Charles's mother, Anne of Denmark, and completed for his wife in 1635. It was originally designed as a house in two parts, one part, within the precincts of Greenwich Palace, the other in the Park. The two parts were joined by a bridge which crossed the road between them. In 1661, however, the two parts were closed up to provide more accommodation.

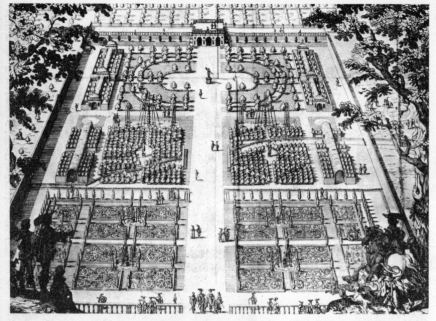

The garden at Wilton House (*below*) as it was laid out by Isaac de Caux for Philip, 4th Earl of Pembroke, and illustrated by him in *Wilton House* (1645).

Wilton House (*opposite*), built between 1633 and 1640 for the Earl of
Pembroke to designs of Isaac de Caux. De Caux was recommended to Lord
Pembroke by Inigo Jones. Charles and Henrietta Maria 'loved Wilton above all
places and went there every summer'. Its beautiful Double Cube room (*above*)
contains portraits of them both by Van Dyck.

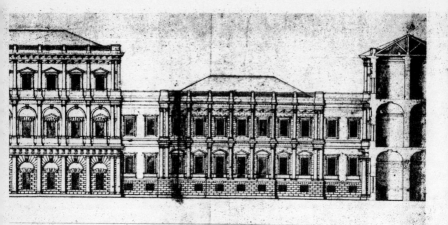

(*above*) Inigo Jones's design for the west front of St Paul's. St Paul's was
extensively repaired in the 1630s by Inigo Jones, who cased most of it with
ashlar masonry at a cost of £100,000 providing it with this new portico,
destroyed with the rest of the cathedral in the Great Fire of 1666.

(*opposite*) Inigo Jones's design for Whitehall Palace showing the Banqueting House. The Palace designs were never realised. The Banqueting House (1619–22), the best known of all the architect's works, an imposing, if small-scale Italianate *palazzo* in the manner of Palladio, struck many a contemporary Londoner as absurdly incongruous amongst its Tudor and Jacobean neighbours. Almost the whole of the old Whitehall Palace was destroyed in the fire of 1689, but the Banqueting House survived.

Inigo Jones's design for stables at Newmarket where James I had built himself a house for the hunting.

Lamport Hall, a country house in Northamptonshire built to the designs of John Webb (1611–74) in 1654–7.

Coleshill House, a purely classical country house in Berkshire, was designed for his cousin by Sir Roger Pratt (1620–84) in 1649 after a long period of study on the Continent which Pratt undertook during the Civil War.

(*opposite, below*) The portico of The Vyne, Hampshire, designed by John Webb, a pupil of Inigo Jones. It is the the earliest classical portico to a country house in England.

The staircase at Ham House (1637–8), an early example of a staircase with carved and pierced panels instead of balusters, which reached its fullest development after the Restoration.

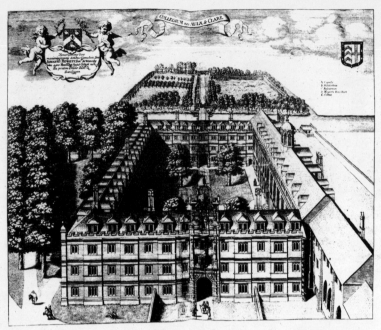

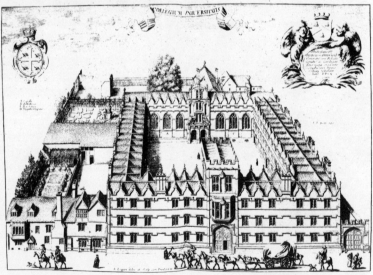

Considerable building at Oxford and Cambridge was undertaken during the period. These views from *Oxonia Illustrata* (1675) and *Cantabrica Illustrata* (1690) show Christ's College, Cambridge, (*opposite, above*) Clare College, Cambridge, (*above*) University College, Oxford and (*opposite, below*) Oriel College, Oxford. The building at Oxford owes much to the influence of William Laud.

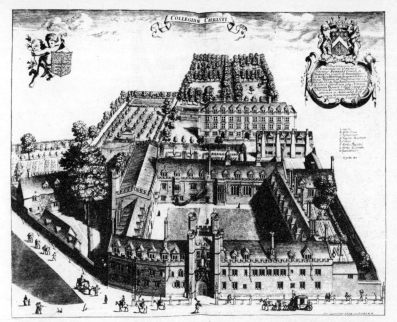

COLLEGIVM CHRISTI

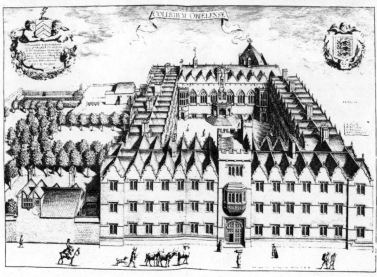

COLLEGIVM ORIELENSE

Designs for monograms for Charles I by Inigo Jones.

It included the staffs of the Royal Mews at Charing Cross and of the other royal stables, the Bargemen and Watermen, Messengers and Musicians, Huntsmen, Harriers and Falconers, Gentlemen Pensioners and Yeomen of the Guard, as well as all those officials below stairs with such appointments as Pages of the Scalding House, Breadbearers of the Pantry and Groom Cooks, the officials of the Great Wardrobe, which supplied furnishings as well as clothing, and of the Chamber, which, under the direction of the Lord Chamberlain, found posts, often honorific, for that type of man more usually associated with the word courtier.

The King still ruled as well as reigned, so the Court, in addition to providing for the comfort and ensuring the dignity of his Majesty, had to provide him with the means of government. Many, if not most, members of the Council held Court appointments and the Secretaries of State were very much the King's servants whose attendances at Court was essential to their duties.

These duties were considerable, for Charles himself did as little work as he could. He had neither taste nor talent for administration, declining to apply himself to problems of government which could not be solved by reference to his own fixed ideas, preferring the company of men whose cheerful optimism encouraged his own delusive hope that the country was as well run as the Court, and becoming either inattentive or irritable when obliged to concentrate his slow-moving mind on an uncongenial topic. 'The King is more willing *not* to hear than to hear,' complained William Laud after an exasperating attempt to make Charles understand a particular problem. 'He neither is,' grumbled Laud on a later occasion, 'nor knows how to be great.'

Hours, days even, that should have been spent facing the difficulties of government were passed playing bowls and tennis and golf, in swimming and riding and hunting, in theological discussion, in conducting visitors round the treasures of his palaces, in singing or playing the viol da gamba, or in supervising the preparations for Court entertainments and Court masques.

The masque – a kind of stylised pageant, allegorical and spectacular, whose complicated symbolism was expressed in verse, song, dance, theatrically extravagant movement, intricate mechanical devices, and by the declamations of fantastically costumed courtiers – had been one of the main delights of Charles's mother. At Denmark

F

House and at Whitehall Palace enormous sums had been spent on these diversions in which she could indulge her passion for display and dressing-up.

The first of Queen Anne's masques, the *Masque of Blackness*, had been performed in the Elizabethan Banqueting House at Whitehall on Twelfth Night 1605. Its magical theme and setting were characteristic of numerous other masques which were to be performed in various London and country palaces over the next thirty-five years. It told the fantastic story of the twelve daughters of Niger, the great Aethiopian river-god, and of their introduction to Albion. Blackamoors and nymphs, tritons and mermaids, monsters and nereids cavorted and sang, appearing from the raging waves in huge conches and disappearing into the fathomless depths of the ocean, all dressed in a variety of costumes, bejewelled and magnificent.

The *Masque of Blackness* – with which King James was 'not a little delighted' – was written by Ben Jonson whose collaboration with its designer, Inigo Jones, produced for the Court of King Charles, as well as for that of his father, as fine a series of entertainments as had ever dazzled the audiences at the Medici Court in Florence. It was followed by the *Masque of Beauty*, the *Masque of Queens*, *Chloridia*, in which Henrietta Maria herself played the part of Chloris, and by many other gorgeous productions – some of them lasting for over twelve hours and costing almost as many thousands of pounds – in which the beauty of the verse was matched by the inventiveness of the costumes and settings and by those marvellous contrivances by which mountains were made to move, angels to fly, devils to sink into Hell. To Jonson, indeed, it seemed that Inigo Jones's costumes and settings, mechanical devices and movable scenery were considered more important – certainly by Jones himself – than his own contributions to their joint enterprises. The final break between the two men came in 1631 when Jonson published the text of *Love's Triumph through Callipolis*, with his name as its author taking precedence on the title page before that of Inigo Jones. For Jones, this was the ultimate insult. Arrogant, self-centred and inordinately vain, an '*huomo vanissimo e molto vantatore*' in the Papal agent's opinion, he protested indignantly at this suggestion that his own ingenious contrivances, brilliant settings and splendid costumes – the *sine qua non* of any successful masque – should be considered of less merit than Jonson's versifications. Thereafter Jonson, quite as arrogant and as much given to self-commendation as his rival, lost Court patronage. Jones worked with other poets; with Aurelian Townsend, Thomas May and Thomas Carew, and with Sir William D'Avenant whose *Salmacida Spolia* was the last masque to be performed at Whitehall before the Civil War brought all such delights and extravagances to an end.

At the time of his break with Jonson, Inigo Jones was at the height of his powers, the self-appointed arbiter of taste at Court, a man often to be seen in the company of Charles and Henrietta, dogmatically asserting the relative worth of various royal treasures, attributing pictures to appropriate painters and congratulating himself when the attributions proved to be correct. His emphatic self-confidence and the high opinion he entertained of his own qualities and accomplishments were not ill-founded. It was as an extremely talented designer and painter that he had first achieved recognition at Queen Anne's Court; but by the accession of Queen Anne's son he had been recognised as an architect of genius.

He was born in 1573, the son of a Smithfield clothworker. Apprenticed to a joiner in St Paul's churchyard on leaving school, he travelled abroad after his father's death to 'study the Arts of Design'; and by 1608, having achieved some reputation as a 'picture-maker' at Court, he was making architectural drawings which reveal his fascination with the great Italian masters. In 1610 he was appointed Surveyor to the Prince of Wales; and a few years later visited Italy again, this time in the suite of Thomas Howard, Earl of Arundel, a well-known courtier, art connoisseur and collector, who had performed in several of Jones's masques. Imbued with a passion for the classical style in architecture as exemplified by the illustrations in *Quattro libri dell' architettura* by the great Paduan architect, Andrea Palladio, he returned to London to take up the duties of Surveyor of the King's Works. Soon classical buildings designed by him or designed by others under his influence were springing up all over London and in the country.

There were houses and churches, stables, lodgings and out-buildings, staircases, galleries, watergates and archways; for the King there were new works at Newmarket and Theobalds, Whitehall and Oatlands, a new Banqueting House to replace the brick and timber structure burned down in 1619; for the King's friend, the Duke of Buckingham, a new Thameside mansion; for the Queen a new chapel at St James's. Later, in 1630, work was resumed on the Queen's House at Greenwich for Henrietta Maria; also for her Jones frequently turned his attention to improvements and decorations at Denmark House, in the Strand. In 1631 – before William Laud had left the see of London for Canterbury but was already strongly advocating the rebuilding and beautifying of England's churches – a new Royal Commission was appointed to restore the decayed St Paul's, used for years as a market, register office, children's playground, meeting-place for lawyers and as a rubbish dump by citizens who tipped their refuse into the crypt. Within little more than a decade of the Commission's appointment, a virtually new cathedral had appeared, with a porticoed west front which, in the words of his talented assistant John Webb, contracted for its architect 'the envy of all *Christendom*, for a Piece of Architecture, not to be parallell'd in these last Ages of the World'.

As Surveyor of King Charles's Works, Inigo Jones was responsible not only for royal and public buildings but for the supervision of private developments by landowners and speculators who managed to obtain a royal licence. And it was soon clear that only those developers who could afford to add to the 'uniformitie and Decency' of any particular area would be granted a licence, and that the designs of all new buildings in London would be closely scrutinised in Jones's office. Some of these buildings were actually designed by Inigo Jones himself whose artistry has been recognised in at least one of the houses, Lindsey House, on the west side of Lincoln's Inn Fields, an open space which was developed – much to the annoyance of the lawyers who lived around it – by a Bedfordshire builder, William Newton, in Charles's reign.

In Covent Garden, which was developed by royal licence in the 1630s, Inigo Jones was responsible for the entire layout, the design of the terraced houses around a central piazza and of the Tuscan church on its western side. The licence, bought by the owner of the Covent Garden estate, the fourth Earl of Bedford, for a fee of two thousand pounds, provided for the building of houses 'fitt for habitacons of Gentlemen and men of ability'. The development when completed – delightful as it appeared to those who shared the taste of Bedford and his distinguished architect – seemed a disgraceful blight to those accustomed to the irregularities and informalities of Tudor and Jacobean vernacular, the homely sixteenth-century brickwork, sloping tiled roofs and exposed timber beams of which

London was still largely composed. This new, foreign style of architecture, blossoming under the patronage of the Court, was to most Londoners thoroughly distasteful. They had little sympathy for the ambition, shared by the King and his Surveyor, to make a new and far more imposing capital city, to erect ranges of classical buildings, even a massive new Whitehall Palace, twice the size of the Escorial, which would be worthy of the greatest town in Europe. They far preferred the old familiar mullions and gables, barge-boards and brackets, to all these Italian ideas of construction which seemed to them 'like Bug-beares or Gorgon heads'; they saw in this new Court architecture the desecration and ruin of old England's streets.

But neither Charles's encouragement of such classical Italianate architects as Inigo Jones and of such Italianate master masons as Nicolas Stone, nor even his wife's extravagant patronage of Court masques, seemed as reprehensible to many of his subjects as his support and maintenance of foreign artists, his outrageously lavish expenditure on Continental works of art, his 'squandering away millions of pounds upon old rotten pictures and broken nosed marbles'.

Charles's interest in fine art – intensified, no doubt, by visits to the splendid galleries of the King of Spain during his visit to Madrid – seems to have been first aroused both by those rich patrons like the Earl of Arundel who attended the Court of his brother, Prince Henry, and, more decisively, by the Duke of Buckingham whose country house at Burley-on-the-Hill near Oakham contained as fine a collection of treasures as any house in England. Many of them were bought for him by Sir Henry Wotton, the learned and discriminating English Ambassador at Venice for the better part of twenty years, and by Balthazar Gerbier, the Flemish artist and diplomatist to whom the design of the York Watergate, the only surviving part of the Duke's London mansion, has been recently ascribed. Before being burned down in the Civil War – during which most of its valuable contents were purchased for the galleries of the Archduke Leopold at Prague – Buckingham's house at Burley-on-the-Hill contained no less than nineteen pictures by Titian (for one of which, the *Ecce Homo*, its owner was reputed to have refused an offer of £7,000), thirteen by Veronese, twenty-one by Bassano and thirteen by Rubens, including a magnificent portrait of the Duke now in the Uffizi Gallery at Florence.

Buckingham had met Rubens in Paris in 1625. There was at that time no more famous painter in Europe. Born at Siegen in Westphalia in 1577, Rubens had first studied under Flemish masters and then had spent eight years in the household of Vincenzo Gonzago, Duke of Mantua; thereafter he had been appointed painter in ordinary at the Court of the Archduke Albrecht in Antwerp. Employed by his patrons as a diplomatist as well as a painter he came to England on a diplomatic mission in 1629, and immediately found a new patron in King Charles for whom he executed several works. These included the painted panels for the ceiling of Inigo Jones's Banqueting House, which represent the union of England and Scotland, the benefits of the government of James I and his apotheosis.

Rubens was but one of a number of artists from the low countries whose work was commissioned by the English Court. Daniel Mytens was already working in England when Charles became King; Cornelius Janssen, born in London in 1593, worked here until his retirement to Holland in 1643; Gerard van Honthorst painted numerous pictures for Charles in England in the 1620s and later at his home in Utrecht; and after Van Dyck's arrival in London in 1632, Jan van Reyn, Adrian Hanneman, Jan van Bockhorst, Remi van Leemput and Peter Thys all soon followed him.

Van Dyck, like his former master Rubens, was welcomed immediately by the English King who knighted him, as he had knighted Rubens, soon after his arrival, found him a studio at Blackfriars, and sat for him for hours on end for those remarkable portraits – sad, wistful, withdrawn, idealized yet perceptive – which were to become so integral a part of the legend of the Martyr King.

Three years before he came to settle in England, which he had visited before at the invitation of the Countess of Arundel, Van Dyck had been approached by one of Charles's agents, Endymion Porter, with a commission to paint the picture *Rinaldo and Armida*. For it was one of the main duties of travelling agents like Porter, Toby Mathew, Kenelm Digby, and Balthazar Gerbier – as well as of resident diplomatists such as Sir Henry Wotton at Venice, and Sir Dudley Carleton, English envoy at the Hague, and of connoisseurs and occasional envoys like the Earl of Arundel and Lord Dorchester – to commission works from promising artists and established masters, and to begin negotiations for the purchase of single masterpieces or whole collections.

So gradually with the help of these men – and of Abraham van der Doort, the Dutch Keeper of the King's Cabinet at White-hall, and Gregorio Panzani, a papal envoy in London, whose patron, Cardinal Barberini, was quite prepared for his protégé to rob Rome of her most valuable ornaments, if, in exchange, 'we might be so happy as to have the King of England's name among those princes who submit to the Holy See' – Charles's own collection grew into one of the finest in Europe, certainly the finest ever assembled by an English King. On the walls of his twenty-four royal residences, from palaces to hunting lodges, ranged in splendid profusion, were the works of every Flemish painter of repute from Rubens and Van Dyck to Jakob Jordaens and Peter van der Faes; of Van Dyck's most talented English pupil William Dobson, who succeeded Van Dyck as Serjeant-Painter to the King, and of numerous Italian masters; Leonardo, Titian, Raphael, Tintoretto, Correggio, Mantegna, Georgione, and Romano.

Amongst the pictures were coins and marbles, medals and cameos, the intricate work of master goldsmiths, silversmiths and jewellers, treasures from the ruins of Apollo's temple at Delos, tapestries from the flourishing works at Mortlake, busts by Bernini and Nicholas Stone, etchings by Wenceslaus Hollar, the royal children's Bohemian drawing master, the entire collection of the Duke of Mantua (purchased for £25,000), 'a chess board, said to be Queen Elizabeth's, inlaid with gold and pearl', 'a conjuring drum from Lapland', 'a Saxon King's mace', and so many statues that 'a whole army of old foreign emperors, captains and senators [were landed] on his coasts to do the King homage and attend him in his palaces'.

But Charles was not just a collector. He had a true appreciation of art, particularly painting. He could make an attribution and date a picture with as much authority as Arundel or Inigo Jones, though with a gracious diffidence that was in pleasant contrast to Jones's complacent dogmatism. Rubens, on whose advice he bought the Raphael cartoons – among the few masterpieces in his collection to escape the sales held after his death by the Commonwealth – described him as '*le prince le plus amateur de la peinture qui soit au monde*'. In London, which could boast of so few native artists of talent, he helped to found a school in Covent Garden where those 'who could prove themselves gentlemen' could be instructed in painting, architecture and antiquities as well as in those subjects to be encountered in the more narrow curricula of schools and universities, including some of a scientific nature.

For Charles's interests extended also to science. He gave his patronage to William Harvey, who discovered the circulation of the blood, and to Sir Theodore Turquet de Mayerne, the great and kindly physician, whom his father had invited from France, the man who first established in England the clinical study of medicine. He encouraged the studies of those of his courtiers who manifested an interest in mathematics, engineering or invention: Edward Somerset who had installed a hydraulic lift in his father's castle, and Lord Herbert who had invented a new type of gun-carriage, both found the King interested and helpful.

Yet, for all this gracious interest in the work of his protégés and servants, for all the exquisite courtesy of his manner towards them, his gentleness and constancy, his innate goodness, Charles was more revered and respected than loved. His grave reserve, fastidious constraint, and lack of humour were barriers to intimacy that all but a very few found it impossible to cross. His slight stammer which, in another man might have been appealing, was in him merely a defect which made it the more difficult for him to put strangers at their ease, seeming to emphasise the atmosphere of melancholy that surrounded him. This atmosphere was reflected in the normally sad expression of his face, an expression so well conveyed in Van Dyck's *Charles I in Three Positions* that when Bernini saw it he described the countenance depicted as a countenance 'doomed'. 'Never,' the sculptor said, 'never have I beheld features more unfortunate.'

Underlying the melancholy there was a certain lack of sympathy in the King's responses, a defensive rejection of an intimacy that might reveal him as a less assured man than he tried to be. Few men ever felt that Charles really liked them. Few servants ever felt that their services were truly appreciated: if they did not do their duty they were politely dismissed; if they *did* do their duty they were doing what was expected of them, they were treated well but rarely with a hint of warmth or affection.

Charles was a studious man rather than an intelligent one; he understood books better than people. Moreover, he seemed incapable of making that sort of contact with his subjects which ensured for his eldest son, despite all his manifest faults, a far greater personal popularity and following.

7

Politics and Puritans
1629–40

WHEN Charles got rid of Parliament in 1629 – the last Parliament to meet for more than eleven years – he persuaded himself that his political problems were over. The expedition which the Duke of Buckingham had been preparing at the time of his death in Portsmouth, in the forlorn hope of recapturing his lost popularity by a military triumph in defence of Protestantism, had sailed in September 1628, under the direction of the Earl of Lindsey, and had proved yet another failure. But on 18 October the Huguenot defenders of La Rochelle surrendered, and Charles was able to make peace. Declining to break that peace, even for the sake of his sister, thus sparing himself the heavy and extraordinary expenses of a Continental war, he was able to pay his way for several years without the necessity of calling a Parliament.

For the ordinary costs of government he and his ministers resorted to a number of devices, some of doubtful legality and none of them popular. Customs duties were collected as of right; Crown lands were managed with exigent severity; medieval laws were resuscitated to extend the limits of royal forests, and to fine encroachers, trespassers and all those owners of freehold land worth £40 a year or more who had not applied for knighthood at Charles's coronation; prosecutions were instituted with a view to the collection of dues from various bodies which had infringed the letter of their charters; monopolies were sold to companies and corporations since the law forbade their sale to individuals; country gentlemen living in London who did not own a London house were fined for contravening a proclamation – issued in 1617 and since repeated – which required them to return to their estates and concentrate on local government; lands in Scotland which had formerly belonged to the Crown but had since been alienated were taken back into royal hands.

Such measures could not but fail to antagonise all those who felt themselves, their lands, or pockets hard and unjustly treated. Nor did the King win back their loyalty by the benefits conferred upon the country as a whole during this period of his personal rule, even though these benefits were considerable. New roads were built and old ones improved; canals were dug and swamps were drained; ale-houses were regulated; a postal service was started; the vagrancy laws were enforced; poor rates were levied; a real attempt was made to make local government effective and to find work for the unemployed. But while those who benefited the most from these public works and social reforms had reason to be thankful, the more wealthy and influential classes felt less gratitude than irritation at the Crown's overbearing interference and high-handed intrusion into local affairs. Certainly the ministers and officials most closely associated with the Government's policy provoked a widespread distrust of its purpose.

Richard Weston, the Treasurer, on whose administration and devices the King's revenues depended between 1628 and 1635, was a nervous, disputatious and dishonest man, quick to take offence and ready to give it, unsure of himself, discontented, hesitant and inquisitive. William Noy, the Attorney-General, who had once been a Parliament-man, was quite as disliked as Weston. His clumsy manner, combined with an aloof reserve, gloomy expression and malicious humour, ensured his unpopularity at Court, while his defection to Whitehall and his wily ingenuity in arguing the King's case rendered him suspect in the country at large. Weston's successor, William Juxon, Bishop of London, was admitted to be an honest man, but he had been appointed largely because the King was reluctant to offend those courtiers and servants who would stand to lose so much money by the more rigid controls of the royal revenues that a sterner official might introduce. The Chancellor of the Exchequer, the cheerful and amusing Lord Cottington, was far too easy-going to introduce them; Sir John Coke, the senior Secretary of State, was too old now to be bothered to introduce them; Sir Francis Windebanke, the other Secretary of State, and Sir Henry Vane, Comptroller of the Household, profited too much from the lack of them ever to think of introducing them. From the unscrupulous and pretentious Lord Finch, Chief Justice since 1635 and – thanks to the Queen's influence – Lord Keeper from 1640, nothing good had ever been expected.

Thomas Wentworth, President of the Council of the North and later Lord Deputy of Ireland, laboured under the same mistrust as a defector to the Court from Parliament as did William Noy. A tall, stooping man whose sallow, hard, worn face was swiftly transformed by a smile of rare charm and whose beautiful voice and hands seemed to belong to a far gentler personality, Wentworth was the owner of huge estates in Yorkshire. He had, as Member for Pontefract, been one of the King's most accomplished opponents in the early Parliaments until ambition, a strong taste for order, unity, thoroughness and authority – and a complementary distaste for the kind of Puritan enthusiasm associated with Sir John Eliot – had brought him over to the King's side. On his taking up office as his Majesty's viceroy at York he had expressed the now firmly held conviction that 'the authority of a King is the keystone - which closeth up the arch of order and government'.

Although Charles had no First Minister after Buckingham's death, nor indeed any intimate friend, Wentworth was by far the most talented of those who served him. Hard, intelligent, energetic, impatient and determined, he had all the authoritarian's self-confidence, tenacity of purpose and devotion to discipline. Yet, despite an intimidating brusqueness with strangers, a charmless manner with acquaintances, an alarmingly bad temper, and a strong capacity for self-deception and self-congratulation, he was not a dislikeable man. He was emotional and generous, an affectionate father, and a fond husband to three successive wives all of whom appear to have been devoted to him. Although he had few friends he was loyal to those he did make and always ready to do what he could to help them. He was a pleasant companion with a ready if childish humour and a well-developed gift for anecdote.

The King who recognised and respected his qualities could never bring himself to like him, while Wentworth was never so much attached to the person of the King as to the idea of kingship. Twice he asked Charles for an earldom so that his position would be lent the more authority, and twice he was refused. 'I desire you not to think that I am displeased with the asking,' the King replied to his first request, 'though for the present I grant it not. For I acknowledge that noble minds are always accompanied with noble ambitions.' 'The marks of my Favours that stop malicious tongues are neither Places nor titles,' Wentworth was told on the second occasion, 'but the little welcome I give to accusers, and the willing ear I give to my servants.'

'I will serve His Majesty with the same diligence, labour and faith as formerly,' he confessed in a letter written after this second refusal; 'yet to confess a plain truth . . . with less cheerfulness in myself hereafter.'

The confession was made to William Laud, Archbishop of Canterbury, with whom, as Wentworth said, he 'neither must nor ever [could] dissemble.' There was, in truth, a real and deep understanding between them. Their backgrounds were widely different; the one, the son of an ancient family from Wentworth Woodhouse, had been born to great wealth which he had greatly increased by none too scrupulous methods; the other, the son of a Reading clothier, was described by Sir Simonds D'Ewes as 'a little low red-faced man of mean parentage'. Those who disliked the look of Laud's alert flushed face and his clever, sardonic eyes, referred to him disdainfully as 'The Shrimp' or that 'little meddling hocus-pocus'.

The two men shared few interests in common; Wentworth found relaxation with his hawks and falcons, the Archbishop in his study. Yet their letters reveal the depth of their mutual affection and sympathy, the extent to which they both rested their faith in discipline, unity, order and thoroughness as virtues in the government both of the State and of the Church; and in applying the same principles to the restoration of 'decent order' and unity to the Anglican Church as Wentworth did to the suppression of abuses in the north-and disorders in Ireland, Laud aroused as much fear as hostility.

Overworked, fussy, unimaginative and outspoken, sometimes irritable and often rude, Laud made many enemies. He was scholarly and devout, withdrawing seven times a day, however pressing his business, to kneel in prayer; his letters and diaries reveal, beneath the intolerance and superstitious anxiety, a man of simple, innate goodness; yet those who had been victims of his sharp retorts and reprimands, who had seen his eyes flash with sudden and alarming fury, who had been shouted down by him in argument, who had suffered at his hands in the Star Chamber or in the Court of High Commission, had good cause to fear and dislike him.

Closing his mind to the possibility that the Puritans within the Anglican Church held opinions as strong and sincere as his own, deeply mistrusting their passion for sermons, he attacked their faith as though it were a 'wolf to be held by the ears'. He introduced measures which effectively reduced the numbers of those who preached Puritanism while appointing to vacant sees bishops who were prepared to endorse his own views on conformity, the use of the prayer book and surplice, the proper position of the Communion table as an altar at the east end of the church rather than as a mere slab of wood in the middle, the need to make services more reverent and churches more beautiful.

'It is called superstition nowadays,' he once indignantly complained, 'for any man to come with more reverence into a church, than a tinker and his dog into an ale-house.'

There was certainly much truth in Laud's strictures, much need for reform. All over the country there were filthy churches, churches without windows, churches with mud floors, churches occupied by squatters or used for business meetings and parties. Countrymen took their dogs in with them, let their pigs root about in the graveyard, shot birds in the nave, used the gravestones as cheese presses. Townsmen put their hats on the altar, or kept them on their heads as a sign of their superiority over the parson. Some clergy were known to wish the mayor good morning in the middle of reading the lesson; others cut up their surplices for towels or referred to the bishops in their sermons as 'upstart mushrumps'.

Yet to his opponents Laud's insistence on the necessity for making churches more beautiful and services more orderly, on ritual, vestments and organs, his sometimes brutal methods of enforcing obedience to his ideas, his determination to restore to the Church some of the wealth which it had lost at the Reformation, and his canvassing for the appointment of ecclesiastics to important secular offices, all smacked strongly of popery. But if he could infuriate the Lord Chief Justice by openly attacking him for being too lenient to Puritans, if he could approve the sentence passed by the Star Chamber upon a knight who, for libelling the Bishops of London, was to be degraded from his rank and to have his ears cropped, Laud could react with scarcely less angry indignation to the numbers of conversions to Roman Catholicism that took place at Court under the influence of a foreign and Roman Catholic Queen. It was true that he did not consider Roman Catholicism as so great a threat to the soul and the true Church as such errors as Presbyterianism, but more than once he warned Charles of the dangers to the Church from the 'Queen's party', and from men like George Con, the Vatican's agent in England, a charming, cultivated Scotsman with whom

Charles delighted to discuss religion and art.

Laud – like Wentworth, very English and insular in his outlook – set great store by the Englishness of the established Church, the Church which had kept itself free from the deviations of the medieval popes, which remained the true Church of Christendom. He conceived it to be his duty under God to maintain it upon that course, to keep it strictly organised, its services conducted according to a settled, standard ritual, to ensure that it continued to steer that 'middle way', as the King described it, 'between the pomp of superstitious tyranny and the meanness of fantastick anarchy', and that it continued to be in the control of and at the service of the secular State.

This view of the meaning and importance of the English Church offended both Catholic and Puritan, yet it could not be said that the jointly held beliefs of the King and the Archbishop were imposed upon a wholly antagonistic people, a people, for the most part, sincerely religious, sharing the belief that true religion was the basis of good government. There was much in 'Laudism', and not only in its nationalistic overtones, which appealed strongly to all classes.

Indeed, during these eleven years when Charles ruled the country without reference to Parliament, there were men enough to be found who believed the country in general, as well as its Church in particular, was set upon a fair and encouraging course. Admittedly, Charles's Government could not claim all or even a large proportion of the credit. Its foreign policy, for instance, was neither successful nor popular. Charles's devious attempts to support the Protestant cause in Europe by a *rapprochement* with Spain was widely mistrusted or misunderstood; while his efforts to repair and strengthen the Navy, by the imposition and extension of the tax known as Ship Money, were strongly resisted when it became clear that the new and refitted ships were being used not only against pirates and England's traditional maritime enemies but for operations along the continental coast which left the country's territorial waters unpatrolled and unprotected. Nonetheless, for most of the 1630s England was prosperous and at peace, trade boomed and the voices of protest were temporarily silent. Edward Hyde, then a successful young lawyer, went so far as to suggest that in 1639 'England enjoyed the greatest measure of felicity it had ever known'. But then, Hyde continued, in the midst of this scene of happiness and plenty 'a small, scarce discernible cloud arose in the

North, which was shortly after attended with such a storm, that even rooted up the greatest and tallest cedars of the three nations; blasted all its beauty and fruitfulness; brought its strength to decay, and its glory to reproach'.

The cloud had first appeared in Scotland, where in their determination to bring back 'beauty and order' into the plain services of the Scottish Church, the King and Laud introduced a new prayer-book designed along Anglican lines. When this new liturgy was introduced in St Giles's Cathedral in Edinburgh there was a riot. The congregation, mostly women and implacably Calvinist, drowned the bishop's words in shouts of protest and outrage. One of them, overhearing the word 'Amen' above the hubbub, turned round in fury, struck the offender over the head with her Bible, shouting, 'Traitor! Dost thous say Mass at my ear?' Another, a stouthearted woman named Jenny Geddes, picked up her stool and hurled it at the Bishop's head, narrowly missing the Dean. Both Bishop and Dean were forced to flee from the church, followed by their attendant clergy, to seek refuge in sanctuary.

It seemed an alarming though scarcely significant incident; but feeling in Scotland against the King and his Archbishop was already hot and strong. The nobility could not forget Charles's resumption of the Crown's rights to properties which they had encroached upon and alienated in past reigns, and they dreaded that his policy might be extended to the further damage of their pockets and estates. The Presbyterian congregations of the Kirk could not forget that when the King had come to Scotland for his coronation in Edinburgh in June 1633, he had shown, even then, his determination to inflict upon them the alien ways of the south; that he had himself crowned with all the trammels of popery – with music and anthems, rich vestments, kneeling chaplains, bowing bishops, and anointing oil – that he had appointed the Archbishop of St Andrews to the Chancellorship, the most important political office in the country and one that had not been held by an ecclesiastic since the Reformation; that he had created an unwelcome precedent by appointing several bishops Privy Councillors and Lords of Session; that the popish Laud, who had accompanied him, had insulted a Presbyterian preacher and the very Kirk itself. The King might have a Scottish name and a Scottish accent, he might have Scottish servants and be of Scottish birth, but it was generally supposed in Scotland that he was at heart an Englishman; neither he nor his Councillors ever bothered to discuss Scottish affairs, leaving them in the hands of such men as the Marquess of Hamilton, a Scotsman who had spent his youth at the English Court and had married the English niece of the Duke of Buckingham.

As the riots which broke out in Edinburgh on the occasion of the first reading of the new liturgy spread to other Scottish towns, thousands of petitioners gathered in the capital to protest against the intolerable innovation; a bishop suspected of concealing a crucifix beneath his vestments, was chased through the streets by an angry mob of three hundred women; a representative of the King's Government in Edinburgh who went to the Bishop's assistance, only to have his hat knocked off and his cloak torn from his back, reported bluntly to London that Charles must choose between abandoning his prayer-book and forcing it down the Presbyterians' throats with the help of an army of forty thousand men.

It was the Scots, however, who were the first to fly to arms, swearing to oppose the liturgy, to fight for a restriction of the bishops' powers and for the right of the Kirk, and the Kirk alone, to decide in free assembly what religious alterations could be made in Scotland. Their aims were expressed in a National Covenant signed by all classes of Scottish Protestant from noblemen to workers, from old market-women to fiery young apprentices who cut their arms with dirks to make their mark on the roll in blood. The forces they enrolled to defend that Covenant were not mere bands of untrained citizens. They included, to be sure, excitable men and women ready to fight on the barricades with knives and pitchforks; but there were among them great numbers of clansmen trained to battle, of troops experienced in continental wars. They combined to form a national rebel army, inspired by patriotism and religious faith, and commanded by a skilfully wily 'old little crooked soldier', Alexander Leslie.

Against them the King could bring but a ragged array of discontented raw recruits neither inspired by their cause nor encouraged by the prospects of good pay. At first, after an outburst of anger at these ungrateful Scottish subjects of his who refused to appreciate what he was trying to do for them, Charles had been inclined to negotiate. But the Marquess of Hamilton had failed to come to terms with them, and after months of exasperating negotiations, the King had returned to his original intention of reducing

G

them to obedience by force. But no sufficient force could be raised without money; and scarcely any money was forthcoming. The City of London, when asked to contribute, 'most monstrously scandalized' Wentworth by offering the derisory sum of £5,000. 'Our army is but weak,' complained one of Charles's courtiers, Sir Edmund Verney, when a few ill-equipped regiments had at last been raised. 'Our purse is weaker; and if we fight with these forces and early in the year we shall have our throats cut, and to delay fighting long we cannot for want of money to keep our army together.'

At Berwick, in June 1639, before a single engagement had been fought, Charles was obliged to make peace and to agree that a Scottish Parliament and Assembly should settle the difference between the two sides. The differences, though, were too marked for settlement. The King refused to allow his bishops to be subordinated to the Assembly; the Scots refused to give way on this intractable episcopal issue. The Scottish Parliament was dissolved and war seemed inevitable once more.

In Whitehall, Charles's natural indecision was aggravated by the conflicting advice his ministers offered him. His principal Secretary of State, a friend of the opportunist Marquess of Hamilton and an assiduous courtier of the Queen, was now Sir Henry Vane, the former Comptroller of the Household. Vane was smooth, cunning and equivocal, 'a busy and bustling man who cared for no man otherwise than as he found it very convenient to himself'. His views – on the rare occasions when they were formulated and expressed – contrasted sharply with the sternly straightforward, bold and thorough methods advocated by Laud and Wentworth. Vane's antagonism to Wentworth was based on a personal grudge, for not only had Wentworth opposed his appointment – believing that his predecessor, the aged Sir John Coke, was still capable of doing the work – but some years before, when Wentworth had been raised to the peerage, he had chosen a courtesy title which he well knew Vane had long wanted for himself. Vane had never forgiven the slight and had long nourished a wish to be revenged for it. His advice to the King was strongly influenced by its rankling memory.

As the months passed it was the opinions of Wentworth, however, which made the deeper impression on the King's mind, particularly as the Queen – who had been so frightened at first by the news of the riots in Scotland that she had urged her husband to give way – now recognised in the forbidding yet somehow re-assuring figure of the Lord Deputy the one man who might save them from disaster. Like her husband, she had always found it difficult to like him. He was too masterful, too ugly, too *écrasant*; but he was the man for the hour.

In the autumn of 1639 he was recalled from Ireland to advise the King in person. In pain, limping from gout and weakened by dysentry, he came home irritable and in apprehension, deeply conscious of the danger in which the Kingdom stood. For too long its Government had been allowed to drift, for too long the King had kept him out of the country, and Laud confined to the business of the Church, while incompetent and ill-chosen ministers like Sir Henry Vane were allowed to remain in office, temporising, pro-crastinating, telling his Majesty what he wanted to hear rather than what he ought to know.

In Wentworth's decided view the only remedy was decisive, efficient and if necessary ruthless action. Such a despotic policy had brought law and order, even some prosperity to Ireland. If practised in England the Kingdom could yet be saved. First the rebellion in Scotland must be crushed; to crush it a large sum of money must be raised; and to raise the money a new Parliament must be called. In trepidation the dangerous advice was accepted. The writs for a new Parliament were issued, together with commissions for a new army. In January 1640 Wentworth received at last the earldom for which he had waited and petitioned so long, and became the Earl of Strafford. Three months later the newly elected Members of Parliament assembled in the chamber of the House which had remained empty and silent for over eleven years.

8

Parliament and Traitors
1640–2

O N the opening day of the session, the Members of what was
to become known as the Short Parliament looked about the
chamber, gazing upon each other, in the words of one of them,
'looking who should begin'. Their leaders in the past were either
dead, like Sir John Eliot, or had entered into the service of the
Crown, as the recently created Earl of Strafford had done; John
Hampden, who had risen to fame by his refusal to pay Ship Money,
had spoken little in previous Parliaments and had shown more
aptitude for committee work than for public debate. Most of the
other Members had taken their seats for the first time that day, and
anxiously waited for a more experienced Member to break the ice.
At length a thickset, rather scholarly-looking figure in late middle
age stood up and began to address them. His name was John Pym.

He was Member for Calne, and had made his maiden speech
several years before in the reign of James I. Like Eliot and Hampden
and so many other Parliamentary leaders of his time, Pym was a
member of an ancient country family who had gone to Oxford and
thereafter studied law. An intense and studious man, with a rough
and shaggy appearance which was to gain him at Court the nickname of 'Ox', he was rigid in his opinions and as ruthlessly determined to gain his ends as any man of far more formidable
appearance. He had none of Eliot's frantic rhetoric, displayed
little of his passionate feeling, yet when he sat down on 17 April,
having spoken for two hours, he was immediately recognised as
the new leader of the House.

His speech had been temperate in tone. But Charles and Strafford
were alike appalled by its content. Before the Commons met
Strafford had gone back to Ireland to ensure that the Irish Parliament
fulfilled its function of voting a reasonable share of the money
required for a war against the Scottish Protestants. The Irish
Catholic vote and Stafford's dominating presence secured enough
money to raise a substantial army in Ireland. Now, on his return to
London, Strafford – already dreadfully dispirited by a recurrence of

dysentery which a stormy crossing of the Irish Sea had so aggravated he had almost died on his journey south – discovered that the House of Commons were refusing to follow this satisfactory example. On Pym's advice they were declining to vote any money at all until the country's grievances, unheeded for so long, had been considered and satisfied; and not until the King, on Strafford's advice, had agreed to stop collecting Ship Money did a compromise begin to seem possible. The slender chance of a settlement was lost, however, by Sir Henry Vane who conducted the negotiations in so incompetent a manner that it was widely believed he had dispelled the hope of an understanding merely to discredit the detested 'Black Tom' Strafford.

Certainly, Strafford himself, at a meeting of the Committee for Scottish affairs on 5 May, felt obliged to advise the King to abandon the restraint he had formerly recommended. A few hours earlier, the Council had agreed on the dissolution of Parliament. Strafford had hesitated before casting his vote; it was on his advice that Parliament had been called. But now that the decision had been taken, the King's course was clear. It was not merely that the Commons were proving difficult over supplies, they were, so reports strongly indicated, in touch with the Scots. They were, in fact, behaving in such a way that Charles, 'being reduced to extreme necessity', was obliged to act decisively in defence of his prerogative rights. Charles, who had spoken in such a way himself when there was still a chance of a compromise on the lines Strafford had advocated, seems now to have recoiled from his Minister's uncompromising counsel. But Strafford persisted. The Scots must be subdued and if a strong enough army could not be raised in England, well then there was the army in Ireland to use against them. 'You have an army in Ireland,' he reminded Charles in words which were later to have a fearful significance. 'You may employ them here to reduce this Kingdom.' Sir Henry Vane, realising perhaps how ambiguous the remark would sound if taken out of the context of the discussion, made a note of it and locked up the paper on which he had recorded it in a drawer of his desk.

After the dissolution of Parliament, Strafford continued to urge that the strongest measures should be taken against the Government's opponents. The situation, he insisted, was getting out of hand. There was rioting in the City where apprentices, mariners and dock hands had raged through the streets, shouting, beating drums and breaking into a prison to release some of their fellows who had been arrested; a mob had roared from Southwark towards Lambeth Palace forcing Archbishop Laud to flee across the river in his barge to seek shelter in Whitehall; the City aldermen were refusing to contribute to a loan which was essential to the continuance of the Scottish war. For such conduct Stafford had simple remedies. 'Unless you hang up some of them,' he told Charles, referring to the recalcitrant aldermen, 'you will do no good with them.' On his advice, two young rioters *were* hanged, one of them being tortured before his execution, tortured on the rack, the last time that instrument was used in England. Viciously repressive measures like this brought temporary quiet; but they did not produce money for the war.

So it was an underpaid and ill-supplied army, 'scanty and in no sort of order', that moved north that summer against the Scottish rebels who had by now crossed the border, routed an English detachment at Newburn and encamped themselves in Northumberland, occupying Newcastle. The Commander-in-Chief, the Earl of Northumberland, dreaded the thought of taking his near-mutinous troops into battle against an enemy for whom he felt much sympathy and was relieved beyond measure when a sudden illness prevented him from doing so. Strafford, too, was ill once more, suffering again from dysentery; yet he took over the command and was carried north in a litter. 'Pity me,' he wrote to a friend, 'for no man ever came to so lost a business.'

Charles, too, travelled north, and in York, forced to recognise how completely lost the business was, he summoned a Great Council of the peerage and wearily accepted their advice to offer terms to the Scots and to summon yet another Parliament. The terms agreed with the Scottish representatives at Ripon were humiliating: the rebels were to be left in control of Northumberland and Durham and their army was to be paid a monthly subsidy until their claims to compensation were settled by Parliament.

It was with these mortifying terms weighing heavily upon his mind that Charles awaited the assembly of this Parliament, the last of his reign, the Long Parliament which was not to be dissolved – and then of its own accord – for twenty years.

Its Members met in determined mood; this time the King would not dismiss them so arbitrarily; this time they, instead, would rid the Court of those 'evil counsellors' to whom Pym had previously referred in the debates of the Short Parliament and to whom he now referred as having broken the 'fundamental laws' of the country. There was no doubt whom Pym had principally in mind. The Earl of Strafford had once been his friend; but it was now his duty, as he conceived it, to destroy him just as it had been the duty of the martyred Eliot to destroy Buckingham. For Strafford personified all the evils that the English people had long been compelled to undergo; he was the one man of real ability upon whom the King could now rely.

Charles was aware of Strafford's danger, but he had come to depend on him; he needed the reassurance of his advice and he asked him to come down from Yorkshire to be near him. Strafford did not hesitate. He left for London 'with more danger beset,' he believed, 'than ever man went with out of Yorkshire'. Yet his 'heart [was] good'; there was 'nothing cold' in him. At least he might turn the tables upon his accusers by charging them with 'treasonable correspondence with the Scotch'.

The day after his arrival in London, on 10 November, Pym made the first strike in the duel for Strafford's life. Followed by a number of his supporters, who had quickly agreed on the charges behind the locked doors of the House of Commons, he marched to the Lords to deliver his accusations. Strafford declined the opportunity to escape and went to look his 'accusers in the face'. 'With speed he comes to the house', a Member recalled. 'He calls rudely at the door. James Maxwell, Keeper of the Black Rod, opens; his Lordship, with a proud glooming countenance, makes towards his place at the board head.' But he was refused permission to speak, ordered to kneel to hear the charge against him, arrested and relieved of his sword. 'This done, he makes through a number of people towards his coach, all gazing, no man capping to him, before whom, that morning, the greatest of England would have stood uncovered.'

With Strafford encarcerated in the Tower, Charles endeavoured as best he could to stem the tide of the Long Parliament's demands by promises and prevarications, by standing his ground as long as possible and only at the last moment giving way – and giving way, as usually happened, with a sulky ill-grace which was as embarrassing to his supporters as it was irritating to his opponents.

He was becoming increasingly anxious and touchy. He had little doubt that God would ensure his ultimate victory, yet he could not but be affected by Henrietta's frequent outbursts of tears and sobbing lamentations. Her lovely and intelligent little daughter Anne had just died, a short time before her third birthday, and she had been overwhelmed with grief at her loss. Now, sleeping badly, losing weight and feeling ill, she devoted herself with a kind of frenzy to the salvation of the throne for her husband and her son. She adopted Strafford's policies as her own, badgering Charles not to give way to the Commons, vehemently urging him not to disband the Irish army, intriguing with various young courtiers and officers of the English army who were conspiring to rescue Strafford from the Tower and to seize power in a wild plot that was betrayed to Parliament, making advances to foreign powers for military and financial help, asking the Pope's nephew for half a million crowns with which to bribe various Members of the Commons. At the same time, she endeavoured to placate the Protestants by reducing the number of Roman Catholics in her Household and by arranging for the marriage of her eldest daughter, the nine-year-old Mary, to the Prince of Orange, whose requests for the hand of her second daughter, Elizabeth, had previously been rejected with scorn.

Apart from Henrietta, Charles had few advisers left. Archbishop Laud had been impeached and hustled off to the Tower in Strafford's wake; less courageous Councillors such as Sir Francis Windebanke and Lord Finch had discreetly gone abroad; most of those few reliable courtiers who had contrived to get themselves elected to the Long Parliament had been squeezed out of it on various pretexts.

Charles's policy, such as it was in these alarming months, was to wait upon events, to rest in hope that time would bring some relief, to try to persuade the Commons that their revolutionary measures threatened to bring the whole country to disaster, and that, as he put it to them himself, a skilful watchmaker might improve the working of a watch by taking it to pieces and cleaning it, provided that when he put it together again he left 'not one pin out of it'. There was little else, indeed, that he could have done, even if he had been capable of envisaging and maintaining a settled programme of endeavour; for Strafford's determination – encouraged and supported by Henrietta – to rot away in the Tower rather than allow the King to surrender to Parliament in exchange for his freedom, made a reconciliation with the Commons difficult to achieve, while the need to pay the Scottish rebels their regular subsidy to prevent them advancing further south rendered a break with the Commons impossible to contemplate. So Charles felt unable to resist a Parliament which was to introduce a whole series of measures declaring monopolies and taxes levied without parliamentary consent illegal, condemning 'Laudism', abolishing prerogative courts, reversing the judgements in various Ship Money cases and in cases that had come before the Star Chamber and forcing him to call a Parliament every three years. He had to listen to the roaring cheers of welcome that greeted the prisoners released by the wholesale revocation of sentences, the excited acclamations given to men like William Prynne – the fanatical Calvinist lawyer who had his ears sawn off by the hangman for issuing a libel on the Queen and had been branded for writing and preaching against the bishops – and John Lilburne, a gentleman from Durham, who had been whipped at the cart's tail from the Fleet Prison to Palace Yard, pilloried, gagged and starved almost to death in prison for refusing to take an oath in the Star Chamber. In March 1641 there came the worst tribulation of all: his servant Strafford was brought to trial in Westminster Hall on a charge of High Treason.

A small curtained room at the back of the throne in the hall was provided for the royal family. The King tore the curtain down on the first day of the trial so that everyone in Court should see him and be ashamed that they presumed to try his servant to whom he had shown, and continued to show, all honour. But he was 'little more regarded' than if he had not been there; even the peers kept their hats on.

Strafford conducted his own defence with the greatest skill. Each day as he was rowed in a barge to Whitehall and mounted the river stairs he was reviled by the mob; each day he had to answer the charges made against him in a restless and impatient atmosphere. Throughout the trial, a witness recorded, there was 'too loud clattering' and 'much public eating, not only of confections but of flesh and bread and bottles of beer and wine, going thick from mouth to mouth without cups, and all this in the king's eye'. Both spectators and members of the Court sauntered about, talking and calling to each other while the prisoner turned his face to the wall and tried to concentrate on scribbling the notes for the refutation of the charges made against him. He was ill, tired, and prematurely old at forty-eight; his beard was grey now, his back more bent than ever; but only once or twice did he lose control of his temper, quickly mastering it. It soon became clear that there was no real substance in the prosecution's case, and Charles began to believe that Strafford would be acquitted. The most damning accusation against him was the advice he was alleged to have given the King at the meeting of the Committee for Scottish Affairs on the afternoon of 5 May when – according to Sir Henry Vane's evidence – he had said, 'You have an army in Ireland, which you may employ here to reduce this Kingdom'. The prosecution insisted that 'this Kingdom' meant England not Scotland. But Vane was a nervous and hesitant witness; he protested too earnestly and repeatedly that in all his life he never 'loved to tell an untruth'; the other Councillors present at the meeting that afternoon could not remember that Strafford had given any such advice to the King; and Strafford was able sarcastically to congratulate his enemy on his powers of recollection, superior to those of 'the party that spake the words, or any man in the company besides'.

Strafford continually scored such points throughout the trial, continually filled his supporters, and even his critics, with admiration for his skill and courage. On 10 April, amidst confused shouts of 'Withdraw! Withdraw! Adjourn! Adjourn!', he caught the King's eye and laughed.

Yet the more extreme and impatient Members of the Commons were determined not to lose their prey. An atmosphere almost of panic had by now been created by the reports of the plots being hatched by the army and the Court; and when a board creaked in a tense moment in the House there was a shout of warning from one Member that he smelled gunpowder and the rest followed him running desperately for safety out of the Chamber. In such an atmosphere it was not difficult for the House to be persuaded that if a trial on a charge of High Treason would not serve their purposes, a Bill of Attainder would do so instead. Provided that Parliament as a whole would pass it and the King would give his assent to it, a Bill of Attainder would ensure Strafford's execution by declaring that his death was necessary to the safety of the country.

In his efforts to gain supporters for the Bill, Pym assured the House that he had additional evidence in corroboration of Sir Henry Vane's testimony: it was a copy of the note which Sir Henry had made at the time. It had been discovered by Sir Henry's sternly Puritan son in his father's desk in a velvet box, and had been handed over to Pym with the bland protestation that the 'tenderness of his conscience towards his common parent, his country', had 'provoked' young Vane to 'trespass against his natural father'.

Sir Henry affected great concern at his son's betrayal, but soon appeared consoled. The Bill of Attainder was read in the House that day.

On 13 April Strafford made his final speech in Westminster Hall, a brilliant performance which ended with the tears streaming down his face. Pym's short speech that followed it was far less impressive; and in the Tower that night Strafford could be heard walking up and down in his cell, singing psalms of thanksgiving. But the victory, in the end, was Pym's.

Although many Members stayed away rather than be involved, and many others voted against it, the Commons passed the Bill by a majority of 204, one of its supporters declaring that there was no need to discuss whether or not it was a legal measure because it was never accounted cruel or foul play to 'knock foxes and wolves on the head' for they too, were beasts of prey.

The Lord's majority was seven. Most Members had not attended the debate, fearful of the mob, warned by threatening posters bearing the names of those fifty-four Members of the Commons – 'Straffordians, enemies of justice, betrayers of their country' – who had cast an opposing vote. The bishops, all of them, gratefully accepted the Bishop of Lincoln's artful advice that as they had taken no part in the trial they should not cast a vote now. Many of the twenty-six Lords who voted in favour of the Bill believed that the King would surely not sign it.

Charles had promised Strafford that 'upon the word of a King' he would not let him suffer 'in life, honour or fortune'; and his word had been trusted. But the mob, shouting for the traitor's death, rampaged beneath the palace windows at Whitehall, laughing at a placard which said that the building was to let, threatening to break down its doors. Inside the Catholics made their last confessions; and the Queen, preparing to fly to Portsmouth, was only dissuaded by the fear that people would say she had gone to join her lover, Henry Jermyn.

Before the House of Lords had voted on the Bill, Strafford had written to the King to release him from his promise. 'I do most humbly beseech your Majesty, for the prevention of evils which may happen by your refusal, to pass this Bill.' As for himself Strafford begged only 'that in your goodness you would vouchsafe to cast your gracious regard upon my poor son and his three sisters ... God long preserve your Majesty. Your Majesty's most faithful and humble servant, Strafford.'

But Charles could not bring himself to sacrifice his servant, and for two days he refused to sign the death warrant. On Sunday 9 May, however, the Constable of the Tower declared that if the King continued obstinate he would kill the prisoner himself; messages reached Whitehall that the lives of the Queen and even of the royal children were in danger; and the Queen's friends, fearful of being arrested for what had now become known as the Army Plot, fled abroad. The King called for the advice of the judges and then of various bishops, asking them if they thought he might now break his word. The Irish Archbishop of Armagh, a friend and admirer of Strafford, urged the King to stand firm; so did William Juxon, the Bishop of London; but John Williams, the prodigal, talkative Bishop of Lincoln – a man who held so many benefices he was known as a 'diocese in himself' – appears to have advanced the convenient theory that the King had 'two consciences: a public and a private one'. His private conscience would find the condemnation of Strafford abhorrent; yet his public conscience must be concerned with the danger of further bloodshed.

By nine o'clock that evening Charles had persuaded himself that Williams was right and it was his duty to give way. 'If my own person only were in danger,' he told the Privy Council, 'I would gladly venture it to save Lord Strafford's life, but, seeing my wife, children and all my Kingdom are concerned in it, I am forced to give way unto it.'

The next morning, in tears, he signed a commission for his assent to the Attainder, together with an Act, which he can scarcely have looked at in his agitation, prohibiting the dissolution of Parliament without its own consent. 'My Lord of Strafford's condition,' he said, 'is happier than mine.'

He sent his eldest son to Westminster, entrusting the ten-year-old boy with his first public duty, to carry a message pleading that Strafford should be sentenced to life imprisonment rather than death. 'But if no less than his life can satisfy my people,' he instructed the boy to add, 'I must say *fiat justitia*.'

On 12 May, all efforts to save him having failed, Strafford, clothed all in black as was his custom, marched to the scaffold on

Tower Hill watched by a crowd which a witness thought must number 200,000 people. He walked 'more like a general at the head of an army than like a condemned man to undergo death'. The Lieutenant of the Tower had advised him to go by coach for fear of lynching, but he had replied, 'No, I dare look death in the face and, I hope, the people too. I care not how I die, whether by the hand of the executioner or by the madness and fury of the people. If that may give them better content, it is all one to me.' He had asked for permission to go to Laud's cell to obtain the Archbishop's blessing, but on being told that Parliament's consent would be required for this he disdainfully declined to seek it. As he went to the scaffold, however, he caught sight of his old friend – who was soon himself, at the age of seventy-three, to pass that way to the block – gazing piteously down at him through the bars. Strafford bowed to him. 'My Lord,' he said, 'your prayers and blessings.' Laud raised his hands in benediction, murmured a prayer, and fell back fainting from the window. 'Farewell, my Lord,' said Strafford as he walked on. 'God protect your innocency.'

The English were mad, Cardinal Richelieu decided when he heard the news of the beheading, 'they have killed their wisest man'. An English country gentleman laconically commented that Strafford owed his fate to the two things in the world he most despised: Sir Henry Vane and the people. The King, for his part, believed that he would never forgive himself for what had happened that day, and he never did. 'I sinned against my conscience,' he lamented to the Queen. 'It was a base sinful concession.' And when his own turn came to die, he was to say on the scaffold, 'an unjust sentence that I suffered to take effect, is punished now by an unjust sentence on me.'

In the summer days that followed, the revolutionary measures that Parliament had begun to pass were increased and extended. 'Reformation goes on,' recorded one observer, 'as hot as toast.' For many Members of Parliament, though, it was becoming far too hot. Most of them were not revolutionaries at all. They did not want to alter the government of the country, merely to maintain their 'ancient liberties'. Reform was one thing, the quickening trend to social revolution and the overthrow of the entire constitution was another. Gradually the Commons began to divide themselves into two groups, with moderate men like Edward Hyde, Lord

Falkland, Edmund Waller and Sir John Culpeper, edging slowly but ever further towards the King's side and the more vehement and progressive Members moving to the other. The disputes that most deeply divided them – and most deeply divided the majority of the Commons from the Lords – were religious; and it was in religious debates that the passions of John Pym's supporters were most deeply aroused, their fervour contrasting sharply with the relative languour of their opponents. Lord Falkland 'was wont to say that they who hated bishops hated them worse than the devil, and that they who loved them did not love them so well as their dinner.'

Nevertheless, by the end of the summer of 1641, a party prepared to defend the established Church and the King was emerging in the Commons. Charles, however, rather than foster it, left for Scotland, mistakenly believing that it was there his salvation lay, that, despite the recent war and the religious troubles which had provoked it, there was still strong royalist feeling in the country of his birth. The more wildly zealous of his supporters hoped that he might perhaps come back to London at the head of a strong and loyal army; after all, there were Scots enough in the shortly-to-be-disbanded rebel army in Northumberland who were discontented with their conditions and their pay, ready to sympathise with a Stuart who had quarrelled with those treacherous Englishmen in London.

But Charles was to be sadly disillusioned. His attempts to win over various Scottish nobles at the expense of others failed as disastrously as did his play for the sympathies of the Presbyterians and Covenanters. He returned to London without any of the real support he had hoped to find in Scotland, firmly persuaded that a conciliatory policy would not work any better there than it had worked in England, more convinced than ever that Strafford's death was due not to his having made concessions too late but to his having made any concessions at all.

Support for his opponents' policies had gradually lost ground in his absence. The enormous expense of maintaining an English army in the north as well as paying subsidies to a Scottish one – an expense that by the beginning of June had already amounted to £682,000 – had led to unprecedented levels of taxation for which Parliament rather than the King was now being blamed. Parliament, the Venetian Ambassador reported, 'is losing the great credit which it enjoyed [hitherto], since it appears that instead of relief it has brought expense and discomfort to the people.'

Many people were also becoming exasperated by the extravagant behaviour and outlandish beliefs of the noncomformist sects which the speeches of various Puritan Members of Parliament seemed to encourage. The Adamites – a particularly hysterical body of persons who, following in the traditions of the medieval Brethren and Sisters of the Free Spirit, believed themselves re-established in Adam's state of original innocence and found it appropriate to worship God in his state of nakedness – were not numerous; but artisans and tradesmen who professed themselves capable of interpreting the gospel better than any priest, female preachers leading congregations in extempore prayers, apprentices who chased Anglican parsons down the streets calling them Canterbury whelps or Abbey-lubbers and tearing their gowns from their backs, were all becoming more common every week. Even the less rampantly aggresive of Puritan pamphleteers wrote of bishops as though they were all the sons of Beelzebub; even John Milton castigated the Anglican clergy for stumbling into 'new-vomited paganisme', their bishops for encouraging 'gaming, jigging, wassailing and mixed dancing', their prayer-book for being 'the skeleton of a Mass-book', their railed communion-table for being 'pageanted about, like a dreadful idol'.

Moderate men who had been prepared to welcome Parliament's earlier reforms now shrank back from its support, and in their distaste for the extreme demands of its more vehement supporters began to turn to the King. But before the King could take advantage of this change in his fortunes a rebellion broke out in Ireland, now released from Strafford's firm rule, and the tide turned once more.

For the rebellion was accompanied by a massacre of thousands of British settlers, a massacre – so Protestants across the Irish Sea believed – instigated by Catholic priests and carried out by disbanded Catholic soldiers. According to the pamphleteers, these Catholic soldiers had murdered and mutilated innocent men, raped their wives, and roasted their children on spits. The English Court, it was widely believed, was at the bottom of the fearful business; the King was sure to be implicated; the Queen, who was known to have expressed the belief that all the concessions her husband had recently made had been forced from him under duress and were therefore null and void, was blamed above all. It became known as the Queen's Rebellion.

The need for its immediate repression and the punishment of those responsible for it was overshadowed in the Commons by the determination that the King should be denied control of the new army which must now be raised. Pym, therefore, persuaded his fellow Members to send a message to Charles, informing him that unless he dismissed his present advisers, the origin of all 'mischievous counsels and designs', and unless he appointed in their place Ministers who enjoyed their confidence, they would take over the Irish problem themselves. At the same time Pym hurried through the Commons a Grand Remonstrance, which he and his friends had long had in preparation, a detailed catalogue of their complaints, of the reforms that had so far been achieved and were yet to be carried out. The Remonstrance was presented for the King's attention at the same time as a petition that the bishops should be deprived of their votes in the House of Lords.

Charles was in no mood now to be pushed further along the road to revolution. He came back from Scotland determined to regain the power of which Parliament were trying to deprive him. Encouraged by the reports of the ferocious arguments and drawn swords in the Commons – mainly on religious matters – which had led to the Grand Remonstrance being passed by a mere eleven votes, encouraged, too, by the conviction that the House of Lords was now firmly on his side, and provoked by the return of many Puritans to the Common Council in London, he determined to make a display of power. He replied to the Grand Remonstrance by denying that he had any evil advisers; he refused to concede there was any need for reform in the Church; he dismissed the Puritan Lieutenant of the Tower and replaced him with a man more to his taste; he asked for volunteers for an expedition to Ireland; he took firm action against the rowdy mobs parading the London streets shouting 'No popery! No bishops! No popish lords.' These actions, though as firm as Strafford would have liked them to be, were not excessive. But when the Commons impeached twelve bishops and threatened to impeach the Queen, Charles in his anger and alarm – and, as so often, having waited too long – went too far.

Already he had offended the House of Lords by encouraging the bishops – who had not dared to attend debates for fear of the mob – to insist that no decisions taken by the Lords in their absence were

Politicians and Traitors

The Dominion of the Sea Medal by Nicolas Briot, struck in 1630 in the year that the Treaty of Madrid brought the disastrous foreign policy initiated by Buckingham to a close.

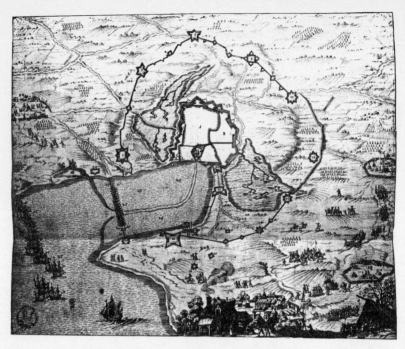

A woodcut showing the town and haven of La Rochelle, home of the Huguenot rebels whom the Duke of Buckingham attempted to assist by his expedition to the Ile de Ré in 1627.

(*opposite*) An etching depicting the murder of the Duke of Buckingham by John Felton, a disgruntled and unbalanced former officer, in August 1628.

'Greate Brittaines Noble and worthy Councell of Warr' showing the members of
the Council in session in April 1624 when war against Spain was being planned.

William Laud (1573–1645). A portrait from Van Dyck's studio.

(*opposite*) An engraving from a broadside showing the execution of Archbishop Laud on Tower Hill in 1645.

The riot in St Giles's Cathedral, Edinburgh, in 1637 when Jenny Geddes threw her stool in protest against the new prayer-book.

PROGNOSTICATION Vpon W: LAVD
bishop of Canterbury written Año: Dom: 1641: which accor:
dingly is come to passe

Denzil Holles, 1st
Baron Holles
(1599–1680), one
of the five
Members of the
Commons whom
Charles attempted
to arrest in 1642.

(opposite) John Pym
(1584–1643) from
the title page
of the publication
of his speech, 1641.

Sir Henry Vane,
the Elder
(1589–1654) from
a portrait by an
unknown artist.

Master *PYM*
HIS SPEECH

In *Parliament*, on *Wednesday*, the
fifth of *January*, 1641,

Concerning the Vote of the House of *Commons*,
for his discharge upon the Accusation of High
Treason, exhibited against himselfe, and the
Lord *Kimbolton*, Mr. *Iohn Hampden*, Sr.
Arthur Haslerig, Mr. *Strowd*,
M. Hollis, by his Maiesty.

The true Effigies of Mr. *Iohn Pym*, Esquire

London Printed for I.W, 1641.

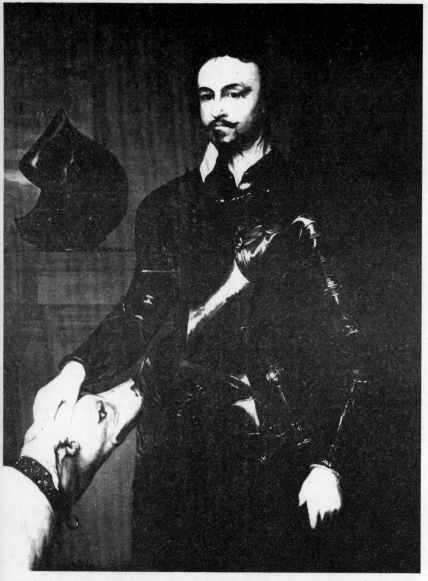

Thomas Wentworth, 1st Earl of Strafford (1593–1641). A portrait after Van Dyck.

(*opposite*) Hollar's engravings of Strafford's trial, which opened in Westminster Hall in March 1641, and of his execution on Tower Hill on 12 May.

A woodcut from 'England's Comfort and London's Joy' (1641) showing
Charles I received in London by the Lord Mayor after his return from Scotland
in 1641.

Hollar's portrayal of the attempted arrest of the five Members in the House of Commons.

1 You ar to accuse those ~~from~~ *six joynt lie & seuerallie.*

2 you ar to referue the power of making additionalls

3 When the Comitie for examination is a naming (wch you must press to be close & under tey of secresie) if eather Essex, Warwick, Holland, Say, ~~████████~~ *, Wharton, or Brooke be named, you must desyre that they may be spared because you ar to examine them as witnesses for me*

A facsimile of Charles's order for the impeachment of the five Members.

Contemporary views of (*above*) the
House of Lords, and (*opposite*)
Charles opening Parliament.

Medal struck in 1641 on the occasion
of the betrothal of Princess Mary to
William of Orange.

Cancellarij sedes

A contemporary view of the House of Commons.

'Times Alteration' dated 8 January 1642. Baron Finch, Speaker of the House of Commons and later Lord Keeper (shown with wings) and Sir Francis Windebanke, secretary of state (a pen behind his ear). Both fled abroad in 1640.

An engraving of Sir Francis
Windebanke (1582–1646).

(*above*) Reverse and
obverse of the Declaration of
Parliament Medal of 1642
when Civil War had become
inevitable, the King had gone
to the North, and Parliament
issued a declaration of its
policy as being 'the safety of the
King's person, the defence of
both Houses of Parliament and
of those who had obeyed
their orders and commands,
and the preservation of the
true Religion, Laws, Liberties,
and Peace of the Kingdom'.

(*right*) Satire on the Parliament,
reduced by Colonel Pride's
Purge to a mere 'Rump', from
Goldsmid's Cavalier Playing
Cards.

*The Rump and dreggs of the house
of Com remaining after the good
members were purged out.*

George, Lord Digby, 'a graceful and beautiful person', a close friend of Charles who appointed him secretary of state on Lord Falkland's death, and a severe trial to Prince Rupert. On his left in this portrait by Van Dyck is William, 5th Earl of Bedford, second but eldest surviving son of Francis, the 4th Earl who developed Covent Garden.

valid. Now, and far more seriously, he enraged the Commons.

In view of the atmosphere in London that Christmas of 1641 Charles's move against his opponents was at least understandable. It was the 'maddest' time that one contemporary witness had ever experienced. New Palace Yard outside Westminster Hall was continually full of citizens walking up and down, arguing and shouting, with swords at their sides. On occasions they marched into the hall affronting anyone who looked like a Court supporter. One day Captain Thomas Lunsford, the new Lieutenant of the Tower, and 'about a dozen other gentlemen . . . drew their swords, chasing the citizens about the Hall and so made their way through those who were in Palace Yard and King Street till they came to Whitehall. The Archbishop of York was beaten by the prentices the same day as he was going into Parliament. The next day they assaulted the Abbey, to pull down the organs and altar, but it was defended by the Archbishop of York and his servants with some other gentlemen who came to them. Divers of the citizens were hurt.'

'I never saw the Court so full of gentlemen,' another officer, Captain Slingsby reported. 'Everyone comes hither with his sword . . . Both factions talk very big and it is a wonder there is no more blood yet spilt, seeing how earnest both sides are.'

It was as much to bring this dangerous state of affairs to an end by decisive action as to punish the Commons for daring to talk of an impeachment of the Queen that on 3 January the King decided to order the arrest of Lord Mandeville, the Earl of Manchester's son and the leading Puritan agitator in the House of Lords, and five Members of the Commons – Pym, Hampden, Denzil Holles, William Strode and Sir Arthur Haselrig, the Member for Leicestershire, who had been closely involved with the introduction of the Bill of Attainder which had declared Strafford guilty of High Treason. The charges against the five Members was that they had attempted to subvert the fundamental laws – the identical though, in fact, meaningless charge that Pym had brought against Strafford – that they had incited the Scots to invade the Kingdom of England, and had raised 'tumults in order to compel Parliament to join them in their treacherous designs'.

Ordering their arrest was, however, a good deal simpler than achieving it. The Lords, to whom the articles of impeachment had

H   177

to be sent, refused to confirm the order; the Commons refused to surrender the five Members. A young courtier and friend of the Queen, Lord Digby, son of the Earl of Bristol and a man who had bravely pleaded for Strafford's life in the Commons, argued that the only solution was for the King to go down to the Commons himself with an armed guard and effect the arrest personally. But Charles hesitated to adopt so drastic a course. It would be a break with all precedent; and if he should fail the consequences would be unthinkable. Why should he fail, though? Lord Digby and Henrietta urged him; and it was the Queen's pleas and final outburst of exasperated temper that evidently made up Charles's mind for him. 'Go, you poltroon!' she is said to have cried out in fury at his indecision. 'Go and pull those rogues out by the ears, or never see my face again.'

It was not the first time that winter that she had threatened to leave him, to go back to France or to retire to a convent, if he would not show his enemies who was the master of his Kingdom. Submissively, he agreed to go, anxious, as always, to show her that he really was the kind of man she wanted him to be. He kissed her and told her that within an hour he would be back, master of his enemies. When the hour was past, Henrietta burst out in relief to her fried, Lucy Carlisle, who had just come into the room, that it was a time for rejoicing for by now the King was 'master in his own state!'

Henrietta had spoken too soon. Charles had been delayed on his way out of the palace by a group of petitioners who wanted to talk to him. Punctiliously, Charles agreed to deal with their cases before going out. It was about three o'clock before he left; and by then – or so Henrietta herself believed – Lucy Carlisle, who delighted in the company of men of power, who had once fallen under the strange spell of the Earl of Strafford, and who had lately developed strongly Puritan tendencies in her admiration for the great John Pym, had sent a message to the Commons warning him and his friends of what she had just overheard in the palace.

Pym had no need of her warning. It was impossible to mistake the tenseness in the capital, impossible to doubt that the King would soon strike. Already Charles had sent a message to the Lord Mayor forbidding him to send out the London Trained Bands to guard Parliament – as two City members had requested – and ordering him instead to authorise the Bands to fire on the mob should there be any further rioting. He had also sent a message to the Inns of Court asking that all their lawyers and students trained to bear arms should hold themselves ready for action. So Pym knew well that the King's action against Parliament could not now be long delayed; it was while having dinner on 4 January that he learned from the Puritan Earl of Essex, and later through the French Ambassador, the timing and form of the King's attack.

Pym had taken his seat in the Commons that morning to provoke the attack, to reveal the King's tyrannous instincts to the world; but he had not wanted to be found sitting there when the soldiers came to arrest him, for with his arrest and that of the four other Members, the Commons would lose their guiding light. The warnings that he received while finishing his dinner came just in time for him and his friends to escape by water into the City.

The King left for Westminster in a coach, accompanied by one of the more truculent of his Scottish courtiers, the Earl of Roxburgh, Prince Charles and the Prince's cousin, the young Elector Palatine. He was followed by four hundred armed troops and a crowd of exited Londoners wondering what was afoot. He alighted from the coach in New Palace Yard, walked through Westminster Hall and boldly entered the House with his nephew. The soldiers stood outside, their pistols cocked, pretending to take aim at the Members in the Chamber, while Lord Roxburgh jauntily leant against the door to keep it open.

Charles, his manners as courteous as ever even now, took off his hat as he walked towards the Speaker's chair, nodding as he went to various silent Members whose faces he recognised.

'Mr Speaker,' he said, 'By your leave, I must for a time make bold with your chair.'

He sat down, explained his presence, and asked for the five Members to come forward. There was no response. The House remained perfectly quiet.

'Is Mr Pym here?'

Still there was silence. He turned to the Speaker, and repeated the question. The Speaker fell upon one knee before him and said, 'Sire, I have neither eyes to see nor tongue to speak in this place but as the House is pleased to direct me.'

''Tis no matter. I think my eyes are as good as another's.'

The King looked along the benches. The Members had already

seen him give a quick glance to the empty seat near the bar of the House which was usually occupied by Pym. He looked back there again; and at length he was forced to admit his attempted coup, on which his whole future depended, had failed. ' Well!' he said with an air of reproach, 'since I see all my birds have flown, I do expect that you will send them unto me as soon as they return hither.'

By the time Charles had returned to Whitehall, where Henrietta expressed her deep repentance for the '*malheureuse indiscretion*' which she believed had been responsible for her husband's failure, London was in uproar. Shops closed their doors and the people came out in their thousands into the streets; it was scarcely safe any more to demonstrate the least loyalty to the Crown. But the King, whose personal courage was never in question, refused to be intimidated. He issued a proclamation ordering the City to surrender the five accused men and drove there himself to demand at a meeting of the Common Council that they should be handed over to him. His words were greeted with shouts of 'Privileges of Parliament! Privileges of Parliament!' to which he replied 'No privilege can protect a traitor from legal trial.'

The cries of 'Privilege!' were repeated on his return to Whitehall by crowds of people who surrounded his coach, shaking their fists as they shouted through the windows. The King was seen to be 'somewhat moved'; but as he said himself was 'driven away by shame more than fear to see the barbarous rudeness of those tumults'.

In the days that followed feelings in London rose to a new pitch, almost to hysteria. Rumours flew about that the Royalists were soon to launch an attack on the City and planned to hang Pym and his supporters outside the Royal Exchange. In reaction, a Committee of Public Safety was formed and a Puritan soldier given overall command of the Trained Bands; barricades were erected in the streets, chains pulled across them; cauldrons of boiling water were held ready to pour down on the heads of the invading troops, cannon were dragged into position to fire at them. Apprentices from the brickfields at Bethnal Green, iron workers from Southwark, watermen from Shoreditch, all poured into the City to offer their services in its defence. The houses of Roman Catholics were attacked; priests were executed. On 11 January Pym and his four friends came out of hiding in Coleman Street and proceeded in triumphant procession up river to Westminster, to be met by cheering citizens and beating drums. As the cavalcade passed Whitehall Palace the derisive shout went up 'Where is the King and his Cavaliers?'

For the King had hurriedly left the day before through a menacing crowd of people, many thousands strong, waving banners and placards on which was scrawled the legend: 'Liberty!' He had gone to Hampton Court where, since no preparation had been made for their arrival, 'the princes were obliged to the inconvenience of sleeping in the same bed with their Majesties'.

Two days later they all moved on to Windsor and soon afterwards the Queen, and Princess Mary who was to join her new husband in Holland, left for Dover in such haste that one Court official had 'never heard of the like for persons of such dignity'. She took with her her dwarf, Jeffrey Hudson, the crown jewels which she hoped to sell or pawn to raise money for her husband's cause, urgent requests for military help from the Prince of Orange and the King of Denmark, and the key to a code in which she was to write a series of letters to Charles urging him to be firm, to stand up for his rights, to put down all opposition, to fulfil the last promise he had made to her before they parted – that he would not come to any understanding with his enemies which was not to the advantage of his family.

The formal parting at Dover was a sad little episode. The spectators cried, Henrietta cried, and Charles, after kissing his wife several times and saying that he felt he would never see his little daughter again, cried too. When the *Lion* sailed away with its precious cargo he rode along the cliffs waving goodbye until the ship was out of sight. Then he returned to Greenwich.

His position was now lamentable and his cause seemed all but lost. London was certainly lost; and the southern counties appeared to be turning against him. He had approved a Bill depriving the bishops of all their temporal positions, giving way on this point, so he said, 'to make it plain that the Queen did not prevent him from consenting to gratify his subjects'. But now Parliament was demanding that he should assent to a Militia Bill which would have put the armed forces of the country under its control. 'By God!' he protested indignantly to the Earl of Pembroke, 'Not for an hour.' And it was this fixed determination never to lose his right to command the army, as much as his determination never to lose the right to choose his own advisers, that resolved Charles to fight.

In March he moved north for Yorkshire, accompanied by a few companions, with an eye on the military supplies which had been stored in Hull since the Scottish rebellion. The governor of Hull, who had agreed to hold the supplies for Parliament, closed the gates of the town and came out onto the ramparts to tell the King he could not enter it. Disgruntled and abashed, yet powerless to enforce his will, Charles retired to York where he was given Parliament's Nineteen Propositions for a settlement. These proposals demanding parliamentary control not only of the army, but of the Church, the royal children and the law, were, in effect, tantamount to a declaration that the King must surrender all executive power. Outraged, he immediately rejected them. Parliament replied by enlisting a force of ten thousand men and placing them under command of the Earl of Essex. The Navy had already been placed in the hands of Essex's cousin, the Puritan Earl of Warwick.

The King's attempts at raising recruits met with far less success than those of Parliament. His appeals in Yorkshire brought few volunteers to his side; and when he turned south for Nottingham he managed to attract few more.

He raised his standard in a field at Nottingham on 22 August 1642, certain that his cause was right, convinced that it was not himself but the rebels in Parliament who were the aggressors, yet wholly without adequate means to fight for his faith.

The Standard unfurled beneath a glowering sky and in a racing wind. A proclamation, declaring that the Commons and its troops were traitors, had been prepared; but at the last minute Charles decided to change its wording which he did so clumsily that his herald could hardly read the alterations and stumbled through it with painful hesitation. Later the wind blew stronger than ever, and threw the standard down.

9
Cavaliers and Roundheads
1642–7

THAT August day in Nottingham, when the Royal standard was raised in the driving rain, there were scarcely more than a thousand men at the King's command. Many even of those who had declared their allegiance to him shared the reluctance of Sir Edmund Verney, shortly to be killed fighting for him in Warwickshire. 'I do not like the Quarrel,' Sir Edmund wrote, 'and do heartily wish the King would yield'. But his conscience was concerned 'in honour and in gratitude'; he had eaten the King's bread 'and served him near thirty Years', and he would not do 'so base a Thing as to foresake him' now.

Yet this simple loyalty to the Crown, whether displayed by men like Verney or by those who would always support the King, right or wrong, was not sufficiently widespread or deeply felt to gain Charles more than a few supporters. Others who might have supported him hung back: it was harvest time, for one thing, and for another, the King was still making overtures to Parliament as though he hoped, even now, to reach a compromise. Men were reluctant to jeopardise their future by openly declaring their support of a cause which might at any moment be abandoned or betrayed.

Charles's behaviour in the months before his arrival in Nottingham had certainly, to say the least, been equivocal. Following the advice of such recent and moderate adherents to his cause as Falkland and Hyde, he had appeared to be willing to accept all the reasonable constitutional reforms which had been introduced, to be concerned to present himself as the upholder of legality and of the Church of England; but at the same time he had shown how ready to be influenced he still was by the firebrands and reactionaries at Court who urged him to crush the rebellion by force, to get help to do this from anyone, foreigners and Catholics included. It was not only his enemies, but also his potential friends who distrusted him. Pym was sure that he would never attract enough support to rise in arms to the provocation that the Nineteen Propositions had given him. In the end it was Parliament itself which allowed him to do so.

For on 6 September its Members declared that all men who did not support it were 'delinquents' and that their property was forfeit. This meant that those who would have been happy to stay neutral were virtually obliged to fight in their own defence; it meant, as the Parliamentarian, Sir Simonds D'Ewes, admitted, that 'not only particular persons of the nobility' but 'whole counties' became 'desperate'. Men whose fortunes might well have been lost had Parliament won, now undertook to raise troops to fight for the King in whose victory their own salvation might be secured; while gentry whose income from land was declining and whose fortunes depended upon the rich perquisites which only the Court could offer, needed no further persuasion to fight.

If self-interest provided the spur for this early surge of support for the Royalist cause, other reasons, no less important, played their part in swelling the numbers of men who eventually decided to throw in their lot with the King. It was not only that the King's majesty was considered by many, including Edmund Verney, to be sacrosanct. 'I beseech you consider,' Verney wrote to his brother who had made up his mind to support Parliament, 'that majesty is sacred; God sayth "Touch not myne anointed."' There was also the strong feeling that the King was the defender of the true Church; and although religion became of much more importance later in the struggle than it was in the beginning, it was even now of grave concern. Moreover, while it was never primarily a class struggle – at least the gentry were fairly equally divided – there was an undeniable fear amongst many of the King's supporters that the lower classes would use this opportunity to turn upon their masters, that the predominantly Puritan merchants and shop-keepers of the towns were intent upon upsetting the structure of power to their own advantage, that the King's opponents represented rebellion and chaos as opposed to law and order. These fears and beliefs were not, of course, general throughout the country; they were strongest in the north, except for the more industrialised parts of Yorkshire and Lancashire, in the west Midlands and Wales and in the West Country. Parliament, on the other hand, derived its strongest support from south-east England and London. But there were no firm lines of division; most trading towns declared for Parliament; many areas endeavoured to remain neutral; a number of landowners changed from side to side with the fortunes of war; hundreds of families were divided in their loyalties as the Verneys were; thousands of country people found themselves drawn into the conflict on the side that their landlords and masters elected to support; thousands more were not too sure what all the fuss was about, or as Sir Arthur Haslerig said, did not really care, what government they lived under 'so long as they may plough and go to market'; some did not even know there was a conflict at all, and only about three men in every hundred took an active part in it. Long after the war had started, long after the first battles had been fought, a Yorkshire farm labourer, when advised to keep out of the line of fire between the King's men and Parliament's, learned for the first time that 'them two had fallen out'.

Charles found such uninvolved countrymen as these of little use as recruits; and often he would dismiss the ragged and disgruntled militiamen of the counties as soon as they were brought in to his headquarters, retaining their weapons for his more interested volunteers.

But these volunteers, although willing enough to use the weapons, had scarcely more experience in doing so than the so-called trained bands of the counties, nearly all of which – with the notable exception of London's eighteen thousand well-drilled citizens – were as ill-organised as they were unskilled. Nor had they enough experienced officers; and when a professional officer who had fought in a foreign army *was* found, it was often difficult to persuade young gentlemen, whose continental tours had included a day or two on the battlefield, to serve under him. Another grave disadvantage was that the troops of cavalry and companies of infantry, raised by wealthy Royalists at their own expense, were considered almost as private armies to be used when, where and how their founders and paymasters decreed. So, while money was not an immediately pressing problem for Charles, discipline was. Thanks to rich well-wishers like the King's cousin, the Duke of Richmond, the Roman Catholic Marquess of Worcester, the Earl of Newcastle (whose losses in the struggle were to amount to an enormous sum), and the universities of Oxford and Cambridge, the King was almost as well off as he had ever been; but the forces their money helped him to raise could not then, or later, be called a well-ordered army. Plunder appeared to many to be its main occupation; and when a town was not plundered it was usually because its citizens had paid money to avoid it. Very early on in the war the citizens of Leicester paid the Royalists five hundred pounds on condition that their town was not plundered. Charles condemned the blackmail; but he kept the money.

Discipline was a problem at first in the Parliamentary forces, too. Before the King withdrew to Nottingham a mob of his opponents, calling itself a regiment, descended on Coventry, poaching and stealing on their way, plundering churches, ducking a whore, and shouting their intent to devour a 'mess of Cavaliers' for their supper. Their action was by no means unusual; it was common enough, indeed, in these early days for Parliamentary units to turn upon each other and fight for plunder or to ransack their officers' quarters for the loot that was stored there.

The stolid, stout and plodding Earl of Essex, the general placed in command of the Parliamentary army, was an amateur soldier whose brief service on the Continent and staunch Puritan sympathies were sufficient to recommend him to John Pym and his friends who had, in fact, a very narrow field of talent from which to make their selection. An honest, taciturn, pipe-smoking man, the maligned husband of that Lady Frances Howard whose passion for the Earl of Somerset had caused him such grief and humiliation, Essex was a popular figure, particularly in London. Even there, however, he had no great reputation as a general.

But then the nominal commander of the Royalist forces, the elderly Earl of Lindsey, was no more experienced than Essex, and had last taken part in a campaign almost fifty years before. It was fortunate for the Royalists, therefore, that when the King's tardy advance on London was checked at Edgehill north of Oxford there had come to join the King's colours a young man of wide experience, remarkable talent and inspiring verve.

Charles's nephew, Prince Rupert of the Rhine, was only twenty-three. The younger brother of the Elector Palatine, he had been born in Prague in 1619 and at the age of ten had entered the University of Leyden. At that age he already knew the pikeman's eighteen postures and the musketeer's thirty-four and could ride a horse with marvellous accomplishment. When he was barely fourteen he had ridden off to join the armies in the low countries and although his mother had summoned him back on that occasion, he had gone off again in 1637 as commander of a cavalry regiment to fight the Emperor in the Thirty Years' War. Within a few months he had been taken prisoner at Lemgo, but by then he had impressed all who came into contact with him with his bravery and resource. He had trained his men to understand that a good regiment of cavalry was not a mere collection of individual horsemen, able to go through the parade-ground movements of thrusting, guarding and parrying with chosen rivals in single combat, but a kind of battering-ram that should thunder down upon its opponents in a powerful mass, overthrowing them and driving them back by the sudden, irresistible force of its impact.

To many who met Prince Rupert for the first time he seemed an intolerable youth. Arrogant, ill-tempered and boorish, he appeared to have no manners and no taste. Before he had left Holland for England he had quarrelled with both Henry Jermyn and George Digby and most of the Queen's other friends who were in exile with her. Henrietta herself wrote to warn Charles, 'He should have someone to advise him for believe me he is yet very young and self-willed . . . . He is a person capable of doing anything he is ordered, but he is not to be trusted to take a single step of his own head'.

It was true that he was impulsive and impatient; it was true, too, that his innate reserve and sensitivity led him to hide behind a mask of dismissive hauteur, that his irritation with the mannered *politesse* of Court behaviour induced him to adopt the manners of the tough sailors and dockers with whom, disguised in old canvas clothes, he had chosen to mix as a student in the taverns of The Hague. Yet Rupert was far more than a rough, handsome soldier of fortune with a taste for fancy clothes, fringed boots, feathered hats, and scarlet sashes; he was more than a cavalry leader of undeniable skill and courage. He was highly intelligent, a remarkable linguist, an artist of uncommon merit, a man with an inventive skill and curiosity of mind that was to give as much pleasure to his later years of sickness and premature old age as the several mistresses who visited him in his rooms at Windsor Castle. Above all, he was a commander whose men obeyed and trusted him.

Henrietta had exaggerated his failings: he may have been incapable of directing a full-scale battle, he was certainly incapable of restraining his own excited enthusiasm after an initial success, but he was an inspiring leader of men in battle and Charles's choice of him as General of the Horse was not misplaced. His tall thin figure, 'clad in scarlet very richly laid in silver lace and mounted on a very gallant Barbary horse', became as inspiring a sight to his own cavalry as it was alarming to his enemies. His life seemed charmed; pistols were fired in his face, but he escaped with powder marks; when his horse was killed under him he walked away 'leisurely without so much as mending his pace' and no harm came to him. The Roundheads – their close-cropped heads which had earned them the soubriquet, in sharp contrast to his own long, curled flowing flocks – accused him of being protected by the devil. They said that the white poodle – which accompanied him everywhere, which would jump in the air at the word 'Charles' and cock his leg when his master said 'Pym' – was a little demon that could make itself invisible, pass through their lines and report their strength and dispositions to its master.

Prince Rupert's value to his uncle's ill-trained amateur army was first demonstrated in the plain below Edgehill ridge on Sunday 23 October 1624. The day had begun badly, with a quarrel between the Prince and the Earl of Lindsey which had ended with Lindsey flinging his baton to the ground in rage at the impertinent young man's criticism of his handling of the infantry. Lindsey had cried out that if he was not considered fit to be a general he would die at the head of a regiment instead, and he had stormed off to do so. Sir Jacob Astley, who had known Rupert as a boy and knew better how to manage him, took over Lindsey's command of the infantry, and having placed them to his satisfaction murmured that brief prayer for which his name was ever afterwards to be remembered: 'O Lord, Thou knowest how busy I must be this day. If I forget Thee do not Thou forget me.'

Charles also prayed, and then, dressed in a black velvet cloak lined with ermine, he spoke to his officers: 'Your King is both your cause, your quarrel and your captain. The foe is in sight. The best encouragement I can give you is this, that come life or death, your King will bear you company, and ever keep this field, this place, and this day's service in his grateful remembrance.'

Rupert, contenting himself with military instructions, urged the cavalry to remember what he had always told his regiment in Germany: to ride in a dense mass holding their fire and to break the enemy line by the force of their impact. And so, when the time came, they did. They charged with shattering force into the Roundheads' left wing, driving it back and forcing it through its reserve, sending it flying a mile beyond the nearest village until stopped at last by a regiment of staunch tenants from John

Hampden's Buckinghamshire estate.

It was undeniably a triumph; but Rupert's excited men had gone too far. By the time they returned to the field, Essex's remaining forces had pushed so deep into the unprotected lines of Royalist infantry that the King's standard was captured, its bearer, Sir Edmund Verney, was killed, and the Earl of Lindsey, swearing to the end that he would never fight with boys again, was mortally wounded. The action had come so close to the Prince of Wales that he cocked his pistol and, crying, 'I fear them not!', would have joined the fight had his attendants not pulled him away.

By nightfall the confused fighting was over. Essex's infantry, exhausted by their unfamiliar exertions, had given ground before Prince Rupert's returning cavalry, and the King's standard had been recaptured by a Royalist officer who dashed into the enemy's ranks wearing one of the orange scarves by which – since they had no regular uniform – the Parliamentary troops were distinguished. Both sides, declining to leave the field, encamped for the night where they were and claimed the victory.

With dead and wounded men lying all around him in the biting cold, the King could not sleep. Before the day's fighting had started he had seemed glad that the time for debate was over, that the problems that beset him were not his to resolve now but in the hands of God. His hesitations and waverings had appeared to be resolved, his wayward self-confidence increased by the knowledge that the time had come for the savage but simple remedies of force. Yet the sudden experience of violence, the sight of so much blood and death, the fearful smells and sounds of battle now brought him once more to doubt and indecision.

It was not that he was afraid, but he was not sure any more. Prince Rupert pressed him to advance on fast to London and forcibly dissolve Parliament; the same advice was urged upon him by the seventy-year-old Earl of Forth, a Scottish officer who had held high command in the Swedish army and, now that the Earl of Lindsey was dead, became the new commander of the infantry. Others more cautious advised him to hold back. Charles wavered, unwilling to commit himself irrevocably, yet reluctant to appear incapable of doing so. He was afraid, he admitted, 'of the temptation of an absolute conquest'.

The Parliamentarians, too, were uncertain how next to proceed. A few hours after claiming the victory, Essex had withdrawn to

Warwick and thence to London, leaving the Royalists free to take
Banbury and re-stock their army from its supplies of clothes and
food; numerous deserters had wandered off after the battle, taking
their weapons with them; an appeal for money in the City had met
with a discouraging response; the mood of the people of the capital
was disquieting: the Trained Bands remained reliable and resolute,
but there were muttered grumbles against Parliament and demands
for a truce. It was decided to suggest to the King that representatives
of both sides should meet to discuss terms for a treaty.

The offer was accepted; but neither side abided by the agreement
for a 'cessation of arms'. Parliament advanced the Trained Bands out
of London, towards the scattered villages beyond the suburbs of
Westminster; the King moved down through Oxford and Reading
towards Brentford which Prince Rupert's cavalry surprised on the
misty morning of 12 November, clattering through the rough
streets of the little town, setting fire to some of its houses, plundering others, driving Denzil Holles's courageous but woefully out-
fought regiment of 'butchers and dyers' into the river.

When Charles reached Brentford the next morning, however,
his nephew's violent attack had roused the Londoners in earnest to
their defence. Thousand upon thousands of citizens, apprentices,
tradesmen, peers and Members of Parliament were ranged across the
road in front of him, standing firm on Turnham Green, shoulder to
shoulder with troops who had fought at Edgehill, well placed
behind hedges and ditches, in orchards and gardens, standing in the
doorways of stables and barns, gazing in nervous defiance from
tavern windows. Behind them there were cannon in the main
streets of the City and at every gate, barricades across the roads in
Westminster and in the northern suburbs, fieldworks in the parks,
armed ships in the river.

To shouts of 'Hey for old Robin!' Essex rode from regiment to
Trained Band and Trained Band to regiment, while his fellow
Puritan, Philip Skippon – an old soldier who had served in the
ranks of the Dutch army and had been entrusted with the Command
of the Trained Bands – cried out, 'Come, my boys, my brave boys,
let us pray heartily and fight heartily, I will run the same fortunes
and hazards with you. Remember the cause is for God!'

There were to be no hazards, though. The day – it was a Sunday –
wore slowly and quietly on. Neither army moved. Each stood
uneasily facing the other, the Londoners being fed in the afternoon

from carts stacked high with 'an hundred loads of all manner of good provisions of victuals, bottles of wine and barrels of beer' which had been loaded up outside taverns and private houses after morning service. Essex wisely refrained from putting this well-fed but ill-assorted army to the test of battle; the Royalists, tired and outnumbered two to one, could not use their cavalry in such confined and treacherous country.

The King had no alternative but to withdraw. By way of Hampton Court, Oatlands and Reading, he rode with his army back to Oxford, thereafter his headquarters and his Court.

Charles established himself at Christ Church. Around him in other colleges, in lodging houses, taverns, rented rooms and attics, cavalry officers and secretaries, chaplains and servants, musicians and ladies of the Court, made new homes for themselves in what cramped quarters they could find in the still largely medieval and Tudor town. Prince Rupert moved into St John's College at which he had been nominally entered as an undergraduate during a visit to England in 1636. All Souls was turned into an arsenal, New College into a magazine, New Inn Hall into a mint. The Council met in Oriel; the Astronomy and Music schools became workrooms for tailors who laboured there to make uniforms for the King's troops; the Law and Logic Schools were piled high with horse fodder; the main quadrangle of Christ Church was used as a cattle pen; Sir Edward Nicholas, who had succeeded Sir Francis Windebanke as principal Secretary of State, settled down with his staff and family at Pembroke College.

By the beginning of the new year, 1643, Oxford was more like a garrison than a university town. Undergraduates, forsaking their books for spades, threw up new earthworks and fortifications; scholars and professors joined the colours; noble students sought leave to put on the gleaming armour of the King's Life Guard; soldiers were drilled in the streets and quadrangles; gunners were trained in the meadows, and when off duty they brawled to such an extent that the sale of drink had to be prohibited after nine o'clock in the evening; duels were so commonplace that scarcely a day passed without an officer being wounded, and Prince Rupert once had to part two furious contestants with a pole-axe.

At the same time the life of the Court went on as though its denizens were still in Whitehall. There were musical entertainments and plays; new sonnets and satires were published; new fashions were paraded through the streets and were copied by the citizens' wives; love affairs were conducted by the river bank and beneath the secluded walls of college gardens; fashionable ladies defied the 'terrible gigantique aspect' and 'sharp, grey eies' of the President of Trinity and walked into his chapel 'half dressed, like angels'; the King appointed a Master of Revels.

Charles himself maintained in public a characteristically wistful dignity. He took walks with Lord Falkland, now his secretary; he talked with his chaplains, with Jeremy Taylor, a Fellow of All Souls, and with Gilbert Sheldon, later to become Archbishop of Canterbury and Chancellor of the University; he attended the services in Christ Church with unfailing regularity; he contrived as best he could – though his own secret intrigues often conducted in direct contradiction of his public statements made him a less than successful mediator – to compose the quarrels which were for ever breaking out between the moderate Edward Hyde and the wild ultra-Royalist George Digby, between Prince Rupert and the capricious courtiers Harry Wilmot and George Goring, between soldiers who fancied themselves as politicians and politicians who fancied themselves as soldiers, between Protestants and Catholics, moderates and reactionaries, husbands, wives and lovers.

Out of all this conflict of interest and ambition there did at least emerge a coherent military strategy, a firm decision to make another attempt upon London by striking towards it from the three areas of the country where support for the King was strongest, from Yorkshire, the West Country and the south-west. The thrust from Yorkshire was entrusted to the Earl of Newcastle, the former governor of the Prince of Wales, a man of tolerant views and expert horsemanship, immensely rich, extremely cultured, exquisitely polite; the approach from Devon and Cornwall was to be conducted by the devoted, Somerset-born Royalist Sir Ralph Hopton who had served in the Thirty Years' War and on Count Mansfeld's ill-fated expedition; the final and consolidating attack was to be led by the King himself.

At first all went well. In Yorkshire, Sir Thomas Fairfax, the most accomplished of Parliament's commanders in the north who had previously captured Leeds and Wakefield with a small force mainly composed of West Riding townsmen, was routed by Newcastle at Adwalton Moor and forced to seek refuge in Hull. In the south-

west, Sir Ralph Hopton's men as decisively defeated the Roundheads at Stratton and advanced through Devon to link up with
another Royalist force under the Marquess of Hertford at Chard in
Somerset. In the Midlands, an advance by Essex, who had captured
Reading in April, was checked by Prince Rupert at Chalgrove Field
where the well-loved John Hampden was mortally wounded. Soon
there followed other Royalist victories in the West Country, at
Landsdown Hill near Bath and on Roundway Down near Devizes;
on 26 July Prince Rupert stormed and captured Bristol, the greatest
port in the country after London. Meanwhile a Royalist uprising in
Kent temporarily threatened London itself.

But then, when it seemed that the Royalist strategy would soon
triumph, the King's forces began to disperse. They were willing
enough to fight in defence of their own counties; they did not want
to be taken too far from their homes. The western army, its numbers
sadly depleted, declined to move further east so long as a Parliamentary garrison still held out at Plymouth, threatening the families they
had left behind; the northern army, having got as far south as
Lincoln, also turned back, refusing to advance while Fairfax's men
were free to plunder Yorkshire from their fortress at Hull.

So Charles, deprived of the possibility of capturing London,
turned his attention to Gloucester, the only garrison the Roundheads had in the west between the Bristol Channel and Lancashire.
Possession of Gloucester, his advisers pointed out to him, would
give him control of the Severn and open up his route to South
Wales where Royalist support was so strong. But to take Gloucester
proved as difficult as to advance on London; its citizens put up a
fierce resistance; and encouraged by their defiance Essex asked the
Trained Bands to volunteer for its relief. They did so, and a hard
march it was. 'At Aynhoe,' wrote one of their number, 'we were
very much scanted of victuals; at Chipping Norton our regiment
stood in the open field all night having neither bread nor water to
refresh ourselves, having also marched the day before without any
sustenance'.

Tired and hungry as they were, they nevertheless helped to turn
the fortunes of the war in Parliament's favour. For at Newbury,
where they came face to face with the Royalists who had been
obliged by their approach to withdraw from the siege of Gloucester,
they gave their opponents a worse mauling than ever yet they had
had. Prince Rupert, a far more prudent general than his enemies

I

allowed or his own behaviour in the heat of battle suggested, had been against giving Essex an opportunity of fighting until more ammunition arrived from Oxford. But he was overruled; and by nightfall on 20 September after a ferocious day-long battle – in which the Royal musketeers exhausted their powder and shot and the Royalist cavalry could not be used to its usual good effect over the constricted ground – the King was obliged to withdraw, mourning the loss of numerous men he had known and of some he had liked. One of these was his secretary, Lord Falkland who, deeply depressed by the breakdown of the peace negotiations and the now spreading war, had ridden to his death as a volunteer in the cavalry.

It was difficult for the Parliamentarians to realise after their sudden successes at Gloucester and Newbury that only a few months before they had come close to collapse. In the summer John Pym, struggling against a peace party on one side and an aggressive war party on the other, had appeared to be losing his grip on Parliament. A mission led by the Earl of Northumberland had been to Oxford to treat for peace but had served only to demostrate that the King could not be induced to give way on matters affecting the Church, the command of the army, or the 'delinquents' who had supported his cause. Yet crowds – angered as much by the financial measures to which Parliament had been driven to resort as by the news of repeated Royalist victories – marched through Palace Yard shouting 'Peace! Peace!'; on 8 August a mob of women, and men disguised as women, banging on the doors of the Commons, and bawling for 'that dog Pym', had to be dispersed by a squadron of cavalry.

Pym was not to be intimidated in this way. He was exhausted by overwork and he was dying of cancer; yet he had one more decisive service to render to his cause. While Essex was marching on Gloucester, he was negotiating for a treaty with Parliament's 'brethren of Scotland'; while the King was vainly intriguing for help from all over Europe and across the Irish Sea, Pym was actually coming to terms with the Scots, formulating with them a Solemn League and Covenant by which the English Parliament swore to maintain the existing structure of the Scottish Church and to reform the Anglican Church, 'according to the Word of God,' in exchange for military help against the King.

Parliament's determination to reform the Church was soon demonstrated by the execution of Archbishop Laud, and Scotland's promise of military aid redeemed less perversely by an invasion of Northumberland. Early in 1644 Alexander Leslie, who had disdainfully brushed aside the English at Newburn four years before, led his troops on into Yorkshire and laid siege to York. The King's hold on the north was now seriously threatened, and Parliament's fortunes were transformed.

Charles returned to Oxford from Newbury in an anxious mood. His failure to win a decisive victory either in 1642 or 1643 was far more of a catastrophe for him than it was for the Parliamentarians, who became relatively stronger with each passing month, whose control of the Navy had allowed them to supply the garrisons of Hull and Plymouth, and the morale of whose soldiers and new recruits was continually improving. He found the Court at Oxford no longer certain of victory, more *intrigant* and quarrelsome than ever.

The arrival of the Queen had added to its dissidence. Henrietta had arrived in Oxford a month before her husband's departure for Gloucester. She had sailed in February from Holland, but after nine tempestuously stormy days at sea her ship had been driven back into Scheveningen and she was taken ashore in a fishing smack. It had been a fearful ordeal, bravely borne: she had never expected to see land again. For days on end she had been unable to leave her little cabin; and, apart from the crew, the only person aboard able even to stand up had been one of her priests who had been a Knight of Malta. Her ladies had been carried ashore too battered, bruised, ill and dizzy to be able to walk, and on landing all their clothing had to be burned. Their only comfort on the way had been their mistress's confident assertion that queens of England were never drowned.

Ten days later they had had to brace themselves for another attempt. On this occasion they had had a perfect crossing and arrived unscathed on the Yorkshire coast at Bridlington where they had seen the Queen to bed in a thatched cottage on the quayside. But their troubles had not yet ended; for Bridlington had come under bombardment from Parliamentary ships in the bay and they had to fly from the village into the open, snow-covered fields inland.

'Tell me now by what road I may come to join you,' Henrietta had written to her husband as soon as she was safe. 'I will not repeat that I am in the greatest impatience in the world to join you.'

It could not be doubted that she was. Her letters from Holland had been full of her desire to come back to him. 'I do not wish to remain in this country,' she had complained. 'I need the air of England, or at least the air where you are.' Her eyes had been giving her pain ever since she had landed on the Continent, and she could not decide whether this was the Dutch atmosphere, all the writing she had to do, or the tears that were 'weighing them down sometimes'. She had sold what jewels she could, the Dutch merchants showing themselves wary of negotiating for the big pieces but giving her something – though but half what they were worth – for the smaller ones; and with the money she had been able to buy arms and send them off to England. This duty done, she had longed desperately to return.

It was not just that she had wanted to be with her husband again, she did not trust him to stand firm when she was away from him. She had dared not think what advice was swaying that pliable, impressionable nature, and had felt it necessary to remind him constantly of his duty to their family and his promises to herself: 'I hope that you are constant in *your resolutions*: you have already learnt *to your cost* that want of *perseverance* in your *designs* has *ruined* you . . . . If you have *broken your resolutions* then there is nothing but *death* for *me* . . . . my whole hope lies in your firmness and constancy, and when I hear anything to the contrary, I am mad . . . . Delays have always ruined you. Take a good resolution and pursue it . . . for to begin and then to stop is your ruin – experience shows it you. It is not enough to declare yourself in writing; actions must afterwards be seen . . . I send you this man express, hoping that you have not *passed* the *militia* bill. If you have, I must think about retiring for the present into a convent, for you are no longer capable of protecting anyone, nor even yourself . . . . I am resolved to bear all and to live in some place where I shall fancy myself a country girl, and leave you to follow the counsel of those who are wiser than I, as they think . . . .'

Although she understood her husband's weaknesses well enough, her counsel to him in his adversity was rarely as realistic as she fancied; and now that she had returned to England Charles's more responsible advisers had cause to be apprehensive.

For the first few months, however, she had remained in the north, riding with Newcastle's army, priding herself on her hardihood, styling herself 'Generalissima' as, with the indispensable

Henry Jermyn as colonel of her guards, she led 'three thousand foot, thirty companies of horses and dragoons ... with a hundred and fifty waggons of baggage to govern in case of battle'. And it was not until July that, slipping past the cavalry that Essex had sent to intercept her, she came down, through Ashby-de-la-Zouch and King's Norton, to Stratford-on-Avon where she stayed the night in the handsome house of William Shakespeare's granddaughter.

Charles – accompanied by the Prince of Wales now thirteen and her second son James aged ten – met her at Edgehill, cheerfully granting her first request that Henry Jermyn should be given a peerage. Delighted to be with her again, he rode back with her to Oxford where the Warden's lodgings at Merton College had been set aside for her.

The happy atmosphere was soon overclouded: Henrietta's return, while a solace to the King, exacerbated all the old quarrels between the 'Queen's party' and the rest of the Court, between Digby of whom the Queen was fond and Prince Rupert whom she distrusted and disliked, between Protestants and Catholics. The King mournfully complained that the quarrels of his friends caused him as much pain as the attacks of his enemies.

As summer turned to an autumn of fogs and floods he had further grounds for complaint. Prince Rupert fell in love with Mary Villiers, the Duke of Buckingham's daughter, now the wife of the Duke of Richmond; Lord Holland, who was always in the Queen's rooms at Merton when her husband wanted to be alone with her, felt intolerably slighted when the Marquess of Hertford instead of himself was made Groom of the Stole and he went off to London to join the other side; other courtiers also abandoned the King, losing faith in his chances of success and dreading another winter in the overcrowded and typhus-ridden town; a Parliament which Charles summoned to Oxford – promising a free pardon to any previously elected Members of the Parliament at Westminster who would attend it – was so sad a failure that his enemies named it the 'Antick-Parliament' and the King himself condemned it as a 'mongrel'.

Henrietta began to lose heart. She was suffering from a perpetual racking cough for which she blamed the damp Thames Valley air; she was suffering, too, from spasmodic and violent pains which she felt could not be attributed to her being pregnant – though pregnant she was, with her ninth child. It was considered that she must be moved from Oxford, particularly as the Scottish army was now threatening the Earl of Newcastle's forces in the north; and so, on 17 April, Henrietta, escorted by Lord Jermyn, left Oxford for the West Country.

Charles accompanied her as far as Abingdon and said goodbye to her there. She was convinced that she was going to die, that she would never see her husband again. Her doctor said that she was hysterical.

She did not die; her baby, a healthy daughter, was born at Exeter on 16 June and was given her mother's name; but the Queen was right in one respect: she never did see her husband again. By the time of her confinement Exeter was threatened by Parliamentary troops and, as soon as she could travel, dangerously ill now with puerperal sepsis, she crept out of the town, accompanied only by a priest, one of her ladies and her doctor who, so he complained, had to walk 'most of the way into Cornwall'. The night before she sailed for France from Falmouth she wrote to her husband, 'Adieu, my dear heart. If I die, believe that you will lose a person who has never been other than entirely yours, and who by her affection has deserved that you shall not forget her'.

Charles, campaigning once again with his western army, moved down into Devonshire and arrived at Exeter a fortnight after the Queen had gone. The distress her last pitiful letter had caused him was cruelly aggravated when news reached him of a catastrophe that had overtaken his army in the north.

'If York be lost,' Charles had written to Prince Rupert a month before, 'I shall esteem my crown little less [than lost] . . . wherefore I command and conjure you . . . that, all new enterprise laid aside, you immediately march according to your first intention, with all your force to the relief of York.'

With this letter in his pocket, Rupert had ridden fast to the Marquess of Newcatle's help, collecting volunteers on his way through Lancashire, taking under his command a thousand horsemen who had come down from Cumberland, skilfully outflanking a body of troops sent to block his passage at Knaresborough, moving north to cross the river Ouse at Boroughbridge and the Swale at Thornton Bridge, then turning quickly south to threaten York's unguarded northern gate. The swift and daring manoeuvre was completely successful; and the Marquess of Newcastle, with customary urbanity, wrote to congratulate the 'Redeemer of the

North and the Saviour of the Crown'.

But Rupert was not satisfied merely to relieve York. He determined to defeat the armies that had been besieging it before returning to the King. Issuing a peremptory order to Newcastle to be ready to march at four o'clock in the morning, he rode away in search of his quarry without waiting for a response. Newcastle, suppressing his indignation at the offhand manner in which the young Prince had treated him, set off after him and caught him up on Marston Moor. 'My Lord,' Rupert greeted him briskly, 'I wish you had come sooner with your forces, but I hope we shall yet have a glorious day.'

Rupert, indeed, seemed to have a little doubt that the coming day would bring him in another victory and a greater one than any he had yet won. Only once that morning had he shown a passing apprehension when, interrogating a Parliamentary trooper who had been taken prisoner, he asked him the single question: 'Is Cromwell there?'

One November day four years before a genial Member of Parliament, Philip Warwick, had entered the House of Commons during one of the Long Parliament's early debates. 'I came into the house well-clad,' he recollected in his memoirs, '(we courtiers valued ourselves much upon our good clothes) . . . and perceived a gentleman speaking (whom I knew not), very ordinarily apparelled; for it was a plain cloth suit, which seemed to have been made by an ill country-tailor. His linen was plain and not very clean; and I remember a speck or two of blood upon his little band, which was not much larger than his collar. His hat was without a hat band. His stature was of a good size, his sword stuck close to his side; his countenance swollen and reddish; his voice sharp and untunable, and his eloquence full of fervour.'

This was Oliver Cromwell, Member of Parliament for the city of Cambridge, forty-one years old.

He had been born in Huntingdon, the son of Robert Cromwell, former Member of Parliament for Huntingdon, and the nephew of Sir Oliver Cromwell, the head of the family, a family of partly Welsh descent that owned a large part of the county and had been long in the King's service as Sheriffs and Justices of the Peace. Young Oliver had been sent to the local free school where under the strict guidance of the sternly Puritan schoolmaster, Thomas Beard – who was also rector of the parish – he had shown more aptitude for games than for study, more interest in 'tennis, wrestling, running, swimming, handling weapons, riding, hunting, dancing and shooting with the long bow' than in the religious instruction which formed so large a part of Dr Beard's curriculum. At Cambridge these preferences remained marked. The tall strong young undergraduate became 'one of the chief match-makers and players at Foot-ball, cudgels or any other boisterous game or sport'. On his father's death, he left without taking a degree to manage the small family estate in Huntingdon which had been left to his charge; and at the age of twenty-one he married the daughter of a well-to-do London merchant, a woman older than himself, who within the next eight years bore him several children. Five of these children, four sons and a daughter, survived – he was later to have three more daughters – and they all lived together in the stone house at the end of Huntingdon High Street. Also living with them there were Oliver's unmarried sisters as well as their mother to whom he was devoted and from who he was never to be parted until she died in her ninetieth year, giving her son, the great all-powerful Protector of England, her last, loving blessing: 'My dear son, I leave my heart with thee.'

Oliver was not happy at Huntingdon. Perhaps it was the constricting, crowded house that was to blame, the oppressively constraining almost claustrophobic domesticity that made him long to escape from it to the society of male companions in the tavern, to the dicing table, to company more exciting and less genteel than that of Elizabeth his wife. A placid and submissive woman, his wife was to play so little part in the years ahead that long after her husband's death a petition to Charles II – in which she pleaded that she had never interfered with politics and knew nothing about his Majesty's jewels – was succinctly labelled by a secretary as having come from 'old Mrs Cromwell. Noll's wife.' It was virtually all that was known of her.

Stories of Cromwell's dissipations were, of course, afterwards exaggerated if not invented by his enemies. The sins of which he himself felt conscious seem to have been sins of the spirit; the memory of them was always painful; 'O I lived in darkness and hated light. I was a chief – the chief – of sinners. This is true. I hated godliness.' He admitted also that he had as little ambition as godliness. He entered Parliament as Member for Huntingdon in 1628;

but this, after all, was the sort of thing his family did: soon he was to have nine relatives in the House, including John Hampden his first cousin. Although he spoke on occasions, his speeches lacked the fire and persuasion that were later to characterise them; and when he returned to the country after the dissolution of 1629 he disappeared once more into the Fenland mists. For a time he rented a farm at St Ives but 'scarce half a crop ever reared itself upon his grounds'; then he inherited property from an uncle and moved to Ely but, so a friend wrote of him, he was restlessly discontented in 'very great troubles of soul, lying a long time under sore terrors and temptations, and at the same time in a very low condition'. A doctor whom he had consulted in London, Sir Theodore Mayerne, the only physician whom James I would trust, had noted in his case-book that the patient was 'excessively melancholic'. This condition was alleged to have been noted also by a local doctor who added that he was 'a most splenetic man and had fancies about the Cross in the town', and that he called for treatment at midnight 'and such unreasonable hours, very many times, upon a strong fancy that made him believe he was then dying.' He appeared in church at St Ives – with a red flannel round his neck as a comfort for his chronically inflamed throat – brooding and miserable; his farm workers were summoned to long prayers with his family before starting work in the morning and again after their midday meal, but he himself appeared to derive little comfort from these devotions. And then at last 'his will was broken into submission to the Will of God'.

It was as though at last Cromwell had found both peace of mind and a purpose in life in overcoming all his objections to the Puritan faith with which Dr Beard had tried to discipline him as a boy. Beard had taught that God was intimately involved in every detail and every seemingly insignificant action in life, that He watched the daily deeds and punished the daily sins of all men, that the Pope was Anti-Christ, above all, that the Elect, those who obeyed God's laws and 'consequently the laws of man and nature' would be saved. By prayer and torment, through misery and distrust, Cromwell had come to believe – as so many of his contemporaries believed – not merely that everything that happened in the world was due to the anger or favour of God, that the Bible was His direct word, that those who 'are instructed in the science of truth by the Holy Scriptures know the beginning of the world and its end', but that he himself was so instructed, that he was one of the

Elect. It was his duty, he saw now, to devote himself to God's fight and to the establishment of His Kingdom on earth. He did so from then on with an ever-burning zeal, an unswerving fixity of purpose, a ruthless, powerful dedication and self-confident patriotism that forced men to recognise that there had risen amongst them in the shape of this middle-aged, clumsy, East Anglican farmer with his rough-skinned reddish face and conspicuous mole beneath his lower lip, a man of destiny.

'Pray, Mr Hampden,' the Member for Wendover was once asked by a colleague, 'who is that sloven?'

'That sloven, that sloven whom you see before you hath no ornament in his speech; but that sloven, I say, if we should ever come to a breach with the King (which God forbid!) in such a case, I say, that sloven will be the greatest man in England.'

When the breach with the King did come, Cromwell reacted with that forceful determined spirit which was, indeed, to make him the greatest man in England. He rushed from Westminster to Cambridge, collecting recruits on the way; placed pickets on the roads leading out of the town to prevent further supplies of college plate being sent to the King; captured the castle and its ammunition; arrested the Royalists who had come to the town to read the King's Commission of Array. He then enlisted and – out of his own slender resources equipped and paid – a troop of horsemen to fight for the 'preservation of the true religion, the laws, liberty and peace of the Kingdom', explaining to his recruits that he would have nothing to do with Parliament's refusal to admit that they were fighting the King, their specious protests that they were taking arms for the 'safety of the King's person' and the 'defence of both Houses of Parliament' against his Majesty's 'evil counsellors'. He would not deceive or cozen them by such expressions, he bluntly told his troopers. If the King happened to be in the body of the enemy that he was to charge, he would fire his 'pistol upon him as at any other private person', and if their conscience did not allow them to do the same, he advised them 'not to list themselves in his troop or under his command'.

With sixty men prepared to fire their pistols at the King, Captain Cromwell of the 67th Troop of Horse had ridden off to place himself under the orders of the Earl of Essex; and it was while he was serving under Essex's command that the Parliamentary cavalry had been driven off the field of Edgehill by the furious charge of Prince Rupert's cavaliers.

'Your troopers,' he had said to John Hampden after the battle, '*your* troopers are most of them old decayed serving-men and tapsters and such kind of fellows. *Their* troopers are gentlemen's sons, younger sons and persons of quality. Do you think that the spirits of such base and mean fellows will ever be able to encounter gentlemen that have honour and courage and resolution in them? You must get men of a spirit – and take it not ill what I say – I know you will not – of a spirit that is likely to go on as far as gentlemen will go, or else I am sure you will be beaten still.'

For his part, Cromwell had gone home to East Anglia to raise and train the sort of cavalry who might one day prove a match for Rupert's cavaliers. Welcoming Parliament's decision to unite the counties under its control in various Associations, he had become the leading spirit of the Eastern Association of Norfolk, Suffolk, Essex, Cambridgeshire and Hertfordshire, and later of Huntingdon-shire and Lincolnshire, organising the Association's resources, training its men, issuing orders which brooked no opposition – 'let me assure you it's necessary, and therefore to be done . . . Raise all your hands . . . Get what volunteers you can . . . Hasten your horses . . . You must act lively . . . Do it without distraction . . . . Neglect no means . . . . Send at once . . . . Remember who tells you . . . .' He had enlisted men and commissioned officers eager to fight not for adventure or for pay – though they were paid more regularly than any other large body of troops on either side – but for their faith: 'such men,' as he described them himself, 'as had the fear of God before them and as made some conscience of what they did'. For he would far rather have 'a plain russet-coated captain that knows what he fights for and loves what he knows, than that which you call "a gentleman" and is nothing else'.

His men were freeholders for the most part, and freeholders' sons, 'who upon a matter of conscience engaged in this quarrel'. Their minds being well armed by their consciences, their bodies by 'good iron arms, they would as one man stand firmly and charge desperately'. They were forbidden to plunder, to get drunk, to go whoring, even to swear, but such prohibitions were scarcely necessary. 'I have a lovely company,' he had written proudly to his cousin, Oliver St John, 'They are honest sober Christians. You would respect them, did you know them. They expect to be used as men.'

Near Winceby in Lincolnshire on 11 October 1643, in conjunction with Sir Thomas Fairfax, whose cavalry had ·been ferried across the Humber from Hull, he and his men – well trained not merely to charge in a mass but to rally quickly after either victory or defeat – routed the Royalist troops. 'Colonel Cromwell fell with brave resolution on the enemy', ran a contemporary report. 'His horse was killed under him at the first charge and fell down upon him; and, as he rose, he was knocked down again . . . but afterwards he recovered a poor horse in a soldier's hands, and bravely mounted himself again. Truly, this first charge was performed with so much admirable courage and resolution by our troops that the enemy stood not another.'

Three months later Cromwell had been appointed Lieutenant-General of the Eastern Association, under the Earl of Manchester, the former Lord Mandeville; and it was as Manchester's second in command, and in control of all the Association's cavalry, that Cromwell now faced Rupert on Marston Moor.

General Cromwell's cavalry was on the left of the Parliamentary line, Sir Thomas Fairfax's troopers of the northern army on the right; the infantry stood in the centre with the musketeers and pikemen of the Scottish army. There were twenty-thousand foot soldiers and seven thousand horsemen.

The Royalist army, beyond the ditch that cut through Marston Field beneath the slope of Marston Hill, had rather more than five thousand cavalry – Prince Rupert's own horse being drawn up opposite General Cromwell's – but the infantry, no more than eleven thousand of them, were greatly outnumbered.

Between four and five o'clock in the afternoon the two armies had settled down in positions within close sight of one another, the cavalry on the wings being less than a quarter of a mile apart, able to see every movement in the opposing lines, every musketeer and pikeman in the leading ranks, every colour flapping in the intermittent showers of rain. As the Royalists waited for the first attack they heard their opponents raise their voices in the singing of a psalm.

When the sun began to go down Prince Rupert decided there would be no battle, after all, that day. It was surely too late now for an engagement involving so many troops. Intending to attack in the morning, he left the lines and settled down to his supper; the

Marquess of Newcastle went back to his coach to smoke his pipe.

Then at about half past seven, as the clouds darkened and the damp and heavy air rumbled with the distant roar of thunder, the Parliament forces moved down the slope of Marston Hill trampling the wet rye underfoot. At first it seemed that, despite their few numbers, the Royalists would gain the victory. Fairfax's cavalry were driven off the field by Lord Goring; the Roundhead infantry faltered beneath the determined attack of Lord Newcastle's 'whitecoats' – so called because of the undyed woollen cloth of which their uniforms were made – and half the Scots, with cries of 'Wae's us. We are all undone', retreated to the south. On the right of the Royalist line, however, Cromwell's cavalry were proving their courage and skill against Rupert's cavaliers. Charged both in front and flank they had 'a hard pull of it' to start with, so one of their officers wrote, hacking to right and left in their struggle to hold their ground, 'but at last (it so pleased God) Cromwell broke through them scattering them before him like a little dust'. Soon all Rupert's right wing was 'flying along by Wilstrop Wood as fast and as thick as could be'. It was then that Cromwell's men reaped the reward of their stern and assiduous training. Instead of giving way to the temptation to pursue the flying horsemen, they rallied, wheeled and re-formed to gallop back to the help of those brave Scotsmen who were still holding to their ground.

Within less than two hours, before it was yet dark, the fighting was over. Prince Rupert's poodle lay dead on the field, his owner – forced to hide for a time in a beanfield – rode back to York along a road strewn with the dead and dying bodies of Royalist soldiers cut down in retreat. His enemies returned to the field of their victory to offer thanks to God for their triumph and, having prayed, to strip naked the corpses of the enemy dead. Next morning a captured Royalist officer was taken round to inspect the thousands of partly clothed and unclothed bodies, to decide which deserved a burial more decent than being tipped into the huge common pits, and he could not hold back his tears. 'Alas for King Charles!' he murmured. 'Unhappy King Charles!'

Charles, to be sure, had cause enough for grief. He had not only lost the north, but the Marquess of Newcastle, unwilling to be any longer associated with so forlorn a cause, had sailed for Holland. Prince Rupert had tried to dissuade him, but Newcastle had been adamant. No, he certainly would not stay to 'endure the laughter of the Court'.

As the days passed, however, it became clear that the King's cause was not yet lost. Prince Rupert managed to escape from Yorkshire by way of the western dales with six thousand men; and the three armies which had combined to defeat him, following a precedent which the Civil War had long since made familiar, went their separate ways on isolated and local operations: the Scots went north to besiege Newcastle, Sir Thomas Fairfax remained in Yorkshire to reduce those Royalist strongholds, like Pontefract and Scarborough, that still held out against him, while the Earl of Manchester took the Eastern Association back to Lincolnshire where he showed himself unwilling to pursue the war with vigour, being in the words of Cromwell's later accusation, 'always indisposed and backward to engagements'.

In the south-west the Earl of Essex, too, seemed incapable of following up the northern victory. He allowed his communications with London to be cut and his troops to be surrounded in Cornwall; he himself escaped by sea, and his cavalry broke through the blockade at Lostwithiel, but six thousand of his infantry were starved into surrender by the encircling posts which the King had established around them. At the same time in Scotland the Marquess of Montrose was winning a series of decisive victories for the King over the Scottish Presbyterians.

Charles had more than military success to sustain him. There were reports of growing discontent with Parliament in the country as a whole and in London in particular. Admittedly, the plundering of his own troops caused dismay, but the taxes by which Parliament maintained theirs aroused quite as wide a resentment amongst those who fell liable for assessment; while the very rules against plundering and other rewarding pleasures of the military life led many soldiers to desert Parliament's army for his own.

Yet once again, when the tide of war seemed to be running in the King's favour, Cromwell turned it. After Marston Moor, Rupert in reluctant admiration of his enemy's hard tenacity had called him Ironsides and the nickname was soon applied to all the fine troops he commanded. But Cromwell realised that, reliable as his own men were, victory could not be won until far more of Parliament's forces were as well organised and trained as the Ironsides were. Pursuing with relentless determination Sir William Waller's idea that Parliament should have a standing army 'merely of their own', Cromwell urged the creation of a New Model Army, a truly professional, regularly paid force under the firm control of a single commander. No good soldier should be excluded from this new army, Cromwell insisted, merely because his own way to God differed from the orthodox way of the Presbyterians. He had been exasperated in the past when men and officers had been criticised, punished or even dismissed from their regiments not because of any military lapse or incapacity, but because they happened to hold some sectarian view. The new army must not on any account deny itself the services of Independents (men who held views which may be compared to those of the later Congregationalists), nor must it deny promotion to them; certainly it must not be placed under the command of the officers of the old school, like Essex and Manchester, who had proved not only their incapacity but also their unwillingness to bring the King to final and total military defeat 'through the ending of the war by the sword'.

To get rid of such officers without undue ill feeling – they had, after all, had the courage to make a stand against the King from the beginning of the war – Cromwell pushed through Parliament the Self-Denying Ordinance which obliged all Members to resign any military command they might be holding. The Ordinance applied to Cromwell himself, of course, as much as to Essex and Manchester, but it did not preclude the possibility of a former officer being reappointed to his command; and so Parliament, naturally unwilling to lose an officer of such talents at so critical a stage of the war, agreed that he could retain his old command as General of the Horse so long as the House of Commons could dispense with his services. In July 1645, therefore, Cromwell, as Lieutenant-General of the New Model Army, left for Northamptonshire to join Sir Thomas Fairfax whose appointment as Commander-in-Chief of Parliament's forces in the Earl of Manchester's place he had so successfully engineered.

The King had done what he could to take advantage of the respite afforded him by the Earl of Essex's defeat in Cornwall and the Earl of Manchester's dallying at Lincoln. 'If we beat the King ninety-nine times,' Manchester had complained, 'yet he is King still, and so will his posterity be after him, but if the King beats us, we shall all be hanged and our posterity made slaves.' Well aware of such thoughts in the minds of his opponents who, like Manchester, dreaded the consequences of outright and decisive victory over the King, Charles returned to Oxford in hopes of arranging a negotiated peace on favourable terms. He knew that the Scots were dismayed by the dismissal of the Presbyterian Manchester in favour of that 'darling of the sectaries', Oliver Cromwell, a man who should, in the opinion of the Scots, himself have been dismissed for his religious beliefs; Charles knew, too, that the Self-Denying Ordinance, the establishment of the New Model Army and all that they both entailed, were not at all to the liking of many Presbyterians in the House of Commons and most of the old school in the House of Lords.

He had been cheered by his victory over Essex in Cornwall, and had come back to Oxford with a sense of pride in his military skill, though Essex's defeat had been achieved more by the Earl's incompetence than by his own dexterity. On his way back, at Newbury, he had come up against the Earl of Manchester, who had moved slowly and belatedly to the help of the western army; and there, also, any reason he had for self-congratulation was due not so much to his own generalship as to his enemies' mistakes and their commander's reluctance to fight. They had greatly outnumbered him, for most of the Cornishmen had deserted his colours as soon as they realised how far away from their own county they were being taken, and a considerable part of the Royalist cavalry had been detached to relieve the besieged garrison at Banbury. The Parliamentarians could certainly have overwhelmed him. But a plan to attack his defensive position simultaneously from east and west had been ruined by Manchester who had held back the eastern attack until an hour after the signal had been given and the sun had already set. The King's forces extricated themselves and slipped away in the darkness.

And so, in that spring of 1645, Charles began to hope once more that satisfactory terms for peace might be arranged. The two sides must stop 'fighting like beasts' and talk together like men whose strength 'should be more in their understandings than in their limbs'. But as in the past, the negotiations broke down before the King's unalterable views on episcopacy and the command of the army. The quarrel after all had still to be settled by force. It was settled on 14 June at Naseby.

Cavaliers and Roundheads

'The King's Declaration to his Gentry and Army' in September 1642.

Robert Earle of Essex, his Excellency, Generall of y Army, Imployed for y defence of the Protestant Religion, y safety of his Maᵗⁱᵉˢ Person, & of y Parliament: y preservation of y Lawes Liberties & Peace of y Kingdome, & protection of his Maᵗⁱᵉˢ subiects from violence & oppression.

Sʳ Wᵐ Waller.

(*left*) Robert Devereux, 3rd Earl of Essex (1591–1646), commander of the parliamentary army until April 1646, a few months before his death, from an engraving by an unknown artist,

(*right*) Oliver Cromwell (1599–1658). A portrait b Samuel Cooper.

Sir William Waller (1597–1668), parliamentary general. A portrait attributed to Edward Bower.

Prince Rupert (1619–82). A portrait of the King's cavalry commander attributed to Gerard von Honthorst.

A List of his Majesties Navie Royall, and Merchants Ships,

Their Names, Captaines and Lievtenants, their Men and Burthens in every one, now setting forth for the Guard of the narrow Seas, and for IRELAND this yeare, 1642.

With an Order, for the speedy Rigging of the Navie for the Defence of the KINGDOME.

ALGERNON PERCY, Earle of Northumberland, Lord Percy, Lucy, Poynings, &c. Knight of the most Noble Order of the Garter, and one of his Majesties most Honourable Privy Counsell, Lord high Admirall of ENGLAND, and Lord Generall of his Majesties Navy Royall.

The Kings Maiesties Ships; the Names of Captaines and Lievtenants, Ships, Men, and Burthens.

1. IN the Iames, *Robert* Earle of Warwick, Vice Admirall, Master *Slingesby* Lievtenant, 26c. men, burthen 875. tun.
2. In the Saint George *William Batten* Captaine, Master *william Smith* Lievtenant, 26o. men, burthen 792. tunne.
3. In the Rainbow, Sir *John Meanes* Captaine, Master *Lucas* Lievtenant, 26o. men, burthen 721. tunne.
4. In the Reformation, Sir *David Murrey* Captaine, Master *Stansby* Lievtenant, 26o. men, burthen 751. tunne.
5. Victory, Captaine *Fogge* Captaine, Master *Fogge* Lievtenant, 24c. men, burthen 762. tun.
6. *Henrietta Maria*, Captaine *Hatch* Captaine, Master *Wattes* Lievtenant, 25o. men, burthen 792. tunne.
7. Unicorne Captaine *Frenchsield* Captaine, Master *Sommersson* Lievtenant, 25o. men, burthen 767. tunne.
8. *Charles Swanley* Captaine, Master *Darcy* Captaine, 25o. men, burthen 81o. tun.
9. Vanguard, Captaine *Blith* Captaine, Mr. *Blith* Lievtenant, 25o. men, burthen 751. tunne.
10. Entrance, Captaine *Owen* Captaine, Master *Bonus* Lievtenant, 16o. men, burthen 539. tun.
11. Garland, Captaine *Slingesby* Captaine, Master *Wakers* Lievtenant, 17o. men, burthen 767.
12. Lion, Captaine *Prisse* Captaine, Master *Hill* Lievtenant, 170. men, 60c tunne.

13. Antelope, Captaine *Barley* Captaine, Master *wilkley* Lievtenant, 16o. men, burthen 512.tun.
14. Mary Rose, Captaine *Fox* Captaine, 10o. men, burthen 331. tunne.
15. Expedition, Captaine *Wake* Captaine, 10o. men, burthen 30t. tunne.
16. Greyhound, Captaine *Wisher* Captaine, 50. men, burthen 126. tunne.

Merchants Ships.

1. In the Marrane, Captaine *George Marrane* Captaine, Master *Holsinger* Lievtenant, 21o. men, b. 7oo. tunne.
2. Samson, Captaine *Ashby* Captaines Master *Andrew* Lievtenant, 18o. men, bunell 6oo. tunne.
3. Cesar, Captaine *Elias Jordan* Captaine, Master *Nevves* Lievtenant, 18o. men, b. 6oo. tunne.
4. London, Captaine *John Seriphrast* Captaine, Master *Pomrey* Lievtenant 18o. men, b. 6oo. tunne.
5. Unicorne, Captaine *Edward Johnson* Captaine, 143. men, b. 475. tunne.
6. May Flower, Captaine *Peter Andrew* Captaine, 121. men, b. 450. tunne.
7. Bonny Venter, Captaine *George Swanly* Captaine, 12o. men, b. 4oo. tunne.
8. The Prosperous, Captaine *William Driver* Captaine, 12o. men, b 4oo. tunne.
9. Hurclins, Captaine *Mover* Captaine, 15o. men, b. 25o.tun.
10. Paragon, Captaine *Leonard Harris* Captaine, 105. men, b. 35o tunne.

NORTHUMBERLAND · HONORATISS: — PERCY COM. D. ALGERNON

The right Honourable and most noble ALGERNON PERCY Earle of Northumberland, Lord, Poynings, Fitz-warine & Brian, &c. of the Garter, Admirall Generall of his Navall, &c.

11. Hopefull Luke, Captaine *Lee* Captaine, 105. men, b. 250 tunne.
12. Golden Angel, Captaine *Walker* Captaine, 105. men, b. 350. tunne.
13. Exchange, Captaine *Lucas* Captaine, 89. men, b. 325. tunne.
14. Mayden-head, Captaine *Lerson* Captaine, 90. men, b. 3oo. tunne.
15. Providence, Captaine *william Swanly* Captaine, 81. men, b. 271. tunne.
16. Jocelyn, Captaine *Partridge* Captaine, 6o. men, 2oo. tunne.

His Maiesties Ships for the Irish Seas.

1. The Swalow, Captaine *Thos: Kenley*, 15o. men, 16o. tunne.
2. Bonny Venture, Captaine *Henry Stradling*, 16o. men, 357. tunne.

Merchants Ships.

1. Discovery, Captaine *John*

Brab-heror, 144. men, 38o. tunne.
2. Ruth, Captaine *Robert Constable*, 12o. men, 4oo. tunne.
3. Employment, Captaine *Thos: Ash*, 122 men, 44o. tunne.
4. Peter, Captaine *Peter Strong* 81. men, 27o. tunne.
5. Pennington, Captaine *Joseph Jordan*, 36o. men, 135. tunne.
6. Fellowship, Captaine *Thomas Colle*, 8o. men, 29o. tunne.
7. Mary, Captaine *william Capell*, 30. men, 103. tunne.
8. John, Captaine *John Thomas*, 15. men, 50. tunne.

Die Mercurii. 2. Martii. 1641.

THE Lords and Commons in this present Parliament assembled, having received advertisement of extraordinary preparations, made by the neighbouring Princes, both by Land and Sea: the Intentions whereof have beene so represented, as to raise an apprehension in both Houses, that the publicke Honour, Peace, and Safety of his Majestie, and his Kingdome cannot be secured, unlesse a timely course be taken for the putting of this Kingdome into a condition of Defence, at Sea as well as Land. It is therefore ordered by the Lords and Commons aforesaid, that the Earle of *Northumberland*, Lord high Admirall of England, doe forthwith give effectuall direction, and Order, that all and every the ships belonging to his Majesties Navy, which are fit for service, and not already abroad, nor designed for this Summers Fleet, be with all speed rigged and put in such a readinesse, as that they may be soone fitted for the Sea; and that his Lordship doe also make knowne unto all the Masters, and Owners of such ships as now are in, or about any the Harbours of this Kingdome, and may be of use for the publicke defence thereof, that it will be an acceptable service to the King, and Parliament. If they likewise will cause their Ships to be rigged, and so farre put in readinesse, as they may be at a short warning set forth to Sea, upon any immergent occasion, which will be a meanes of great security to his Majesty, and his Dominions.

IT is ordered, that the Masters of the Merchants Ships, shall be allowed after the rate of ten shillings a moneth, so every one of his men for rigging of the Ships, and 31. shillings a moneth for every one of the men when they are at Sea, and to have one third part of the mony in hand and another part at foure moneths end and the last pa. ment at five moneths end, being the expiration of the time, for which they are imployd, or when they come to Barc-Wife. and to have three Colours and Surgion, Chests furnisshed at the Kings charge, out of the Kings Store-house, and prest and demand them, but if any Ship chance to be cast away in the Kings service, they are to have no allowance, but the Kings pay for five moneths.

Printed for *John Aswhell*. 1642.

Robert Rich, Earl of Warwick (1587–1658), brother of Henry Rich, Earl of Holland, and commander of the navy for Parliament.

Oliver Cromwell's watch.

A pair of spurs which belonged to Charles I.

Soldiers of the New Model Army as shown on wooden figures from the oak staircase at Cromwell House, Highgate. The house was built in 1637, but has no associations with Oliver Cromwell.

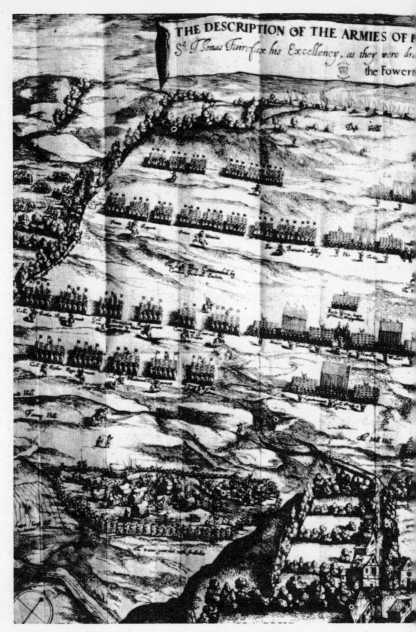

The opposing armies at the battle of Naseby as shown in an engraving in Joshua Sprigge's *Anglia Rediviva* (1647).

Charles I dictating despatches to one of his aides, Sir Edward Walker, by an unknown artist.

A silver crown, *c.* $\frac{3}{2}$, minted at Oxford (seen at left, under the horse), Charles's headquarters, in 1644.

GLIVERIVS MAGNÆ BRITANNIÆ HIBERNIÆ   ET TOTIVS ANGLICI IMPERII PROTECTOR
HANC SVMMI ET TOTO TERRARVM   ORBE CELEBERRIMI HEROIS
EFFICIEM SVPREMO SVÆ CELSITVDINIS   CONSILIO D.D.D.

Oliver Cromwell in an engraving by Lombart.

(*opposite*) An engraving by Abraham Bosse of a fighting cavalier.

How to fire from horseback. An engraving from Captain Nathaniel Burt's *Military Instructions* (1644).

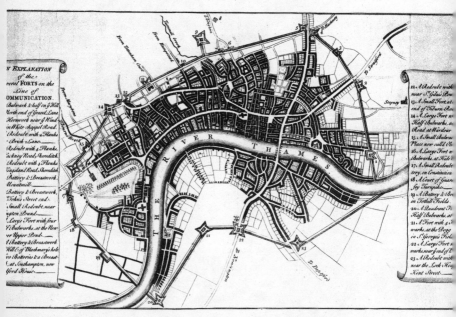

Fortifications erected around London by order of Parliament in 1642–3. There were twenty-four forts in all and eighteen miles of linked trenches.

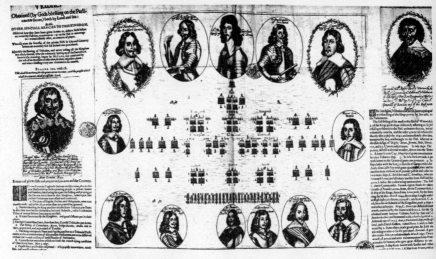

'Victories obtained by God's blessing on the Parliament's forces both by land and sea.' An engraved broadside with portraits of Parliamentary commanders.

A coin minted as a siege-piece in 1648 at Colchester.

A medal commemorating the Battle of Edgehill, 1642.

His
Excellencie
Sr Thomas Fairfax K
Generall of the forces
raised by the
Parliament.

Printed for John Partridg   Edua Bower fecit   W. Marshall Sculpsit

Thomas, 3rd Baron Fairfax (1612–71). An engraving of the parliamentary general
who succeeded Essex in supreme command from *Anglia Rediviva* (1647).

In the weeks before the Battle of Naseby, Charles had appeared as confident of ultimate victory as he had been ever since the war began. He still controlled the south-west; he could still recruit troops in Wales; he could still hope for assistance from the Continent; he could still expect that the Marquess of Ormonde would successfully conclude his negotiations for help from Ireland; he could comfort himself with reports of Montrose's continuing success in Scotland and of unrest in the New Model Army whose discipline was threatened by religious quarrels and whose numbers included thousands of unwilling soldiers forced into service by the press-gang.

On 7 May Charles left Oxford for the summer campaign in excellent heart. He was accompanied by Prince Rupert, who had brought up his troops from the West Country two days before; he had an army of eleven thousand men at his disposal and good hopes of greatly enlarging it within the next few days. 'We have great unanimity among ourselves,' Lord Digby wrote, reflecting the King's own views, 'and the rebels great distractions.'

The news that Sir Thomas Fairfax was marching up towards him from the west and that Cromwell was also on the move towards Oxford disturbed Charles not at all. Rupert advised him to draw the two Parliamentary armies away from Oxford by marching into the east Midlands and threatening the enemy's strongholds there. If the Royalist army could fall upon Fairfax before Cromwell had joined him, the King would be certain of victory, and free to march off on a campaign to regain the north. 'On my conscience,' exclaimed Digby, for once in his life in agreement with Rupert, 'On my conscience, it will be the last blow in the business.'

The first part of Rupert's plan was achieved by an assault on Leicester at the end of May. At three o'clock on the afternoon of 30 May his gunners opened fire on the medieval walls of Leicester whose inhabitants had declined an offer of pardon if they surrendered. After three hours' bombardment the wall was breached by that part of the town known as the Newark, and at midnight an assaulting party rushed the gap, while two other attacks were made with scaling ladders on the northern and eastern walls. An hour later the defenders had been overcome after a desperate resistance and the cavalry and Welsh infantry poured into the town. The losses on both sides were heavy, and the sack of the town which followed the surrender of its last defenders in the market-place was fearful. Several of those who laid down their arms were killed out-right by Royalist troops whose night-long plunder of the town was unchecked by either the King or any of his senior officers. By morning every cottage in Leicester had been broken into, every shop had been raided, every church had been pillaged; soldiers marched out of the town next day their knapsacks stuffed with stolen goods, their pockets bulging with coins. One of them, so it appeared when the Mayor came to attend Charles to morning prayers, had even taken the mayoral mace.

Charles's optimism continued unabated. The capture of Leicester was followed by the news that Sir Thomas Fairfax, who had settled down before the walls of Oxford a week before, had abandoned the siege. The King looked forward happily to what would now turn out to be 'probably a merry winter'. 'My affairs,' he told Henrietta in a contented letter, 'were never in so fair and hopeful a way.'

Rupert could not share his serene confidence. He recognised what a good general Thomas Fairfax was; he did not give so much credit as the King and Digby and other cheerful courtiers did to the rumours of all these quarrels in the Parliamentary camp, of stories that Fairfax had actually come to blows with one of his major-generals. He knew that if Fairfax – whose forces even without Cromwell's were greater than the Royalists could at present muster – attacked before the King's army was joined by the troops still in the West Country and Wales under Lord Goring and Sir Charles Gerrard, Charles might well be defeated. Rupert argued that it would be far better to avoid battle with Fairfax and to continue the northward march. But Digby, once back on familiar ground in opposition to the Prince's views, disagreed; he carried the more excitable and vociferous of the courtiers, and the King himself, with him.

Fairfax was now as anxious to fight the Royalists as Rupert was to avoid him. For, not only had he been joined by Cromwell whose seven hundred horse had been greeted by a 'mighty shout for joy', but he had intercepted a letter to Rupert which gave him the information that Lord Goring was still far away in the west and intended to remain away. Now was Fairfax's chance. He quickly marched towards Market Harborough, where the King was reported to be. He came upon him south of the town, just across the Northamptonshire boundary not far from the village of Naseby.

Fairfax drew up his forces on Naseby ridge, a grassy shoulder of land which rose gently above the marshy lower ground between himself and the more northerly ridge on which the Royalists chose to make their stand. He had fourteen thousand men under his command, five thousand more than the enemy; but his infantry, he knew, were less reliable and less experienced than the enemy's and he took what measures he could to spare them the sight of the glittering array of the King's army manoeuvring into position in the summer morning sunlight.

The Royalist troops were certainly an impressive and alarming sight as they marched across the New Model Army's front – their colours flying and arms gleaming, the King himself in full and shining gilt armour riding a Flemish horse – taking up a position which would give them the advantage of the strong north-west wind that would otherwise blow back the smoke from muskets and cannon into their eyes. And it was probably to keep this unnerving muster out of sight of his impresssionable soldiers – 'poor ignorant men' as Cromwell called them – that Fairfax ordered the whole of his line a hundred yards back behind the brow of the ridge.

They did not have to wait there long, for Rupert, remembering the delay that had lost him the advantage at Marston Moor, determined to attack as soon as his men were ready. Shortly after ten o'clock the first charge of his cavalry was made. Led in person by himself and his brother, Prince Maurice, the Cavaliers came thundering down the slopes, 'very stately' at first, then gathering speed, keeping well together, under fire from a regiment of dragoons which Cromwell had concealed behind a hedge on their right, but making straight for the New Model Army's left wing. The cavalry here, outnumbering Rupert's three to two, was commanded by Henry Ireton, the clever, determined young Nottinghamshire lawyer who was soon to marry one of Cromwell's daughters.

Ireton was wounded in the thigh and face as Rupert's charge struck home. He saw the Cavaliers break triumphantly through the left wing, scattering parts of it and sending two regiments, 'better armed than hearted', 'clear away to Northampton'. Ireton could not rally his men; but nor could Rupert, and the Cavaliers went chasing off, as was their habit after victory, until they came up with Fairfax's baggage train a mile behind the lines. Here Rupert, wearing a red *montera* like the one Fairfax wore, was mistaken by the baggage commander for his own general. He went up to him, cap in hand, to ask how the battle went. Rupert answered him by abruptly demanding he and his men should surrender. Soon recovering from their surprise, they shouted 'No!' and opened fire on him with their muskets; and Rupert, taking advantage of the incident to rally his excited men, led them back to the field. He was appalled by the situation he found there.

Soon after his cavalry had charged into Ireton's men, the Royalist infantry, wearing beanstalks in their hats as a field sign, had lunged into the centre of the New Model Army's line, firing but one volley from their muskets, before gripping them by the barrels and wielding them as clubs. Although these musketeers had had to advance uphill, and had marched hard both that morning and the day before with little sleep or food, they and their supporting pikemen had soon gained the upper hand and had begun to drive the enemy back. Philip Skippon, in command of the wavering Roundhead infantry, had been wounded by a musket-ball which pierced his breastplate; and, although he had managed to stay in his saddle, he had not been able to prevent his first line breaking and his men falling back onto the second line. Lord Astley, commander of the Royalist infantry, had begun to hope that victory would soon be his – as well it might have been had it not been for the Ironsides on his left.

Cromwell had led his Ironsides in a charge on the Royalist left wing which had proved as successful as Rupert's. He had broken right through the line and suddenly appeared, like a *deus ex machina*, before the King's reserve which stood on Dust Hill behind Lord Astley's shouting, brawling ranks on the moor below. The King, nominally Commander-in-Chief, had now had his first opportunity to take an active part in the battle. He lined up his Life Guards and would have led them against the Ironsides had not the Earl of Carnwarth, one of his Scottish friends, grabbed hold of his bridle, shouting above the din, 'Will you go upon your death', and led the horse away.

Cromwell, declining the opportunity to chase the Life Guards off the field, had reformed his well-disciplined regiments and had taken them down the slope again to charge into Lord Astley's unprotected infantry. Fairfax had joined him in the charge and with these two leaders at their head the Ironsides had so transformed the aspect of the battle by the time of Rupert's return to the field that there was nothing he could do but cover the retreat of the King through Leicester to Ashby-de-la-Zouch.

Between four and five thousand Royalist troops were captured on the field and most of those not seriously wounded were herded into Market Harborough church. Their companions, endeavouring frantically to escape along the road to Leicester, were cut down mercilessly in a vigorous pursuit as they tried to run away weighed down by plunder or as they paused to scoop up the coins which had tumbled onto the road from the upturned wagons of the baggage-train.

Before Leicester was reached the pursuers caught up with the royal coaches, the sumpter-wagons and hundreds of women, officers' mistresses and soldiers' wives, camp followers, whores and 'leaguer-bitches'. Those with money or jewels paid the soldiers not to kill them, but many of the poor wives and the slatterns who could not afford to buy mercy were murdered or had their cheeks and noses slashed to the bone.

The King's enemies felt no need to apologise for this gross violence. It was, they said, well known that hundreds of Irish-women followed the royal armies – though in fact most of the victims were more likely to have been wives of the Welsh recruits – and that Irishwomen murdered good Protestants as soon as look at them. The outrage, in any event, was soon forgotten. For captured in the retreat was the King's secret correspondence, all the letters he had received from the Queen, copies of all the letters he had written to her, all the evidence necessary to show how anxious they had both been to bring over foreigners and papists from the Continent and Ireland to help him in the struggle. After the publication of this correspondence, many Englishmen who had formerly felt some sympathy for the King's cause now turned their backs on him.

As before the battle, so after it, Charles preferred to listen to Lord Digby and to reflect his cheerful optimism than to pay attention to the irritable, energetic Rupert who urged him to recognise how hard a blow had been dealt to his cause at Naseby, who was for ever harassing him with plans to retrieve the situation without delay. Charles gave Rupert's ideas little encouragement. He preferred to wait until more Welsh infantry had been recruited to take the place of those who had surrendered at Naseby, and to rest his hopes on ɪlvation from Ireland. 'The consequences . . . of the unfortunate loss of a most hopeful battle . . . will have no great extent,' Digby wrote unconcernedly to the Marquess of Ormonde; and Charles shared his complacently sanguine view. 'I am nowise disheartened by our late misfortune,' he assured the Earl of Glamorgan. 'I hope shortly to recover my late loss with advantage . . .'

He proceeded with Digby, the Duke of Richmond, the young Earl of Lindsey and other of his more favoured courtiers from Ashby-de-la-Zouch through Lichfield, Wolverhampton and Hereford, to stay with the Earl of Glamorgan's father at Raglan Castle. Here he led a quiet country life as though oblivious to the danger that threatened him, leaving Rupert to go down into the West Country to discuss with the Prince of Wales – who had been sent to the relative safety of Bristol before the Battle of Naseby – the measures to be taken for the defence of the diminishing areas under Royalist control.

Charles at Raglan seemed to have dismissed all such disagreeable thoughts from his mind. He played bowls every day, went to the village church every week, talked amicably to his friends, read poetry. 'We were all lulled asleep with sports and entertainments,' wrote one of his companions, 'as if no crown had been at stake or in danger to be lost.'

Reports came of the defeat of Lord Goring by Fairfax and Cromwell at Langport in Somerset where seven hundred resolute horsemen of the New Model Army, with some help from artillery-men and musketeers, had ridden down all opposition in the burning town, defeated a force of far greater strength, and taken two thousand prisoners. Reports came, too, of the surrender of Bridgwater, between Bristol and Taunton, and the consequent cutting of the road between the Royalists' main stronghold in the west and their remaining armies in the field.

In Wales the situation was deteriorating fast. The Welsh, peasantry and gentry alike, had for months been incensed by the drunken indiscipline and ruffianly behaviour of the troops of the local commander, Sir Charles Gerrard. Nor had they been appeased by the ultimate dismissal of Gerrard who had been granted a barony by the King as a recompense and allowed to answer their charges in words which they found insulting. The publication of the King's correspondence with the Queen had increased the Welsh people's discontent, and all over South Wales the people 'began to be saucy'. The Parliamentary general, Rowland Laugharne, who had once been the Earl of Essex's page, had little difficulty in defeating the King's Welsh army at Colby Moor and occupying the important Pembrokeshire centre of Haverfordwest. Yet the King still refused to have any 'melancholy men' about him, and continued to insist that 'God will not suffer rebels and traitors to prosper, nor this cause to be overthrown.'

These phrases were contained in a letter to the exasperated Prince Rupert, confirming the King's extraordinary intention of going to Scotland, where he hoped that an alliance might be made with the Scottish Covenanters, more and more dismayed by the spreading influence of the Independents in the Parliamentary army. Rupert, who was not told of the King's secret plans but soon learned what they were, begged the Duke of Richmond to dissuade his cousin from pursuing this 'strange resolution'. Considering the state of the war in England and the unlikelihood of his ever getting to Scotland, anyway, it seemed to Rupert a mad proposal. 'If I were desired to deliver my opinion, which your Lordship may declare to the King,' Rupert wrote to Richmond, 'His Majesty hath now no way left to preserve his posterity, Kingdom and nobility, but by a treaty. I believe it a more prudent way to retain something than to lose all.'

But Charles, determined to go to Scotland, refused to contemplate the possibility of compromise, just because his fortunes might momentarily be in decline. He was 'resolved' against a submission 'whatever it cost' him; for, as he replied, 'I know my obligation to be, both in conscience and honour, neither to abandon God's cause, injure my successors, nor forsake my friends . . . . He that will stay with me at this time must expect and resolve either to die for a good cause or (which is worse) to live as miserable in maintaining it as the violence of insulting rebels can make him.'

And so, accompanied by his Life Guards, the King left for Scotland. He paused at Brecon to send instructions to the Prince of Wales to sail for France if he found himself in danger of falling into rebel hands; but otherwise he displayed little concern at his predicament. He seemed, indeed, to enjoy the march in the fine summer weather, taking his meals outside in the fields or in some such country house as the one at Radnor where, eating chicken and cheese alone in the parlour, he was surprised by the easy-going housewife popping her head round the door to ask 'if he had done with the cheese for the gentlemen without desired it'.

By the time he had reached Yorkshire, having collected two thousand horsemen on the way, he thought his situation was now 'miraculously good' again. Yorkshire, however, was as far as he reached; for near Rotherham he was warned of a large enemy army approaching and was constrained to move south east instead. The countryside was almost bereft of troops, for the New Model Army was still campaigning in the West Country; and Charles was able to enter Huntingdon without opposition. Many of the inhabitants, protesting that they were delighted to see him, came out to greet him 'with much compliment, all hatting and bowing', though here, as elsewhere, they were soon disgusted by the behaviour of Royalist troops who drank pailfuls of ale in the taverns and plundered the town and surrounding farms to such an extent that the King's hanging of two of the worst offenders amongst his soldiers seemed to them scarcely punishment enough.

From Huntingdon the King rode west again for Hereford, forcing the Earl of Leven's Scotsmen to abandon their siege of the town which the Royalists then entered in triumph. It was almost their last success. During the rest of August scarcely a day passed without a fresh disaster being reported. Lord Goring, now drunk for days on end and quarrelling bitterly with the other leaders of the western army, showed no sign of being able to raise the new levies he had promised; Lord Digby's half-brother, Sir Lewis Dyve, was forced by Fairfax's guns to surrender Sherborne Castle which he had been holding for a fortnight with the help of a brave garrison inspired by two hearty gamekeepers who had used their fowling pieces to devastating effect on the enemy's officers; towards the end of the month Prince Rupert's position in Bristol was rumoured to be untenable.

Rupert had brought large stores into Bristol, ammunition, corn and cattle, as well as food for the inhabitants and heavy cannon to hold the walls. He had expressed the hope that he could hold out for four months. But morale in the town was low; plague was rife and the citizens showed themselves prepared to betray the defenders for the sake of their trade. On 10 September, at two o'clock in the morning, Fairfax's four huge siege pieces opened up on the walls and the assault began. Six hours later Rupert's garrison in the castle was separated from the troops still fighting on the walls by Cromwell's cavalry which had come charging through the broken defences. Hopelessly outnumbered Rupert felt obliged to surrender and, under the generous terms which Fairfax allowed him, he marched away to Oxford with his men and his horses, his colours flying, his sword by his side, but followed by the people's angry shouts of 'Give him no quarter! Give him no quarter!', miserably aware that with the loss of Bristol the King's last hope had gone.

Charles, himself, felt not so much downcast as indignant: he felt sure he had been betrayed. Rupert's surrender, he wrote to his Secretary of State, Sir Edward Nicholas, in Oxford, was 'strange and most inexcusable'. Digby had always warned him of his nephew's unreliability; now there seemed proof of it. In his bitter disappointment at the fall of Bristol into the hands of the rebels, he began to believe all the stories he had ever been told about Rupert. There was surely something sinister in his being allowed to march out of the town with all his men and, except for cannon and muskets, all his weapons and baggage; there was surely a sinister connection between this and his scheming eldest brother's being voted a handsome pension by Parliament such a very short time before; there was surely something alarming in Rupert's move on Oxford where the governor, Colonel Legge, was a close friend of his and where the King's younger son, the Duke of York, lay open to his schemes to wrest power from the ashes of defeat.

Convinced that Rupert was, indeed, about to stage some sort of *coup*, Charles issued orders to Edward Nicholas for the immediate dismissal of Colonel Legge, and for the revocation of the Prince's commission. In a personal letter to Rupert he further ordered him to consider himself expelled from the country. The surrender of Bristol, Charles wrote, 'is the greatest trial of my constancy that hath yet befallen me; for what is to be done, after one that is so near to me as you are both in blood and friendship, submits himself to so mean an action (I give it the easiest term)? I have so much to say, that I will say no more of it, lest rashness of judgement be laid to my charge . . . You assured me that, if no mutiny happened, you would keep Bristol for four months. Did you keep it four days? Was there anything like a mutiny? More questions might be asked, but now I confess to little purpose. My conclusion is, to desire you to keep your subsistence (until it shall please God to determine of my condition) somewhere beyond the sea, to which end I send you herewith a pass.'

Having dealt with what he supposed to be Rupert's treachery, the King moved north once more. With Bristol lost and with Rowland

Laugharne triumphant in South Wales, he could remain no longer either in Hereford or at Raglan Castle, and so rode off through the Welsh hills in the vague hope of reaching Montrose. He did not even reach the Cheshire Plain, for hearing that Chester – so vital if help from Ireland were ever to reach him – was on the point of collapse, he turned to its assistance. On 24 September his cavalry rode out to drive the besiegers off. Intercepted by horsemen of the New Model Army commanded by a skilful and vigorous officer trained in Germany, it was they themselves, however, who were driven off; and in the encounter the King's cousin, Lord Bernard Stuart, the Duke of Richmond's younger brother, was killed. 'O Lord! O Lord!', Charles lamented, 'What have I done that should cause my people to deal thus with me?'

He abandoned his northward march and rode instead through the Derbyshire dales and Sherwood Forest to Newark where reports of fresh disasters reached him from every side. He was told of Royalist garrisons falling to Cromwell in Wiltshire and Hampshire, of the surrender of Devizes and Winchester, then, and most cruelly, of Montrose's defeat at Philiphaugh on 13 September, and, in the middle of October, of Cromwell's assault on the Marquess of Winchester's enormous and strongly fortified mansion, Basing House.

Numerous Royalists had withdrawn to Basing House for safety, including Wenceslaus Hollar, several Jesuit priests, a giant, said to be nine feet tall, and Inigo Jones who had been 'gotten thither for help' in planning the defences of the house. The Marquess had claimed that his garrison, which had successfully resisted previous sieges, could hold out 'for ever'. But on 15 October the outer walls were broken down by Cromwell's ceaselessly pounding shot and the Roundheads poured into the gardens and courts, then into the house, firing in all directions without discrimination, lashing out with their swords at armed defenders and civilian refugees alike, killing several of the priests and a woman who tried to protect her father, murdering Robbins, the comedian, stripping Inigo Jones – that 'famous Surveyor and great Enemy of St Grigory', the 'contriver of scenes for the Queen's Dancing Barne', and leaving him to be carried away in a blanket – stripping the Marquess of Winchester, also and abandoning him to the denunciations of Cromwell's rabid chaplain, Hugh Peter – tearing down tapestries and hangings, burning religious pictures and papist-looking books, carting away furniture and plate, even roofing lead and window bars, to sell to London dealers. 'We have had little loss.' ran Cromwell's laconic report. 'Most of the enemy our men put to the sword, and some officers of quality, most of the rest we have prisoners.'

With these and other military defeats a daily burden to him, Charles soon had further problems with which to contend. For Prince Rupert, refusing to be dismissed from the King's service without a hearing, rode to Newark, accompanied by his brother Maurice, several loyal officers and a troop of horse, to demand an enquiry. Skilfully evading the fifteen hundred Parliamentary horsemen sent out to capture him, the patrolling garrison of Burghley House and the cavalry besieging Belvoir Castle, Rupert arrived at Newark on 16 October. Lord Digby, forewarned of his approach, arranged to leave for a military command in the north shortly before Rupert arrived.

At Newark feeling ran strongly in Rupert's favour. No soldier with any claim to military competence doubted that the Prince had nearly always been right in his arguments with Lord Digby and that Digby had been almost invariably wrong. The Prince was sometimes irritating and overbearing, and his habit of speaking little in councils of war except 'with a pish to neglect all another said' must have been maddening to Digby. But there could be no doubt that Digby's influence over the King – whose military capacity was not in any case pronounced – had been a dangerous one, nor that Prince Rupert had been treated with gross unfairness after the surrender of Bristol. Sir Edward Nicholas had felt so at the time; and had written to the King to assure him that his nephew, far from living in luxury at Oxford on the spoils of plunder and bribery, was in fact very poor. Lord Gerrard and the Governor of Newark, Sir Richard Willis, agreed that Rupert had been unfairly dealt with and, disobeying the King's orders, they went together to greet the Prince as he approached the town gate.

When the Prince arrived and unceremoniously went up to the King to say that he had come to render an account of the loss of Bristol, his uncle would not speak to him. He went in to supper and ignored him throughout the meal. Later, although he was prepared to endorse a Council of War's opinion that there was no evidence of lack of courage or fidelity at Bristol, he still insisted that Rupert might have done more to hold the place longer. Displeased with the findings of the council members who exonerated the Prince from all blame, and concerned by the effect which these unseemly disputes were having on the morale of the Newark garrison, the King dismissed Sir Richard Willis from the governorship, attempting to placate him with the offer of the command of his Life Guards, vacant since Lord Bernard Stuart's death.

But Willis was not to be placated; and accompanied by Lord Gerrard – who also had not been placated by the sop of a barony after his dismissal from command in Wales – by Prince Rupert and Maurice and several other officers who supported him, he burst in upon the King after church on Sunday. Willis demanded an explanation; he had been dishonoured; his fate was being discussed all over Newark. Rupert interrupted him to say that the explanation was simple: Willis had been dismissed because he had shown him sympathy. Then Lord Gerrard spoke, 'This is all Digby's doing, and Digby is a traitor, and I can prove him so'.

The King asked for silence and said that he would speak to Willis privately in the next room. But Willis 'would not, saying that he had received a publicke injury and therefore expected a publicke satisfaction'.

'Say no more,' the King rebuked him, angry as always when his dignity was endangered. 'This is a time unreasonable for you to command here.'

'All that Sir Richard desires is very reasonable,' Gerrard audaciously persisted. 'For if gentlemen must be putt out upon every occasion and aspersion it will discourage all from serving Your Majesty.'

'What does this concern you?'

'I am sure and can prove that Digby was the cause for which I was ousted from my command in Wales.'

Then Rupert broke in again about his own complaint, 'whereat the King sighed and said, "O nephewe," and stopt. Then he would say no more.' And at last he told them all to leave the room.

They left to put Willis's complaint in writing and later returned to present it to the King in person. Someone, with a kind of apology which the others felt far from expressing, hoped that the King would not call this mutiny. Charles would not give it a name, he said, but to him it looked 'very like'.

And very like mutiny it was next morning when Rupert and his men rode into Newark's market-place to protest against the appointment of a new Governor. The King came out to them. Those who were dissatisfied, he told them, his anger well controlled, could leave for Belvoir Castle and disband themselves. He would not do anything to stop them; but on no account would he give way to their demands. Defeated, they rode away south to the Vale of Belvoir.

The King was soon forced to follow them. Digby's forces in the north had disintegrated and he himself had crossed over to the Isle of Man where he wrote with irrepressible buoyancy of his intention of sailing to Ireland and hurrying up the Irish reinforcements which would change the whole course of the conflict. But not even the most sanguine of his friends could believe him any more. The remaining strongholds in the south-west were falling fast. The fall of Carmarthen was followed by the occupation of Chepstow, the occupation of Chepstow by the fall of Monmouth. More threatening to the King's own person, two armies, one English, the other Scottish, were converging fast on Newark. On the night of 3 September Charles rode out of the town for Oxford.

Back at Oxford, once more soothed by the deferential and decorous atmosphere of Court life, Charles comforted himself with the hope that his enemies' quarrels and dissensions were more rancorous and went deeper than those in his own party, with plans and plots to deepen the growing distrust between the rebels' political and religious factions. He envisaged ways of separating Presbyterians from Independents, Englishmen from Scotsmen, of negotiating with one side at the expense of the other, of winning present help by promises of future favours. But his schemes never worked out as he planned they should, since it was a sad, inescapable fact that the King's promises were not believed any more, either in the country or outside it; he was not trusted to stand by his word even if he had the power and the means to do what he promised to do.

Yet if he could persuade himself that diplomatic bargaining might even now save him from defeat, he could not ignore the succession of military disasters that rendered victory in the field inconceivable. Nor could the return of an apologetic Prince Rupert to Oxford alter that bleak prospect of military defeat, for not only was the Prince given no command by the King who had been reluctant at first to receive his nephew back into favour at all, but there were scarcely any forces left for him to be given. The remaining Midland garrisons were being battered into submission one by one. In the west the Royalist armies scarcely existed any more; Goring had abandoned them for the pleasures and peace of France. In Devon, Fairfax's capture of Tiverton Castle had induced the Prince of Wales's custodians to take him even farther down the Cornish peninsula to Truro where he indignantly rejected a polite summons to surrender his troops and himself to Parliament with the explosive comment 'Rogues and rebels! Are they not content to be rebels themselves but they must have me of their number?'

Shortly before Christmas, in biting cold weather that froze the Thames and Severn and crippled soldiers with frostbite, Hereford fell to an army of volunteers from Parliamentary garrisons in Somerset and Gloucestershire. After Christmas Chester surrendered at last; then Dartmouth and Torrington were taken by Fairfax, and Ralph Hopton was driven out of Truro from which the Prince of Wales had already fled to the Isles of Scilly. In South Wales, Laughorne occupied Cardiff; in the Midlands, Belvoir Castle, Lichfield and Ashby-de-la-Zouch were all occupied by the besieging forces of the New Model Army. On 21 March 1646 Lord Astley, commanding the King's last army in the field, was defeated near Stow-in-the Wold. Over fifteen hundred of his infantry, mostly young Welsh recruits, surrendered after a half-hearted fight. The cavalry galloped away for the safety of Oxford. Sitting on a drum, old Astley, who had fought bravely for the King since the Battle of Edgehill three and a half years before, gave up his sword to a Parliamentary soldier. 'You have done your work, boys,' he said. 'You may go play, unless you fall out among yourselves.'

Three weeks later Fairfax captured Exeter taking prisoner the little Princess Henrietta who had been left there with a governess when her mother escaped to France. 'The Western War,' wrote Fairfax, 'I trust in the Lord, is finished.'

At Oxford, Charles recognised now, as he told the Queen in a letter written the day after Lord Astley's surrender at Stow-in-the-Wold, that he had 'neither force enough to resist nor sufficient to escape to any secure place'. For months now deserters in their hundreds had been abandoning his cause and going over to the New Model Army; Hopton's force at the end had been nothing but a 'dissolute, undisciplined, wicked' army; everywhere Royalist officers and troopers were abandoning themselves to what pleasures could still be enjoyed or taking to a life of crime: in future years travellers on the roads of England were to be in constant danger from highwaymen who had once been in the service of the King, men like Zachary Howard who had mortgaged his estate for £20,000 to raise a troop of horse. Everywhere, too, Royalists were taking advantage of Parliament's offer of a peaceful settlement by compounding for their estates, paying fines proportionate to their value, saving from the wreck what they could while they could.

Without any army left to fight for him in England, Charles turned for help to the Scots. He knew that the Scottish Covenanters felt themselves ill-used by the English Parliament which had been thankful enough to enlist their help when the Royalists seemed likely to triumph but which now seemed as ready to neglect the unpaid Scottish army as to go back upon the promises contained in the Solemn League and Covenant. If Charles could play on this dissatisfaction, if he could aggravate Scottish fears of the growing influence of the Independents in the English Parliamentary army, if he could arouse their sympathy for one who was, after all, a Scottish King and persuade them to agree to defend his interests against his rebellious English subjects, he might yet retrieve his fortunes.

He left Oxford in an attempt to do so on 27 April, He took with him but two companions, one of his chaplains, and Jack Ashburnham, a Groom of his Bedchamber. With his long hair trimmed, wearing a false beard and a suit of ordinary clothes, he travelled disguised as his companions' servant, riding by night, eating, and sleeping in strange taverns and ale-houses.

On the morning of 6 May, he rode into the courtyard of the Saracen's Head at Southwell close by the Scottish army head-quarters between Nottingham and Newark. The Scots, anxious to get him out of the way of the English, took him north to Newcastle where day in and day out for almost eight months they tried to persuade him to accept the Presbyterian system as outlined in the Solemn League and Covenant, to reform religion in England 'according to the Word of God' and 'the example of the best reformed Churches'. Every conceivable argument was advanced to him by an assortment of Scottish ministers who, singly and to-gether, pleaded with him, argued with him, quarrelled with him, pitied his ignorance, flattered his intellect, condemned his stubborn-ness in an attempt to break down his intractable resistance, his obstinate beliefs. They could not believe that he had come to the Scottish camp without intending to support the Scots on the

Presbyterian issue, and they refused to be defeated by his obduracy.

Deprived of the reassuring comfort and consoling, attentive flattery of his Gentlemen and courtiers, deserted even by his chaplain and Jack Ashburnham who had come with him to Newcastle but had been advised to leave him there to avoid being handed over as prisoners to the English, Charles was quite alone. He was permitted to go out to 'the Shield Field without the Walls' to play an occasional game of golf, watched by Scottish sentinels; but golf and chess were almost his only relaxations from the tedious discussions with the Presbyterian divines who hung about him so persistently that he was 'never wanting new vexations'. He remained placid, only once showing a flash of anger when he abruptly cut short a long extempore grace of more than usual tedium by falling to his meat with the comment that he did not intend to let it grow cold while the minister 'stood whistling for the spirit'. Normally, however, Charles reserved his complaints for his wife, and in the letters that he managed to send her he told her that he had never known what it was to be 'barborously baited before'. The only comfort he had left was in her love and his own 'clear conscience'.

The Queen had little sympathy with his tiresome conscience; any promises he gave need not be *permanently* binding; she agreed with Lord Jermyn: surely it was better in the end to be a Presbyterian King than no sort of King at all. It was not as if he were a Catholic.

But the King would not give way. His 'clear conscience' would not let him abandon the Anglican Church which he loved; and even now there might be hope. Admittedly the news from England continued to be bad: the few towns that remained in Royalist hands were all falling fast; towards the end of June Oxford surrendered, and Prince Rupert and the Duke of York were captured, the Prince sent into exile, the Duke taken to London to join Princess Henrietta and his six-year-old brother Prince Henry under guard at St James's Palace. But the Prince of Wales had escaped, sailing from Jersey to France on the very day that Oxford capitulated; and from France or from Ireland help might yet come.

Also, his enemies were still far from composing their own quarrels. Parliament's peace terms had now been drafted. They were so harsh both upon the King and his supporters, that when Hyde read them he decided that if Charles accepted them there would in future be no 'seeds left for monarchy to spring out of'. Charles knew this, too; and when Parliament's representatives came to Newcastle he knew that he must reject them. Had they any authority to discuss them with him, he asked the Earl of Pembroke, head of the mission. No, he was told, they had come merely to take back his answer. In which case, the King retorted, their mission might just as well have been entrusted to 'an honest Trumpeter'.

Yet Charles did not want to give them an immediate reply. Delay meant a prolongation of hope; he studied how to make an 'honest denying answer'; he persuaded himself that at least the terms contained clauses that might bring about an open breach between the Scots and the English. All Charles's hopes, in the end, were disappointed and his prevarications of no avail. The Scots, as it turned out, urged him to accept the terms, telling him that if he did not do so the English Parliament would demand that he be handed over to its charge. And this, at last, was what was done.

Understandably refusing to consider the King's proposition that he should agree to the establishment of Presbyterianism for three years – since Charles admitted it would go against his conscience not to use that period to 'lay a ground for a perfect recovery' – the Scots entered into negotiations with the English for the payment of the money due to them for their army's services in the recent war. When this money was paid the Scots prepared to withdraw across the border, leaving the King to fall into the hands of the English Parliamentarians.

Once he had resigned himself to the inevitability of this fate, the King appeared quite tranquil once more. When he was told that the Scots had definitely decided not to receive him in their country, he went on calmly with a game of chess; when he tried and failed to escape he appeared not unduly perturbed; when he heard the figure – £400,000 – which the Scots had agreed, after a deal of haggling, to accept for their military help, he teased them on the poor bargain they had made in selling him; and when the Earl of Pembroke came to Newcastle again as Parliament's messenger to discuss the arrangements for the King's removal south and his detention at Holmby House in Northamptonshire, Charles greeted him politely and consented to go with him.

10

The Prisoner and His Captors
1647–9

CHARLES'S journey south from Newcastle was not so much an ignominious withdrawal as a triumphal entry. Church bells rang in greeting; crowds gathered along the road to wish him well, many kneeling in dutiful submission, others shouting 'God bless your Majesty!' some coming forward to be touched by him and so be cured by his miraculous grace. The troopers guarding him seemed infected by the people's gaiety and reverence and gave them no 'check or disturbance as the King passed . . . (a civility His Majesty was well pleased with)'. On his arrival at Holmby 'very many country gentlemen, gentlewomen and others of ordinary rank, stood ready there, to welcome their King, with joyful countenances and prayers . . . counting him as only able to restore to them their peace and settlement'.

Charles, profoundly reassured, felt a resurgence of hope. Four years of bitter quarrelling, fighting, plundering, loss of rents and wages, disruption of trade and profits, of homes and pleasures, had made men long for the peace and order of the past. Changes in the manners and structures of society, the breaking down of social conventions, the denial of old allegiances, were far from being universally acclaimed. The propaganda of the war, and the experiences of those who had taken part in it, had certainly provoked in the country widespread demands for the reformation of the whole nature of society; but the apprehension such demands occasioned, the fears its advocates aroused, might even now, Charles began to believe, prove his salvation. England was aflame with new ideas and revolutionary doctrines spread by men like John Lilburne, the passionate aggressive champion of radical reform, a kind of Christian communist, Gerrard Winstanley, who demanded that all men should have an 'equal share in the earth', and Colonel Thomas Rainsborough, the extreme Independent who, as an officer in the New Model Army, preached the necessity for manhood suffrage. The horrified opponents of such seditious doctrines were natural allies of the King; and it was to the King that the predominantly

Presbyterian Parliament now turned in its intensifying quarrel with the Independent leaders of the Army.

Cromwell, 'the great Independent', had urged Parliament, after both Naseby and Marston Moor, to remember that the soldiers who had fought, and to whom God had granted victory, had risked their lives not only for the liberty of their country but for religious toleration as well. Now the Presbyterians in Parliament, rigid in their orthodoxy, seemed bent on denying the men's rights to liberty of conscience; and, far from displaying gratitude for the victory which the Army had won for them, they were trying to disband it without back pay. Cromwell strongly pleaded the Army's cause, but, never in sympathy with its wilder spirits, he tried earnestly to reconcile it with Parliament. He satisfied neither side. Lilburne accused him of betraying the Army; Parliament distrusted him and blamed him for the Army's unrest. At last, recognising the impossibility of reconciliation, he decided to throw in his lot with the Army.

Before taking any step he knew that he must secure the King at Holmby House, place him in the Army's care, and so make it impossible for Parliament to come to terms with him. It seems that he sent for George Joyce, a cavalry officer he trusted, to come to his house in Drury Lane where for weeks now he had been keeping open house for army officers and Independents who flocked there 'as to their headquarters with all their projections and were entertained with small beer and bread and butter'. Whether or not they came directly from Cromwell, Joyce's instructions were simple enough: he was to ride with a troop of horsemen to Holmby and secure the King from Parliament's clutches.

The King's life at Holmby was far from unpleasant. 'All the tables were as well-furnished as they used to be when his Majesty was in a peaceful and flourishing state.' He enjoyed a game of chess after meals; he walked in the herb garden with his guardian, the Earl of Pembroke; he played bowls three times a week; he read for two or three hours every day. He was distressed not to be allowed his chaplains, not even when he suggested that Parliament should appoint two out of twenty he would nominate; but he seemed to have a good esteem of the Presbyterian clergymen at Holmby, 'both as to their learning and conversation'. His spirits were, above all, borne up by his conviction that he was now the master of the situation, by playing off one side against the other he could solve all his difficulties and return to Whitehall in triumph.

Cornet Joyce's arrival at Holmby appeared to surprise but not to alarm him. He had been asleep when Joyce came and had been woken by the sound of angry words outside his room. He rang the silver bell which – together with two watches (one silver, one gold), a diamond seal (his arms cut into its face) and a wax lamp – he always kept beside his bed; and when a servant came into the room he asked him what the disturbance was about. The young Cornet, who had been a tailor in civilian life, explained that he had come to take the King away for his own good, assuring him that no harm would come to him, that his servants could accompany him, and that he would be required to do nothing against his conscience.

The next morning Charles got up earlier than usual and at six o'clock was standing on the lawn in front of the house where an escort of five hundred troopers was already paraded. Joyce asked them if they all promised to observe the assurances which he had given the King. They shouted their agreement, 'All!'

'And now Mr Joyce,' Charles said. 'Tell me where your commission is. Have you anything in writing from Sir Thomas Fairfax!' The Cornet hesitated for a moment, unwilling to admit what his orders actually were and from whom they came. Then turning round in his saddle, he pointed to the horsemen behind him. Charles agreed to go with them. 'It is written in characters fair and legible enough,' he conceded. 'A company of as handsome proper gentlemen as I have seen for a long while.'

And so it was that at the beginning of June 1647, the King and Cromwell met for the first time. The meeting took place at Childerley near Cambridge, not far from Fairfax's headquarters at Newmarket. Fairfax (alarmed at what had been done in the Army's name), Cromwell (insisting that if the Army had not acted in this way Parliament would have done), and Ireton (now married to one of Cromwell's daughters and the most influential of his father-in-law's confidants) all rode over together to greet their royal captive. Fairfax kissed Charles's hand. Neither Ireton nor Cromwell felt able to go so far in courtesy as this, but otherwise they 'behaved themselves with good manners towards him'.

He was, in fact, treated with all due deference while terms were prepared by the Army leaders to which he might be persuaded to agree. He was allowed his chaplains back, his closest friend, the

Duke of Richmond, to attend him, and other friends, like Sir John Berkeley, to visit him regularly; he was permitted to visit his former palaces where his old servants waited upon him as though the Civil War had never been. Most gratifying of all, arrangements were made for him to see his younger children.

They were brought to Maidenhead from St James's Palace by the Earl of Northumberland and he met them at the Greyhound Inn. His joy at seeing them was as great as it was unaffected. Cromwell, himself a loving father, was present that day and he looked upon the scene with unconcealed emotion. His own eldest son had died, probably of smallpox when he was a schoolboy at Felsted and he had never recovered from the grief of it. 'It went as a dagger to my heart,' he was to say on his deathbed; 'indeed, it did.' His second son, Oliver, handsome and brave, a 'civil young gentleman and the joy of his father', had left Cambridge to fight in the war and had also died of smallpox. Watching Charles, so happy to be with his two younger sons and his little daughter Elizabeth – who bore the name of Cromwell's own sweet second girl – seeing them all having dinner together at a big table in the tavern parlour, Cromwell's eyes, he afterwards confessed, filled with tears.

When the Army's terms – the Heads of Proposals – were presented to Charles, there was nothing in them to which he could not in all honour have agreed. 'A crown so near lost was never recovered so easily as this would be,' Berkeley said, advising him to accept them. But Charles hesitated. He was distrustful of Cromwell and his stern, resolute son-in-law, and uneasy in their presence. Believing that delay would favour him, that the quarrels between them and Parliament would soon erupt into a crisis which could be manipulated in his favour, he chose to wait and to intrigue. He was, at least, right in supposing that a crisis could not be far distant.

The crisis, when it came, was precipitated by the overwhelmingly Presbyterian City of London whose citizens rioted in protest against the Army's recent actions and against its apparent intentions, in the words of Cromwell's angry threat, to 'purge and purge and purge and never leave purging the Houses till they have made them of such a temper' as to endorse the Proposals which had been presented to the King. The Army's reaction against the riots was prompt and devastating. At the head of eighteen thousand men Cromwell and Fairfax, demanding that the Army's pay should no longer be withheld, rode through London on 6 August, occupying the Tower and establishing their headquarters at Putney.

A week later the King moved down to Hampton Court. He was as happy here as at any time since the Queen had left him that April day at Abingdon. He was not only able to play tennis and billiards, but free to hunt in Richmond Park and, in a 'new tennis suit of wrought coloured satin lined with taffeta', to visit the children, now staying with the Earl of Northumberland at nearby Syon House. He was allowed to worship as he pleased, to talk in private to those who waited upon him in his bedchamber, to write to his wife. They were halcyon days in the memory of one of those who shared them with him; it was almost as though the King's troubles were all over. Cromwell and his wife came to visit him with their daughter, Bridget, and her formidable but handsome husband; and Jack Ashburnham, the charming, gay Groom of the Bedchamber who had accompanied the King to Southwell, took the hand of the good Mrs Cromwell and led her into dinner. The King was still under guard, of course, but not obstrusively so: Colonel Whalley, Cromwell's cousin and the guard's commander, was a tactful man.

Yet Charles, for all his apparent gratitude to the Army leaders for their courteous treatment of him, for all his protestations of being prepared to agree to the Proposals if just a few small details could be amended, was actively and constantly scheming to make a better deal for himself and his successors. He believed himself indispensable to any settlement. The Army's 'liberation' of London had revealed the ineffectiveness of Parliament, but there were still the Scots – a little more time and he might come to terms with *them*.

While the King prevaricated and dissembled, Cromwell's position became more and more difficult to maintain. Attacked by Royalists and anti-Royalists alike, by Presbyterians for his Independent views, and by Independents for not being Independent enough, he was as suspect in the Army for hobnobbing with the King as at the renascent Court for having brought the Army into being.

In the end help for Cromwell came from an unlikely quarter. The King it was who saved him. For in the second week of November Charles brought the meandering negotiations to an end, by escaping from Hampton Court.

The King's determination to fly from the Army's surveillance, to find a hiding-place near the coast, where he could continue his negotiations with the Scots and escape abroad if necessary, may have been recently increased by warnings that his life was in danger and that he would have to be kept a closer prisoner. He had, it is said, been shown a letter from Cromwell to Whalley which began, 'Dear Cousin Whalley, there are rumours abroad of some intended attempt on his Majesty's person. Therefore I pray have a care of your guards . . .' He had also, perhaps, received a letter warning him that certain Levellers had 'resolved for the good of the Kingdom' to take his life away. He was not afraid of death, but, like his father, he *was* afraid of the sudden indignity of an assassination.

He chose to make his escape in the afternoon of 11 November, a Thursday. He usually spent the afternoon of that day writing alone in his room before Evensong at six o'clock, so that with luck he would have at least two hours of darkness before he was missed. He planned to slip out of his room when all was quiet, to creep down the backstairs along an underground passage to the river, and row across to the far bank where Ashburnham and Berkeley would meet him with horses on which they would gallop away to the Hampshire coast.

By eight o'clock Colonel Whalley – who, ever since he had read Cromwell's letter, was 'extreme restless in his thoughts' – was seriously worried. The King had not appeared at Evensong, had not even appeared at supper afterwards. His secretary had said that he had told him that he had a very long letter to write to his daughter, Mary, and that he was, in any case, not feeling very well. But even so, Whalley thought, there should be some sounds to indicate that the King was still in his withdrawing-room. He looked through the keyhole, could see nothing, tried the door which was locked on the inside, and forcing his way into the room by a back entrance, found it empty. Whalley immediately sent out patrols, but he knew that the King by now must be far away.

Before the patrols returned, in fact, Charles was across the Solent in the Isle of Wight in the care of the island's governor at Carisbrooke Castle. The Governor was Colonel Robert Hammond, a known enemy of the Levellers in the Army, a nephew of Henry Hammond, one of Charles's Anglican chaplains, and a distant relative of the Royalist Marquess of Winchester. Though he had fought bravely against the Royalists in the war, and had married John Hampden's youngest daughter, it was felt that he sympathised secretly with the King's cause. And, indeed, though noncommittal in his assurances, Hammond did greet Charles with an encouraging courtesy and respect.

The pleasant relationship did not long survive. For it soon became known to Hammond that Charles was deep in clandestine negotiations with the Scots for a settlement of his problems by force. Cromwell, according to one source, had intercepted letters which revealed the King's true attitude towards him, his endorsement of Henrietta Maria's description of him as a 'traitor', his determination not to be held to any promises he might have made when he had power enough to break them, and his inclination to 'close with the Scotch Presbyterians'.

On Boxing Day 1647 this inclination was confirmed by Charles's signing an 'Engagement' with the Scots by which, in return for the aid of a Scottish army to restore him to his erstwhile powers, he agreed to restore Presbyterianism in England for three years, to suppress 'the opinions and practices of Independents and all such scandalous doctrines', and to appoint to the English Privy Council a 'considerable and competent number of Scotsmen'. This 'Engagement' was wrapped in lead and buried in the garden at Carisbrooke. Two days later Charles officially and at last brought to an end the wearisomely protracted discussions he had been having with the English Army and prepared to leave Carisbrooke.

But it was not now possible for him to do so. His deceitful intrigues had resolved all doubts in Colonel Hammond's mind as to the manner of his treatment. From now on, for the next nine months, he was kept as close a prisoner on the Isle of Wight as ever he had been at Holmby House. His personal attendants and chaplains were dismissed and replaced by four 'Conservators', whose instructions were never to leave his side 'in their courses two at a time, to be always in his presence, except when he retires into his bedchamber; and then they are to repair the one to one door, and the other to the other, and then to continue till the King comes forth again'.

Charles's outward patience and uncomplaining endurance during these months of captivity at Carisbrooke struck most of those who came into contact with him as noble; but Robert Hammond, though still usually polite, could not on occasions hide his exasperation with the gracious little man who seemed so resigned yet was involved in perpetual plots to escape.

Once they had a heated argument. Charles burst out that

Hammond was 'an equivocating gentleman' who used him 'neither like a gentleman nor a christian'; Hammond retorted that he would speak to him when he was in a better temper but, at present, he was 'too high'; and Charles, hoping to end the argument by a joke – he was never very good at making jokes – protested that if he was too high then it must be his shoemaker's fault as all his shoes were meant to be made to the same pattern. On another occasion there seems to have been an even more embarassing encounter. One account of it – a Royalist account – says that they actually came to blows when Hammond searched the room. Whether this story is to be believed or not, it was certainly true that the room was searched.

Hammond had cause enough for both his suspicions about the King and for his sudden outbursts of fretful irritation. No sooner was the King allowed some privilege than he immediately made use of it to try to effect his escape, elaborating the most complicated plans with anyone who came into contact with him, arranging a code based on the names of vegetables with the man who supervised his meals, talking secretly with another servant through a screened hole in his bedchamber wall, concealing cryptic messages in his gloves which could be extracted by the Gentleman Usher whose duty it was to hold them while the King was at the dining-table, entrusting letters to the laundry-woman, the laundry-woman's maid, the woman who emptied the stools, and Jane Whorwood, an attractive and enterprising woman whom Charles had known well in the days when her father had held an appointment at Court. Jane Whorwood found her way into the stool-room inside his bedchamber with both letters and articles useful for his escape including files and aqua fortis to cut through the bar on his bedchamber window. Charles's attempt to escape through this window was, however, foiled; for, believing that he could squeeze through without the removal of the bar, he 'stuck fast,' in the words of one of his accomplices, 'between his breast and shoulders' and, extricating himself with difficulty, he had to signal with a candle to his friends in the grounds outside that the attempt would have to be abandoned.

While not engaged in such attempts to set himself at liberty, Charles played bowls on the green which Hammond had made for him on the castle's barbican, took his dogs – the spaniel, Rogue, and the greyhound, Gypsy – for walks around the castle walls, and dealt gracefully with those suffering from scrofula who approached him begging to be cured of the King's Evil. In the past, the Easter and Michaelmas ceremonies of touching for the King's Evil had been almost the only occasions upon which he came into any sort of contact with the common people, and they had been regulated with the strictest care, none but those who could provide a certificate signed by a justice of the peace, a clergyman and a churchwarden being allowed into his presence. Now the procedure was necessarily less formal, and Charles evidently found the duty a distasteful one.

He seemed far happier in the more congenial company of the Governor's chaplain, a young man whose lesser knowledge of history and inferior powers of disputation and command of logic put the King in a good mood so that 'he always parted merrily from him and was very pleasant'.

Charles also spent long hours writing verses and in reading a great number of books and volumes of verse, from Spenser's *Faerie Queene* and Tasso's *Godfrey of Boulogne*, to Henry Hammond's sermons and Hooker's *Ecclesiastical Polity*. But 'the sacred scripture was the book he most delighted in'; and from the Bible and from his devotions, regular as always, he appeared to derive great comfort and peace of mind. So that, despite the frustrations of his captivity and the interferences of Robert Hammond – whom the devil himself could not 'outgo neither in malice nor cunning' – the months passed without undue distress.

For his supporters in the outside world, though, life was far more difficult and turbulent.

In the early summer war had broken out again. There had been Royalist risings in Wales, in Kent and Essex; and a Scottish army 30,000 strong, had invaded England under command of the Duke of Hamilton in accordance with the 'Engagement' signed at Carisbrooke Castle. Royalist hopes of an early victory had been high. Dissatisfaction with Parliament was general throughout the country; the local rebellions in England were expected to spread; Hamilton's army was reputed to be excellent; while the New Model Army was believed to be split by religious and political dissension.

It was certainly true that at the end of the previous year there had been serious trouble in the New Model Army, that only by promising to look into the complaints of the men and to reform the Parliamentary system had the generals been able to quell what threatened to become a mutiny. Cromwell had had to put down in person a mutiny which actually did break out in a regiment commanded by John Lilburne's brother at Ware. But by the time the Second Civil War had begun, the Army's leaders were in control of their men once more and ready to take them into battle. Fairfax dealt with the troubles in Essex; and Cromwell, having reduced the Royalist stronghold at Pembroke Castle in Wales, marched north and overwhelmed the Scottish army at Preston in a three day battle which ended on 19 August.

When the war was over the reversal of Cromwell's attitude towards the King was complete. A year before he had been as prepared to come to terms with him as the Levellers were; he had nothing against the monarchy as an institution as the republicans had. But this invocation of foreign troops – and to Cromwell the Scots were just as much foreigners as Spaniards and Italians were – was unforgivable. Many good Englishmen had died at Preston. He could never forget them.

Before the fighting had started again, he had agreed with reluctance at a council of officers that the King must be proceeded against as a 'Man of Blood'. Gradually his views had hardened. The more evident it became how far the King was prepared to go in his promises to the Scots, how deeply he and his friends had been deceived, the more Cromwell was convinced that to have any more dealings with Charles was 'to meddle with an accursed thing'.

At the beginning of 1648 Cromwell's condemnation of the King in the House of Commons had been followed by a vote of *No Addresses* by which negotiations with him were broken off; in April, after a serious illness, he attended a great prayer meeting of army officers at Windsor Castle and concluded with the others, most of them in tears, that it was their duty 'if ever the Lord brought [them] back in peace, to call Charles Stuart, that Man of Blood, to an account for the blood that he had shed, and mischief he had done to his utmost, against the Lord's cause and people in these poor nations'. Now, after Preston and after much more blood had been shed, Cromwell's mind was made up.

He heard with disgust that the Presbyterian leaders in Parliament in contradiction of their vote of *No Addresses* and without consulting the Army, were once more in negotiation with the King in the Isle of Wight; he expressed himself 'glad' of the action of Colonel Pride, said to be a former brewer's drayman, who – while Cromwell was on his way to London from his headquarters in Yorkshire – posted himself outside the House of Commons and with the help of Ireton arrested or forcibly turned away all Members out of sympathy with the Army's views. And when the few remaining Members passed an Act setting up a High Court of Justice to try the King and naming Commissioners to serve on it, Cromwell assured his fellow Commissioners – many of whom refused to serve or were doubtful of their legal right to do so – that the time had come to act decisively. 'I tell you,' he cried out in a terrible, unequivocal and memorable phrase, 'We will cut off the King's head with the crown on it'.

By the time Colonel Pride's Purge had turned the Commons into a mere 'Rump', the King had been taken away from Carisbrooke Castle. The negotiations with the representatives of Parliament had been little more than a pitiful farce. The delegates, fearful that the country lay in immediate danger of being subjected to the government of a military dictatorship, had begged the King to try to come to terms with them as soon as he possibly could. But Charles had refused to be hurried. Still hoping and plotting for foreign help, considering the Scottish defeat at Preston not an end to war but a reason for a new one, he had as so often before played for time. Contesting every point at issue, he wore himself and the Parliamentary delegates out. The conference had been expected to last for forty days; but as November drew to a close it still dragged inconclusively on. By the time it had ended, on 25 November, the delegates had long since abandoned hope of any settlement; and, from a sad letter to the Prince of Wales written four days later it appeared that the King now recognised that no settlement would ever be possible; he looked beyond his own life to the future reign of his son.

The morning after this letter was written Charles was moved from the Isle of Wight by order of the Army. One of the Pages of the Bedchamber later described how the 'bloodhounds' who had come to escort him away spent the previous night 'in all places within and without the house, even in his bedchamber', how the King had said to him 'I know not where these people intend to carry me, and I would willingly eat before I go, therefore get me something to eat'.

'And coming myself in half an hour, to tell him it was ready,' the Page went on, 'I met these wretches leading him down the stairs to hurry him away, not suffering him to break his fast.

'I kneeled down to kiss his hand, at which he stopped to give me leave to do so; then they thrust him, saying "Go on, Sir!" and thrust him up into the coach, which was set close to the door.'

One of the officers stepped up into the coach after him without taking his hat off, and the King, infuriated as always by this sort of impudence, burst out in anger, 'It's not come to that yet. Get you out!'

He was taken to Hurst Castle, a fortress built by order of Henry VIII at the furthermost tip of a long strip of sand and shingle by the west entrance to the Solent. It was a gloomy forbidding place, a 'dismal receptacle', according to Sir Thomas Herbert, one of those who accompanied him there. It had 'very thick stone walls . . . and the air was equally noxious, by reason of the marsh grounds that were about, and the unwholsom vapours arising from the Sargasso's and weeds the salt water constantly at tides and storms casts upon the shoar, and by the fogs that those marine places are most subject to . . . The captain of this wretched place stood ready to receive the King with small observance; his look was stern, his hair and large beard were black and bushy, he held a partizan [halberd] in his hand and (Switz-like) had a great basket-hilt sword by his side; hardly could one see a man of a more grim aspect, and no less robust and rude was his behaviour'.

The King was shown to his room, a small, dark place, needing to be lit by the candles even at noon, with a slit of a window looking out across the Solent towards Yarmouth. Charles spent hours looking out at the sea and at the ships that sailed past the Needles through the narrow waters, listening to the cry of the gulls, with the smell of the dank seaweed in his nostrils. Every day he went for a walk, hurrying along the shingle with his usual quick step, leaving his companions far behind him; but he seemed calm and serene, resigned to his fate, even on occasions optimistic again.

Fairfax had given orders that he was to be treated well. Although the Duke of Richmond had not been allowed to come from the Isle of Wight with him, he was permitted the services of two Gentlemen of the Bedchamber and of over ten other servants, including a carver, and cupbearer, two pages and three cooks. He dined beneath a canopy in what forlorn state the dismal fortress would allow and the people of the nearby villages along the coast were admitted to watch the ceremony, crowding round the door.

One morning he rang his silver bell before dawn and called Sir Thomas Herbert into his room. He had heard the drawbridge let down at midnight and the clatter of horsemen entering through the gate. He asked him to go and learn 'what the matter was'. When Sir Thomas came back to tell him that 'it was Major Harrison that came so late into the castle', the King said little in reply and straight away went to his prayers; but it was obvious that he had been deeply perturbed at the mention of Harrison's name. An hour later Sir Thomas joined him again and suddenly burst into tears. What was the matter? Charles asked him. Herbert replied, 'Because I saw your Majesty so much troubled and concerned at the news I brought.'

'"I am not afraid," said the King, "but do you not know that this is the man that intended to assassinate me, as by letter I was informed . . . this is a place fit for such a purpose. Herbert, I trust your care; go again, and make further enquiry into this business."'

Herbert, after further enquiries of the Captain of the guard, was able to assure Charles that Harrison had merely come to make arrangements for his removal from Hurst Castle to Windsor; 'and so soon as the King heard Windsor named, he seemed to rejoice at it'.

Charles was brought to Windsor just before Christmas, passing through villages lined with people some of whom cheered him on his way or called out 'God preserve Your Majesty!' A plot had been prepared for his escape in Windsor Forest on a fast horse, 'the fleetest in all England', which was to be added to the other horses in the troop by Lord Newburgh with whom he was allowed to dine at Bagshot. The King prepared the ground by protesting at the going of his own horse and suggesting a change; but when he was given another mount it was not the horse he had hoped for. Major Harrison, knowing that Lord Newburgh owned some of the most famous race horses in England, had taken care to see that the King could not seize his last chance of escape.

Life at Windsor was not made difficult for him. He was permitted a choice of rooms in the Upper Ward, the freedom to walk all over the castle and along the north terrace; twenty pounds a day were allowed 'for the daily expenses of the King and his attendants'; his meals were still served in some state, trumpets sounding at the approach of his covered dishes, attendants standing by to hold his gloves, present the plates and taste the meat, his Cupbearer waiting upon him on bended knee.

'His Majesty hath three new suits,' *The Perfect Weekly Account* reported, 'two of them are cloth with rich gold and silver lace on them, the other is of black satin, the cloak lined with plush. Since the King came to Windsor he shows little alteration of courage or gesture, and, as he was formerly seldom seen to be very merry, or much transported with any news, either with joy or sorrow; so now, although he expects a severe charge and tryal, yet doth he not shew any great discontent.'

Soon after this report was written, orders came that Charles should be kept more like a prisoner and less like a King. Many of his attendants were dismissed; his meals were simply served; without a chaplain, he was obliged to read the daily services himself; when he attended St George's chapel, stripped now of its beutiful ornaments, he had to listen to the preachings of the garrison chaplain and to the intonations of the Puritan soldiers who prayed standing up. He comforted himself with private prayer, with reading Shakespeare's plays, with fast walks around the castle, up and down 'the long terrace that looks towards the fair college of Eaton', wearing the collar of the Order of the Garter he never took off during the day.

One last attempt was made to come to terms with him. But, after several hours of thought, Charles refused even to see the envoy whom the Army had sent. Knowing what would be required of him, he gave answer that he had already 'conceded too much, 'and even so had failed to give satisfaction, and he was resolved to die rather than lay any further burden on his conscience'.

On New Year's Day, 1649, the purged House of Commons passed without a division the ordinance for the King's trial. 'Charles Stuart, the now King of England' was accused of having entertained 'a wicked design totally to subvert the ancient and fundamental laws and liberties of this nation, and in their place to introduce an arbitrary and tyrannical government; and that, besides all other evil ways and means to bring his design to pass, he hath prosecuted it with fire and sword, levied and maintained a cruel war in the land'. The House declared that a King who prosecuted such a war against his subjects was guilty of treason.

Ever since Charles had been brought from Carisbrooke Castle, Cromwell had been working hard to ensure that the trial should be given an appearance of legality, that the forms of Parliamentary procedure should be observed, that all possible evidence should be collected against the 'Traitorous' King, and that all Members who could be persuaded to agree to his trial should attend the Commons and say so.

For it was not only the Royalists who condemned the Army's decision. The Presbyterians, their voice in Parliament stilled by Colonel Pride, were as strongly opposed to the trial as the Levellers whose leader, John Lilburne, denounced it as a plot by the 'Grandees' and the 'silken Independent', Oliver Cromwell, to use the proceedings as a means of turning attention away from the far more urgent problems of social reform. Also, Fairfax, still nominally the Army's commander, gave Cromwell no active encouragement. A hesitant man when not at war, stammering of speech, with no strong political views apart from a belief in the importance of the land-owning class from which he came, Fairfax whenever possible maintained a discreet silence. He acquiesced in what was done in the Army's name, apparently believing that the threat of trial was intended merely to force the King to give way; he stayed away from London when the crisis came, afterwards maintaining that any action on his part would have plunged the country into a third civil war.

Cromwell had no such qualms. For him the King was 'a man against whom the Lord [had] witnessed'. God had given His sign at Marston Moor, Naseby and Preston; now, since the King would not recognise this, since negotiation with so treacherous a man was impossible, he must be tried and executed. He knew that the Army and the present Parliament that supported it were far more representative of the country as a whole than the Presbyterians or the Royalists pretended to be. He had merely to establish a High Court willing and competent to carry out a distasteful but necessary task.

In this he found great difficulty. The two Chief Justices and the Lord Chief Baron of the Exchequer alike refused to serve, though all three were opponents of the King and had only recently been appointed. Other legal luminaries went into the country or, like the Attorney General, pleaded illness. Eventually the little known and undistinguished Chief Justice of Chester, John Bradshaw, was

The Last Years: Prisoner and Victim

A broadsheet of 1648 showing Charles imprisoned at Carisbrooke Castle,
Isle of Wight, where he remained from November 1647 until his removal to
Hurst Castle in December 1648.

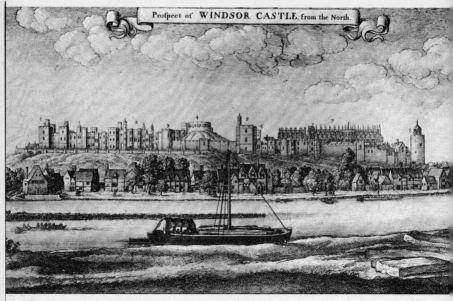

Prospect of **WINDSOR CASTLE**, from the North.

Windsor Castle where Charles was imprisoned during the last Christmas of his life. It had been used as a garrison and prison during the Civil War, having been taken over by Colonel John Venn in the name of Parliament in 1642; and it was here, at a meeting of the general officers of the Army in November 1647, that it was 'resolved that the King should be prosecuted for his life as a criminal person'.

A marble bust of Oliver Cromwell by Joseph Wilton.

The King during his trial. A painting by Edward Bower who obtained a good seat in the Hall, made sketches throughout the trial, and painted this last authentic portrait of the King, several times for different patrons.

(*opposite*) A contemporary engraving of the trial of Charles I in Westminster Hall in January 1649.

The chair, covered with red velvet, in which the King sat during the trial.

The specially reinforced hat made for John Bradshaw, president of the court that tried Charles I.

One of the two shirts which Charles wore at his execution. He put on a second shirt over the top of the first – one is at Windsor the other at Longleat – for it was a cold morning and he was anxious not to shiver on the scaffold and allow people to think that he was afraid.

Whereas Charles Steuart Kinge of England

and other high Crymes, And sentence...

severinge of his head from his body. Of w...

require you to see the said sentence executed

this instant moneth of January betweene t...

day with full effect And for soe doeing this s...

and other the good people of this Nation of E...

Peace

The warrant for Charles's execution signed by fifty-nine of the King's judges.

The execution of Charles I on the scaffold erected outside the Banqueting House on 30 January 1649.

THE
CONFESSION ¹⁴
June 25 OF *1649*
Richard Brandon

The Hangman (upon his Death-bed) concerning His beheading his late Majesty, CHARLES the first, King of Great
Brittain; and his Protestation and Vow touching the same;
the manner how he was terrified in Conscience; the Appa-
ritions and Visions which apeared unto him; the great judg-
ment that befell him three dayes before he dy'd; and the
manner how he was carryed to White-Chappell Churchyard on Thursday night last; the strange Actions that happened thereupon; With the merry conceits of the Crowne
Cook and his providing mourning Cords for the Buriall.

Printed in the year Year, ot the Hang-mans down-fall, 1649.

'The Confession of Richard Brandon'. It was later rumoured by Royalists that
Brandon, the City's principal hangman, had refused to perform his task and that
Hugh Peter, the Army chaplain, or even Cromwell himself had taken his place.

A contemporary Dutch engraving depicting the King's last days.

(*opposite*) A marble bust of William Juxon, Bishop of London (1582–1663) who ministered to the King during his last hours.

(*above*) The Juxon medal, given to the bishop by the King on the scaffold.

The frontispiece to *Eikon Basilike* (Royal Image), the book subtitled *The Pourtraicture of his Sacred Majestie in his Solitudes and Sufferings* published on the day of the King's burial by the devoted Royalist bookseller, Richard Royston. It purported to be meditations by Charles I on the principal events of his reign, though the authorship of it was later claimed by John Gauden who was elevated to the Bishopric of Worcester by Charles II. Numerous copies were illegally sold; it was reprinted thirty times within the year and eventually forty-seven editions of it were published.

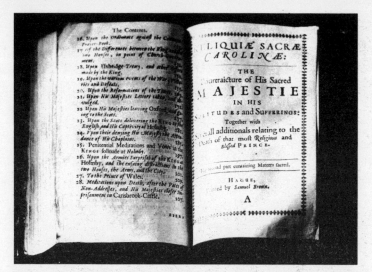

The title page of the copy of *Eikon Basilike* at Carisbrooke castle.

The explanation of the symbolism of the frontispiece of *Eikon Basilike* from the same book at Carisbrooke.

'The Blessed King Charles the Martyr' as he appeared to eighteenth-century Tories. An engraving of 1717 by Faber.

appointed President of the Court; and John Cook, a devoutly religious, republican barrister of Gray's Inn, passionately convinced of Charles Stuart's evil and guilt, was delegated to conduct the prosecution. Most of the judges – there were 135 of them – were equally obscure. They were not all brewers, shoemakers and 'other mechanick persons' as Cromwell's enemies suggested; but, since the Lords had rejected the ordinance for the trial, there were no English peers on a list of names that included those of several highly dubious country gentlemen.

A number of judges, nevertheless, obscure though some of them may have been, acted from purely disinterested motives, sincerely convinced that it was their duty to do so. Fifty-nine of them were eventually to sign the death warrant; and although some did so unwillingly, and others in the hope of gain, most were as certain as Thomas Harrison was, when his own turn came to die as a regicide, that they had acted 'out of conscience to the Lord'.

Certainly, as Harrison protested, 'it was not a thing done in a corner'. The trial was held in Westminster Hall, the President so exposed to public view that he thought it as well to reinforce his hat with steel plates. When the proceedings opened on 20 January, the Hall was so crammed with spectators that some of them were forced to find a seat high above the Court in the embrasures of the windows.

The King had been brought up from Windsor the day before. It was a bitingly cold day, and few people lingered in the streets to watch his coach go by. He spent the first night of his return to London at St James's Palace; but the next afternoon he was taken to Sir Robert Cotton's Thameside mansion which was nearer Westminster Hall.

He was carried across the Park to the river stairs at Whitehall in a closed sedan chair surrounded by guards. At the stairs he was told to get out of the chair and to step into a barge which conveyed him to the garden of Cotton House. The garden was full of soldiers; two hundred of them were accommodated in a temporary guard house erected in the grounds; two long files of them stretched from the river bank to the garden door of the house; inside the house they clattered about from room to room, upstairs and down, leaning in doorways, resting their halberds against the walls, smoking and talking, peering into the King's bedchamber – where some of them slept the first night of the trial so that the King refused to undress or go to bed. Soon after two o'clock a squad of them formed up in the street to escort the prisoner to Westminster Hall.

In the hall an arm-chair covered in red velvet had been placed for him opposite the table at which Bradshaw, the President of the Court, was seated with his clerks. The King entered the Hall, walking with his usual hurried step, and sat down in the chair, looking straight in front of him, showing no emotion.

He was wearing a black velvet cloak, on the left sleeve of which gleamed the embroidered silver star of the Order of the Garter, a broad white lace collar and a tall black hat. Between the fingers of one small white hand was the silver-headed cane with which, so elegantly poised, he had made his gracious entrance into the rooms of his palaces in happier days. Men who had not seen him since the wars were appalled by the change in him; his hair was grey, his cheeks sunken, his eyes deeply shadowed and pouched, his beard thicker and more grizzled than ever it had been in the past. At forty-eight he looked tired, old, and worn.

Yet a strong spirit still burned within him; and even amongst those who hoped to see him condemned to death there were many who could not but admire that spirit, who, within the next few days, were forced to conclude that, traitor or not, Charles Stuart at the end had shown himself to be a man of resolution, conviction and courage. Exasperating those who, believing him to be pliable, had come upon the ultimate bedrock of his obstinacy, angering those who condemned his calm manner as an impudence that ill-behaved a man 'guilty of the blood that hath been shed in this war', he refused to betray his conscience. Always in the past readier to accept the advice of others than to trust in his own opinions, he was not afraid of his judgement now. To his supporters he had never seemed more noble.

He listened in silence as Bradshaw told him that the 'Commons of England, assembled in Parliament, being sensible of the great calamities that have been brought upon this nation' had 'constituted this High Court of Justice . . . according to that duty which they owe to God, to the nation, and to themselves . . . .' He listened, still in silence, as the fervent John Cook, staring him in the face, accused him of 'high treason and high misdemeanours'. It was not until Cook said he would read out the charge and began to unroll the big scroll of parchment on which it was written, that Charles spoke for the first time: 'Hold a little.'

Cook went on unrolling the parchment and Charles, in an effort to attract his attention, tapped him on the arm with his cane. The silver knob fell off. The King made no move to retrieve it; and then, as though suddenly remembering that he had no page now to pick it up for him, he bent down and picked it up himself.

He made no further effort to interrupt as Cook, having at last unravelled the scroll, read the charge inscribed upon it. He sat, apparently indifferent, looking up at his judges, turning round to glance at the spectators behind him, laughing sardonically when Cook impeached him 'as a Tyrant, Traitor and Murderer'. But when the prosecutor had finished and Bradshaw told him that the Court expected his answer, he protested that he did not know by what power or lawful authority he was called upon to make any answer. He spoke with clarity and confidence, quite without the impediment that normally hampered his tongue, insisting that the Court had no right to try him, that he would not submit to it, that he had a trust committed to him by God, 'by old and lawful descent', and that he would not betray it 'to answer a new unlawful authority'.

Answer it he would not, neither that Saturday, nor the following Monday, nor yet the day after that. Each day, having calmly and stubbornly questioned the authority of the Court and refused to recognise its right to try him – their 'lawful King', a king who knew 'as much law as any gentlemen in England' – he was escorted from the hall by the soldiers, symbol of the Court's authority. Cook warned him that, 'according to the known rules of the law of the land', a prisoner who would not plead was regarded as having pleaded guilty; he remained unimpressed. Bradshaw told him to remember that he sat before a Court of justice; he replied, 'I find I am before a power.' He was urged to remember that his accusers were the 'People of England'; the spirited Lady Fairfax, her face masked, stood up in the gallery of the Court that her husband had declined to attend, and made answer for the King: 'Not a quarter of them! Oliver Cromwell is a traitor!'

On 27 January, Charles Stuart, 'as a Tyrant, Traitor, Murderer and a Public Enemy' was condemned to be put to death 'by the severing of his head from his body'.

The King, refusing to accept the injustice of it all, shocked by the sudden ending of the trial, called out loudly, 'Will you hear me a word, Sir?'

'You are not to be heard after the sentence.'

'No, Sir?'

'No, Sir, by your favour, Sir. Guard, withdraw your prisoner.'

'I may speak after the sentence – by your favour, Sir, I may speak after the sentence. By your favour, hold! The sentence, Sir – I say, Sir, I do –'

For the first time in the trial he was incoherent. The soldiers were moving in on him to drag him away if necessary; even if he were allowed to speak now he would scarcely be able to make himself heard above the noise in the Court. 'I am not suffered for to speak,' he said resignedly, once more in control of his emotions. 'Expect what justice other people will have.'

He was not taken back to Cotton House that day; instead he was carried in a sedan chair down King Street, both sides of which were lined with troops, to the more familiar comforts of Whitehall. Some of his guards had called out, upon a signal from their Colonel, 'Execution! Justice! Execution!'; and he had commented wryly, as they breathed tobacco smoke in his face, 'Poor creatures! For sixpence they will say as much of their own commanders'. But the people who looked down upon his quickly moving chair from the windows of King Street were silent.

The following afternoon, after listening to a comforting sermon by William Juxon, the kindly Bishop of London, in the chapel at Whitehall, he was taken back to St James's. Here a letter from the Prince of Wales was brought to him by a former page who fell in tears at his feet, kissing his hand and clasping his feet. 'I do not only pray for your Majesty according to my duty,' the Prince had written, 'but shall always be ready to do all which shall be in my power to deserve that blessing which I now humbly beg of Your Majesty.'

The Prince's brother, the Duke of York, had escaped to Holland disguised as a girl in April the previous year; but two of the King's other children, Princess Elizabeth and the Duke of Gloucester, were still in England at Sion House; and their father's request to see them for the last time was granted.

It was over a year since he had seen them last. Elizabeth was thirteen now, not so pretty as she had been as a baby, a serious, intense girl, with big eyes and thick fair curls, overwhelmed with sadness at being so cruelly separated from her parents for so long.

As soon as she saw her dear father again, she burst into tears and, on her knees before him, she could not stop crying. He bent down to help her to her feet and took her to one side, asking her to try to listen carefully to his words and to remember the important things he had to say. She was to tell her brother James, who was rather jealous of the Prince of Wales, that it was his father's last wish that he should revere his eldest brother 'and be obedient unto him as his sovereign'.

Elizabeth was still weeping so bitterly, 'shedding tears and crying lamentably', as her father talked to her that he said to her in gentle reproach, 'Sweetheart, you will forget this'.

No, she said, 'I will never forget it whilst I live'; she would write it all down that night. And so she did.

'He told me he was glad I was come,' she wrote in her child's hand. 'He wished me not to grieve and torment myself for him, for that would be a glorious death that he should die, it being for the laws and liberties of this land, and for maintaining the true Protestant religion . . . he should die a martyr. He told me he had forgiven all his enemies, and hoped God would forgive them also, and commanded us, and all the rest of my brothers and sisters to forgive them. He bid me tell my mother that his thoughts had never strayed from her, and that his love should be the same to the last . . . . He doubted not but the Lord would settle his throne upon his son, and that we should be all happier than we could have expected to have been if he had lived.'

When he had finished speaking to Elizabeth he turned to Henry and, sitting down, took the chubby, eight-year-old boy on his knee. 'Heed, my child, what I say,' he said to him. 'They will cut off my head, and perhaps make thee a king.' The boy looked up at his father 'very steadfastly'; and Charles went on, 'But mark what I say, you must not be a King so long as your brothers Charles and James do live; for they will cut off your brothers' heads (when they can catch them) and cut off thy head too, at last; and therefore I charge you, do not be made a King by them.'

Henry promised that he would rather be 'torn in pieces first'.

Charles put the boy down and kissed him. He kissed Elizabeth, too, and blessed them both. Then he asked them to go away with Bishop Juxon, and was himself leaving the room for the bedroom next door when a fresh outburst of sobbing from Elizabeth, who was herself to die at Carisbrooke the following year, made him come back to give her a last kiss. He turned away, walked quickly into the bedchamber, and lay down on the bed; his legs were trembling.

Next morning he awoke soon after five o'clock, and 'opened his curtain' to call Sir Thomas Herbert who had spent the night on a pallet-bed by his side. 'I will get up,' he told Herbert, 'having a great work to do this day.'

'This is my second marriage day,' he added when Herbert was helping him to dress, 'I would be as trim to-day as may be, for before to-night I hope to be espoused to my blessed Jesus.'

He put on a second shirt over the top of the first, for it was a bitterly cold morning and he did not want to shiver on the scaffold for the people might think he was afraid. 'I would have no such imputation,' he told Herbert. 'I fear not death. Death is not terrible to me. I bless my God I am prepared.'

When he had finished dressing and Herbert had brushed his hair and fixed his pearl ear-rings in his ears, he went to his prayers with Bishop Juxon and received the Blessed Sacrament. He said that he would have no other food that day; but the bishop persuaded him, as the morning wore on, to eat a piece of bread and drink a glass of claret in case he should faint at the end. He had already taken the precaution of putting an orange stuck with cloves in his pocket. He was not, as he had said, afraid of dying, but he *was* concerned that he might not die with that grace and decorum that had marked his life.

Just before ten o'clock there was a knock on the door; an Army officer came into the room and, 'in trembling manner', told the King it was time to leave. Charles knelt briefly in prayer, then, taking the Bishop's hand, he said, 'Come let us go', and walked out of the palace into the park, his dog, Rogue, running after him.

'The Park had several companies of foot drawn up, who made a guard on either side as the King passed' Herbert remembered. 'And a guard of halberdiers in company went, some before, and some followed; the drums beat, and the noise was so great as one could hardly hear what another spoke.'

As the procession passed through the Spring Garden the King raised his voice to point out a tree that his brother, Henry, had planted over thirty years before.

For almost four hours he had to wait in the palace before the order came for him to mount the black-draped scaffold that had been built outside the Banqueting House. It had been decided that the execution should take place here and not on Tower Hill for the square in front of Inigo Jones's handsome building was small and easily guarded.

Charles walked through the Banqueting House and then out through one of its especially enlarged windows onto the scaffold, Dr Juxon by his side. Two Army colonels were there with a guard of soldiers, a few reporters, and the executioner and his assistant, both of them masked and disguised with false hair and beards.

He could not speak to the crowds in the square, for a line of helmeted soldiers with pikes and halberds separated them from the railings round the scaffold, so he turned to the group of men around the axe and the block. He spoke to them as he might have spoken to the High Court in Westminster Hall had the President allowed him to do so after sentence had been passed upon him. He protested his innocence, explained his own view of the troubles that had brought him there that day, and forgave his enemies. It was, in any event, God's judgement upon him for having let his servant Strafford go through this same agony: 'An unjust sentence that I suffered to take effect, is punished now by an unjust sentence on me.'

He died 'a Christian according to the profession of the Church of England'; he had a good cause and a gracious God; he had no fear, going as he did from 'a corruptible to an incorruptible crown, where no disturbance can be, no disturbance in the world'.

He asked the executioner what he should do about his hair, and with the help of the Bishop he tucked it up under his white satin night cap. Then he asked if the block was fixed firmly and if it could not be raised higher so that he could kneel down in front of it instead of having to lie down. But it had been set low so that it would be easier to kill him should he struggle. 'It can be no higher, Sir,' the executioner said.

Charles stood praying for a short time, looking up at the sky, then he lay down with his neck on the block. The executioner bent down to ensure that no strands of hair had escaped from the night cap to deflect the edge of his blade, and the King said quickly, 'Stay for the sign'. He had arranged that after he had said his last prayer, he would stretch out his hands as a signal that he was ready.

The executioner assured him that he had not forgotten, 'I will, Sir, an' it please Your Majesty'.

As soon as the sign came, the axe fell and Charles's head was severed in a single stroke.

'The blow I saw given,' said a young spectator, 'and can truly say with a sad heart, at the instant whereof, I remember well, there was such a grone by the Thousands then present as I never heard before and desire I may never hear again.'

There were no disturbances in London that night. There had been a short scramble round the scaffold as men and women had run forward to dip their handkerchiefs in the spilled blood, to grab some sort of memento of the scene they had witnessed; but the square in front of the Banqueting House had soon be cleared by mounted troops and by late afternoon London had fallen into a kind of shocked silence. The wars had caused much suffering; trade had been badly hit; the poor were as poor as they had ever been; crippled soldiers and beggars wandered everywhere. Perhaps the death of the King would lead to better times. Certainly it was true that no one in the whole of the teeming, rambling town had risked his life to save him, that many Londoners felt sure that those who had brought him to his death had done their duty to their country and to God.

The King's embalmed body remained at St James's for a week; and long afterwards the legend was created that the Earl of Southampton, while watching over it, had seen a man enter the room 'very much muffled up in his cloak, and his face quite hid in it. He approached the body, considered it very attentively for some time, and then shook his head, sighed out the words "Cruel Necessity!" He then departed in the same slow and concealed manner as he had come. Lord Southampton used to say that he could not distinguish anything of his face; but that by his voice and gait he took him to be Oliver Cromwell.'

In Paris it fell to Henry Jermyn at the Louvre to tell Henrietta Maria that her husband was dead. As gently as he could he broke the news. The Queen, who up till then had been comforting herself with belief in a rumour that Charles had been rescued, suddenly rose from her chair in shock, and then remained standing before him, unable to speak or to move. For over an hour she stayed, transfixed and silent while Jermyn, her priest and her ladies tried to rouse her; but they 'found her deaf and insensible'. Eventually fearing that she might go mad, they sent for the wife of her illegitimate brother, Françoise de Vendôme, a woman she loved and had known since her childhood. Madame de Vendôme arrived, her cheeks wet with weeping, and as she sank to the floor at Henrietta's side, throwing her arms round her knees, the Queen, too, found relief at last in tears.

The King's body, lying in a coffin on which the Duke of Richmond had scratched 'King Charles' and the date of his death, was buried in St George's chapel, Windsor, on 9 February. Richmond was accompanied by the Marquess of Hertford, the Earls of Lindsey and Southampton, Sir Thomas Herbert and Bishop Juxon. The Governor of the Castle refused the Bishop permission to read the service from the Book of Common Prayer the use of which Parliament had forbidden, so he carried it closed in his hands in silence.

Dr. Juxon was in tears when the coffin, covered by a black velvet cloth, was brought down from St George's Hall by soldiers of the garrison. The King's four friends held up the corners of the pall, and he followed behind them. It was as cold as ever; the Thames below the castle windows was frozen over from bank to bank. The sky, earlier serene and clear, now darkened as the coffin approached the west end of the chapel; and then heavy snow began to fall, turning the black pall white.

N

Sources

ALTHOUGH good biographies have been written of his father and of his two elder sons, an adequate, full-length life of Charles I has yet to be written. Of the eight biographies written since 1924 and listed below the most satisfactory are, perhaps, those of F. M. G. Higham and Esmé Wingfield-Stratford. But the best account of him is to be found in the relevant volumes of Samuel Rawson Gardiner's monumental history and in the pages of Miss C. V. Wedgwood's brilliant, and yet to be completed, *The Great Rebellion* which I have, of course, found of great value in the preparation of this brief sketch. Convincing incidental portraits of him may also be found in the works of Hugh Ross-Williamson, David Mathew, M. A. Gibb, Maurice Ashley, Sir Charles Petrie, in J. P. Kenyon's sparkling *The Stuarts: A Study in English Kingship*, and in the masterly biographies of his two greatest servants – C. V. Wedgwood's *Thomas Wentworth, First Earl of Strafford 1593–1641: A Revaluation* and H. R. Trevor-Roper's *Archbishop Laud 1573–1645*.

The history of his wife has been delightfully told by Carola Oman; an excellent account of the Civil War has been recently provided by Austin Woolrych and of the Great Rebellion by Ivan Roots.

ABBOTT, W. C. (Ed.) *The Writings and Speeches of Oliver Cromwell* (Cambridge, Mass., 1937–47)

AIKIN, LUCY *Memoirs of the Court of Charles I* (London, 1833)

ASHLEY, MAURICE *England in the Seventeenth Century* (2nd Edition, Penguin Books, 1954)
Cromwell's Generals (Jonathan Cape, 1954)
The Greatness of Oliver Cromwell (Hodder & Stoughton, 1957)
Life in Stuart England (Batsford, 1964)

AYLMER, G. E. *The King's Servants: The Civil Service of Charles I, 1625–42* (Routledge and Kegan Paul, 1961)
The Struggle for the Constitution (Blandford Press, 1963)

BIRCH, THOMAS *The Court and Times of Charles the First* (London, 1848)

BIRKENHEAD, LORD *Strafford* (London, 1938)

BIRNE, A.H. See Peter Young.

BLOMFIELD, SIR REGINALD *A History of Renaissance Architecture in England* (London, 1901)

BRETT, S. REED *John Pym, 1583–1643* (John Murray, 1940)

BUCHAN, JOHN *Oliver Cromwell* (Hodder and Stoughton, 1934)

CHANCELLOR, E. BERESFORD *Life of Charles I from 1600–25* (London, 1886)

CHARLTON, JOHN *The Banqueting House, Whitehall* (H.M.S.O., 1964)

CLARENDON, EDWARD HYDE, EARL OF *History of the Rebellion and Civil Wars in England* (Ed. W.D. Macray, Oxford, 1888)

COATE, MARY *Social Life in Stuart England* (London, 1924)

COIT, C.W. *The Royal Martyr* (London, 1924)

COOKE, HAROLD P. *Charles I and his Earlier Parliaments* (London, 1939)
Commentaries on the Life and Reign of Charles I (London, 1851)

DAVIES, GODFREY *The Early Stuarts 1603–60* (Oxford University Press, 2nd Edn. 1960)

D'EWES, SIR SIMONDS *The Autobiography and Correspondence of Sir Simonds D'Ewes* (Ed. J.O. Halliwell, London, 1845)
The Journal of Sir Simonds D'Ewes (Ed. Wallace Notestein and Willson Havelock Coates, New Haven, 1923, 1942)

FERGUSSON, BERNARD *Rupert of the Rhine* (1952)

FIRTH, C.H. *Cromwell's Army* (4th Edn Methuen, 1962)
Oliver Cromwell (1900)

FORSTER, JOHN *Sir John Eliot* (London, 1865)

GARDINER, SAMUEL RAWSON *History of England from the Accession of James I to the Outbreak of Civil War, 1603–42,* (London, 1883–4)
History of the Great Civil War (London, 1893)

GIBB, M.A. *Buckingham 1592–1628* (Jonathan Cape, 1935)
The Lord General.

HEXTER, J.H. *The Reign of King Pym* (Cambridge, Mass, 1941)

HIGHAM, F.M.G. *Charles I* (Hamish Hamilton, 1932)

HILL, CHRISTOPHER *The English Revolution, 1640* (3rd Edn

Lawrence & Wishart, 1955)

The Century of Revolution, 1603–1714 (Nelson, 1961)

Economic Problems of the Church from Archbishop Whitgift to the Long Parliament (Oxford, 1956)

Puritanism and Revolution (London, 1958)

Historical and Critical Account of the Life and Writings of Charles I (William Harris, 1758)

HULME, HAROLD *The Life of Sir John Eliot, 1592–1632: Struggle for Parliamentary Freedom* (London, 1957)

HUTCHINSON, LUCY *Memoirs of the Life of Colonel Hutchinson* (Ed. C.H. Firth, 1906)

JOHN, EVAN *King Charles I* (Arthur Barker, n.d.)

JONES, JACK, D. *The Royal Prisoner* (Lutterwort Press, 1965)

KEELER, M.F. *The Long Parliament, 1640–1* (Philadelphia, 1954)

KENYON, J.P. *The Stuart Constitution 1603–88: Documents and Commentary* (Cambridge University Press, 1966)

The Stuarts: A Study in English Kingship (Batsford, 1958)

LOCKYER, ROGER (Ed.) *The Trial of Charles I* (Folio Society, 1959)

MATHEW, DAVID *The Age of Charles I* (Eyre & Spottiswoode, 1951)

James I (Eyre and Spottiswoode, 1967)

Scotland under Charles I (Eyre and Spottiswoode, 1955)

MACALPINE, IDA AND RICHARD HUNTER *Porphyria: A Royal Malady* (British Medical Association, 1968)

MILLAR, OLIVER (See Margaret Whinney)

MORLEY, JOHN VISCOUNT *Oliver Cromwell* (Methuen, 1923)

MORPURGO, J.E. (Ed.) *Life Under the Stuarts* (Falcon Educational Books, 1950)

MUDDIMAN, J.G. *Trial of Charles I* (William Hodge, 1928)

NALSON, JOHN *A True Copy of the Journal of the High Court of Justice* (London, 1684)

NICHOLAS, DONALD *Mr Secretary Nicholas, 1593–1669: His Life and Letters* (Bodley Head, 1955)

NICOLL, ALLARDYCE *Stuart Masques and the Renaissance Stage* (London, 1938)

OMAN, CAROLA *Henrietta Maria* (Hodder & Stoughton, 1936)

PETRIE, SIR CHARLES (Ed.) *The Letters Speeches and Proclamations of King Charles I* (Cassell, 1935)

The Stuarts (Eyre and Spottiswoode, 1958)

PICKEL, MARGARET BARNARD *Charles I as Patron of Poetry and Drama* (Frederick Muller, 1936)

RERESBY, SIR JOHN *Memoirs* (Ed. A. Browning, Glasgow, 1936)

ROOTS, IVAN *The Great Rebellion* (Batsford, 1966)

ROSS-WILLIAMSON, HUGH *Charles and Cromwell* (Duckworth, 1946)
The Day they Killed the King (Frederick Muller, 1957)

RUSHWORTH, JOHN *Historical Collections* (London, 1659 –1701)

STEVENSON, GERTRUDE SCOTT (Ed.) *Charles I in Captivity* (London, 1927)

STRICLAND, AGNES *Lives of the Queens of England vol 8* (London, 1845)

SUMMERSON, JOHN *Inigo Jones* (Penguin, 1966)
Architecture in Britain 1530–1830 (2nd Edn London, 1955)

TREVELYAN, GEORGE MACAULAY *England under the Stuarts* (Methuen, 21st Edn 1949)

TREVOR-ROPER, H. R. *Archbishop Laud* (2nd Edn Macmillan, 1962)
The Gentry (1953)

VERNEY, LADY *Memoirs of the Verney Family During the Civil War* (London, 1892)

WALPOLE, HORACE *Anecdotes of Painting in England* (London, 1849)

WARBURTON, ELIOT *Memoirs of Prince Rupert and the Cavaliers* (London, 1849)

WARWICK, SIR PHILIP *Memoirs of the Reign of King Charles I* (London, 1813)

WATERHOUSE, ELLIS *Painting in Britain: 1530–1790* (Pelican History of Art, London, 1953)

WEBER, KURT *Lucius Cary, Second Viscount Falkland* (Columbia University Press, 1940)

WEDGWOOD, C. V. *Oliver Cromwell* (Duckworth, 1939)
The Great Rebellion: The King's Peace 1637–1641 (Collins, 1955)
The Great Rebellion: The King's War, 1641–1647 (Collins, 1958)
The Trial of Charles I (Collins, 1964)
Thomas Wentworth, First Earl of Strafford, 1593–1641: A Revaluation. (Jonathan Cape, 1961)

WHINNEY, MARGARET AND OLIVER MILLAR *English Art,*

1625–1714 (Oxford History of English Art, 1957)

WHITELOCKE, BULSTRODE *Memorials of the English Affairs.* (London, 1682)

WILKINSON, CLENNELL *Prince Rupert, the Cavalier* (Harrap, (1934)

WILLEY, BASIL *The Seventeenth Century Background* (London, 1934)

WILLSON, D.H. *King James VI and I* (London, 1955)

WINGFIELD-STRATFORD, ESMÉ *Charles King of England* (London, 1949)

King Charles and King Pym (London, 1949)

King Charles and the Conspirators (London, 1937)

King Charles the Martyr (Hollis & Carter, 1950)

WOOLRYCH, AUSTIN *Battles of the English Civil War* (Batsford, 1961)

WORMAID, B.H.G. *Clarendon* (Cambridge University Press 1951)

YOUNG, G.M. *Charles I and Cromwell* (Rupert Hart-Davis, 1950)

YOUNG, PETER AND A.H.BURNE *The Great Civil War* (Eyre and Spottiswoode, 1959)

Edgehill, 1642 (Roundwood, 1967)

Index

READ MORE IN PENGUIN

In every corner of the world, on every subject under the sun, Penguin represents quality and variety – the very best in publishing today.

For complete information about books available from Penguin – including Puffins, Penguin Classics and Arkana – and how to order them, write to us at the appropriate address below. Please note that for copyright reasons the selection of books varies from country to country.

In the United Kingdom: Please write to *Dept. EP, Penguin Books Ltd, Bath Road, Harmondsworth, West Drayton, Middlesex UB7 0DA*

In the United States: Please write to *Consumer Sales, Penguin Putnam Inc., P.O. Box 12289 Dept. B, Newark, New Jersey 07101-5289.* VISA and MasterCard holders call 1-800-788-6262 to order Penguin titles

In Canada: Please write to *Penguin Books Canada Ltd, 10 Alcorn Avenue, Suite 300, Toronto, Ontario M4V 3B2*

In Australia: Please write to *Penguin Books Australia Ltd, P.O. Box 257, Ringwood, Victoria 3134*

In New Zealand: Please write to *Penguin Books (NZ) Ltd, Private Bag 102902, North Shore Mail Centre, Auckland 10*

In India: Please write to *Penguin Books India Pvt Ltd, 11 Community Centre, Panchsheel Park, New Delhi 110017*

In the Netherlands: Please write to *Penguin Books Netherlands bv, Postbus 3507, NL-1001 AH Amsterdam*

In Germany: Please write to *Penguin Books Deutschland GmbH, Metzlerstrasse 26, 60594 Frankfurt am Main*

In Spain: Please write to *Penguin Books S. A., Bravo Murillo 19, 1° B, 28015 Madrid*

In Italy: Please write to *Penguin Italia s.r.l., Via Benedetto Croce 2, 20094 Corsico, Milano*

In France: Please write to *Penguin France, Le Carré Wilson, 62 rue Benjamin Baillaud, 31500 Toulouse*

In Japan: Please write to *Penguin Books Japan Ltd, Kaneko Building, 2-3-25 Koraku, Bunkyo-Ku, Tokyo 112*

In South Africa: Please write to *Penguin Books South Africa (Pty) Ltd, Private Bag X14, Parkview, 2122 Johannesburg*

INSPECTION COPY REQUESTS

Lecturers in the United Kingdom and Ireland wishing to apply for inspection copies of Classic Penguin titles for student group adoptions are invited to apply to:

Inspection Copy Department
Penguin Press Marketing
27 Wrights Lane
LONDON
W8 5TZ

Fax: 020 7416 3274

E-mail: academic@penguin.co.uk

Inspection copies may also be requested via our website at:
www.penguinclassics.com

Please include in your request the author, title and the ISBN of the book(s) in which you are interested, the name of the course on which the books will be used and the expected student numbers.

It is essential that you include with your request your title, first name, surname, position, department name, college or university address, telephone and fax numbers and your e-mail address.

Lecturers outside the United Kingdom and Ireland should address their applications to their local Penguin office.

Inspection copies are supplied at the discretion of Penguin Books

READ MORE IN PENGUIN

PENGUIN CLASSIC MILITARY HISTORY

 This series acknowledges the profound and enduring interest in military history, and the causes and consequences of human conflict. Penguin Classic Military History covers warfare from the earliest times to the age of electronics and encompasses subjects as diverse as classic examples of grand strategy and the precision tactics of Britain's crack SAS Regiment. The series will be enjoyed and valued by students of military history and all who hope to learn from the often disturbing lessons of the past.

Published or forthcoming:

READ MORE IN PENGUIN

PENGUIN CLASSIC HISTORY

Well written narrative history from leading historians such as Paul Kennedy, Alan Moorehead, J. B. Priestley, A. L. Rowse and G. M. Trevelyan. From the Ancient World to the decline of British naval mastery, from twelfth-century France to the Victorian Underworld, the series captures the great turning points in history and chronicles the lives of ordinary people at different times. Penguin Classic History will be enjoyed and valued by everyone who loves the past.

Published or forthcoming:

Ernle Bradford	**The Mediterranean**
Alan Moorehead	**The Fatal Impact**
Samuel Pepys	**The Illustrated Pepys**
J. H. Plumb	**The First Four Georges**
J. B. Priestley	**The Edwardians**
A. L. Rowse	**The Elizabethan Renaissance**
G. M. Trevelyan	**English Social History**
T. H. White	**The Age of Scandal**
Lawrence Wright	**Clean and Decent**
Hans Zinsser	**Rats, Lice and History**

READ MORE IN PENGUIN

PENGUIN CLASSIC BIOGRAPHY

 Highly readable and enjoyable biographies and autobiographies from leading biographers and auto-biographers. The series provides a vital background to the increasing interest in history, historical subjects and people who mattered. The periods and subjects covered include the Roman Empire, Tudor England, the English Civil Wars, the Victorian Era, and characters as diverse Joan of Arc, Jane Austen, Robert Burns and George Melly. Essential reading for everyone interested in the past.

Published or forthcoming:

Ernle Bradford	**Cleopatra**
David Cecil	**A Portrait of Jane Austen**
Roger Fulford	**Royal Dukes**
Christopher Hibbert	**The Making of Charles Dickens**
Christopher Hill	**God's Englishman: Oliver Cromwell**
Edward Lucie-Smith	**Joan of Arc**
George Melly	**Owning Up: The Trilogy**
Lytton Strachey	**Queen Victoria**
	Elizabeth and Essex
Gaius Suetonius	**Lives of the Twelve Caesars, translated by Robert Graves**